9.5 |

RESPONSIBILITY AND
PRACTICAL FREEDOM

RESPONSIBILITY
AND
PRACTICAL FREEDOM

BY

MOIRA ROBERTS

CAMBRIDGE
AT THE UNIVERSITY PRESS
1965

· PUBLISHED BY
THE SYNDICS OF THE CAMBRIDGE UNIVERSITY PRESS

Bentley House, 200 Euston Road, London, N.W.1
American Branch: 32 East 57th Street, New York, N.Y. 10022
West African Office: P.O. Box 33, Ibadan, Nigeria

CAMBRIDGE UNIVERSITY PRESS
1965

Library of Congress Catalogue
Card Number: 65-14347

*Printed in Great Britain by Willmer Brothers Limited
Chester Street, Birkenhead*

PREFACE

Where there is danger of ambiguity in the following pages between a word discussed as a word-form and things, ideas, etc. discussed by means of words, I have used double quotation marks for the former, and single ones for the latter.

As the reading for this book was completed in the summer of 1961 there are no references to many relevant books and articles published since then.

M.R.

January 1964

CONTENTS

I

INTRODUCTORY

One could hardly deny that moral philosophy has fallen upon hard times. There is not so much a widespread interest in moral theory as a widespread concern over the lack of it; for this is an age when the evolutionary development of societies is taken as a fact, and the stages of that development take shape slowly and often painfully in men's minds before they can be realised. The framing of a constitution and the drafting of a new law are simple examples of this process. The future grows out of the present, and becomes the present only when compatible with it in practice. A man who scorns the world about him may be a man who longs for a "better" future, but he is not the man who builds it.

Moral philosophy provides and examines the means whereby a man criticises those ideas about the future which occur to him. He reflects upon the world as it is and as it might be, and out of that contrast emerge his own actions. If a man has no criteria by which he can select from among his own ideas about the future, if he has no way of bringing them together in comparison, then he has no means of acting consistently. He can only do what seems "best" to him on the spur of the moment when decision is forced upon him, or else follow some recognised code of rules without troubling to satisfy himself about its ground or aim.

Any attempt to dissociate moral philosophy from ends must lead to its debasement, for it is a fact of common experience that, when we consider what we should do, we admit into that consideration not only our own ends, but also those of others so far as they are known to us. To include ends in an extended concept of action is only to camouflage, not to deny, their presence.

Ends, when dealt with by philosophical methods of inquiry, inevitably become ultimate ends: for if it is the intention of that inquiry to find criteria for preferring one to another, for setting one above another, it is not permissible to start with a hierarchy, since a hierarchy would itself be the result of the application of the kind of criteria which form the object of the inquiry. No end, accordingly, which can be subsumed to another, is admitted as such. And since ultimacy is a category falling within metaphysics, moral systems have tended to share the recent fate of metaphysical systems in being regarded as logically unsound and valid only as personal rationalisations. Deprived of any grounds, even controversial ones, for the uses of "good", "right", "virtue", etc., philosophers have found themselves left with the *fact* that such uses occur in our daily discourse as applications of moral principles in the moral judgment. It could be argued with some force that the judgment which ends moral deliberation, or which solves a moral problem, is on that account alone, a *moral* judgment: but a simple, contextual explanation of the moral character of the judgment is not in favour. Instead, the same diligent search is now being made for the specifically moral element in the moral judgment as was formerly directed towards the formulation of moral systems.

A spate of theories [1] as to the nature of the moral judgment and the logic of the moral principle has not at all assuaged doubts about the status of moral philosophy. Such theories, for instance those of Stevenson, Hare, Nowell-Smith, and A. C. Ewing,[2] are interesting and skilfully presented yet singularly unsatisfying. It was argued by T. H. Green [3] that since we encounter actual moral effort, the true good 'must be an end in which the effort of a moral agent can really find rest'. But contemporary theories fail to indicate that there might be any end at all, except in the sense that a miscellany of decisions in a seemingly causal world would have a miscellany of effects. Nor does anyone now speak of progress, for "progress" is itself a teleological expression, and, used in moral contexts, might be said to beg the question of ends.

In these circumstances, it may be fruitful to look at those features of philosophy as it is today which appear to discourage the study of moral philosophy as traditionally understood. We should examine them to see upon what grounds, if any, they

---

[1] A theory does not escape being a theory because it is called an "analysis": the result of the analysis must be a theoretical statement, or set of statements.

[2] C. L. Stevenson, *Ethics and Language,* ch. 2.
R. M. Hare, *The Language of Morals,* chs. 9, 10, *passim.*
P. H. Nowell-Smith, *Ethics,* esp. chs. 19, 20.
A. C. Ewing, 'A suggested non-naturalistic analysis of good', in *Mind* (1939).

[3] *Prolegomena to Ethics,* paras. 171-2.

do in fact constitute a threat to moral philosophy in general, or to any section of it. It will suffice to distinguish three trends of thought which have reached and impressed many people who lack the ability to challenge them by reasoned arguments. Within the limits of this first chapter, I shall make only brief comments upon each.

The first is the notion that philosophy is not concerned with the world of things or of action, but is strictly a second-order inquiry into accounts of these. Wittgenstein's remark in *Philosophical Investigations* 124 that philosophy 'leaves everything as it is' has been widely misinterpreted as indicating the practical futility of philosophy. Yet to look carefully into the validity of what is given in an account may not be idle reflection if it leads to a review of evidence; if it does, that is, occur within a wider purpose. That it would not be the business of the philosopher to refer back to the evidence himself, but only to criticise what was conveyed to him in words, may be all that Wittgenstein intended. There is nothing to prevent the philosopher from providing himself with theoretical statements to examine in both political and moral philosophy, so long as he does examine them and does not treat them as assumptions upon which to base more theoretical statements. The usefulness of philosophical inquiry may lie necessarily outside philosophy itself, but so does the usefulness of any science. No one studies genetics for the sake of the genes. Metaphysical problems, such as those of time, space, identity, etc., are not so much the practical worries of philosophers as the perennial pegs upon which to try out methods.

However, if philosophy is not to concern itself with actuality, it is a fair question to ask how it can deal with so intimate and practical a part of our lives as our moral decisions. Disputes about human ends and the complexities of theory, if they are to be considered away from a particular context, must take as their starting point an account of moral behaviour and of moral situations which, once taken, constitutes an unchangeable given. There can be no going back to look at a particular occasion, even if there were one which could be subsumed to the account under discussion. Either we discuss a given world, a description, or we look at the world through defined words: in the former case we are restricted to an arbitrary account, in the latter the scope of our account is limited by arbitrary definitions. The practical situation, as an agent knows it, is summed up and concealed in concepts such as that of 'action'; for when we speak of an action in moral theory, we do not specify whether the action is the first solution that occurs to a man, whether any one of those which intervene, or whether it is the end product of a long series of deliberations, in the course of which many moral criteria have been carefully considered and applied. However excellent an account philosophers may give of the nature of virtuous action, the unfortunate agent in his predicament has no sure means of relating it to his immediate difficulties.

'I hold', wrote Bradley in chapter 4 of *Truth and Reality*, 'that in the end theory and practice are one. I believe in short that each is a one-sided aspect of our nature'. In saying this, Bradley did not mean that theory and practice are complementary, but that to consider one without the other would be to abstract, and thus to withdraw from what is actual. If a theory were so comprehensive and so detailed as to cover every possible contingency, then ideed moral theory would meet our practical needs. It may be that this is another way of saying that if we had full knowledge of our situation, our actions would be adequate to solve our problems. Our practical mistakes would, on this view, reflect or represent the shortcomings of our knowledge. While most philosophers are prepared to admit the limitations of and objections to their own contributions to the subject, it is often overlooked that during their investigations and pending the building up of an adequate theory, the practical moral situation is left almost untouched. This state of affairs might seem reasonable to philosophers if they noticed it, but it does not seem so to the troubled agent, who finds more practical wisdom in the *Ethica Nichomachea* of over two thousand years ago than in any moral treatise of today. Yet Aristotle claimed to extract principles from what lay before him rather than superimpose a system of rules. Many philosophers, sensitive on these points, have disclaimed interest in moral guidance, saying that this is the task of moralists, as distinct from philosophers. But can we take moral questions and divide them up into these two groups? And, if philosophers accept one group as relevant, can we assume that others will concern themselves with the one they repudiate? The supposed division is a division of purposes, and by distinguishing purposes one does not thereby make distinctions among those who have them. There may be no 'You take the high road, and I'll take the low road' in moral philosophy. The dichotomy ignores the difference, clearly seen by Kant, between formal and material guidance; for what a man wants to find out is not *what* rule to follow but *how to know* what rule to follow, how to analyse and assess his situation for himself.

To the agent, in his dilemma, the distinction between the moralist and the moral philosopher is at best unreal, for to add to the number of moralists is merely to add to the number of codes—religious or secular—that compete for his allegiance. What he asks is when, at what point, he is to apply moral criteria, and how, when he has decided what kind of action he ought to take, he should set about making sure he does it, and does not serve some other purpose which has crept in unnoticed. If he goes to the psychologist to ask what he should do, he is encouraged to say what he wants to do, and why. If he says he wants to do what is right, the psychologist has nothing to suggest. Again, playwrights such as Eliot, Marcel, and from time to time also Sartre, tell us that if we want to know what we should do, we ought to get to understand our own natures; but if it should be true, and it is a view very difficult to refute, that there are many men whose nature it is to act from belief in the rightness of what they do, then this kind of information, though desirable, seems in the main irrelevant. A moral problem is often a problem because the natures of others, and hence also their interests and convenience, are of equal importance with our own. In general, if philosophy is not able to supply disciplines suitable to moral inquiry, then it should at least show that its failure to do so rests upon logical grounds, that it is a matter of principle; and further, it should attempt to indicate where such disciplines might be looked for. If there are practical problems, then there must be formal aspects of those problems, and with these, at least, philosophy should be competent to deal.

The second trend that is casting a shadow over moral philosophy is the positivist attitude to ethical concepts. Since ethical sentences, it is argued, do not express anything that can be empirically verified, they do not express propositions, or make statements. To express a proposition is generally held equivalent to making a statement. Philosophy then has to declare ethical concepts to be pseudo-concepts; words such as "good", "right", etc. can only be said to have a sense if it is given to them by means of a theory of values. Their sense thus becomes analytically derivative from the agreed definitions. The propositions of ethics are accordingly pseudo-propositions in that they express *a priori* elucidations of linguistic conventions, in other words they are mere tautologies.

Before giving examples of the positivist contentions, we should pay some attention to the background against which these ideas were introduced, for in this way we shall be able to understand recent developments in ethical thought. The publication of Moore's *Principia Ethica* in 1903 popularised the view that, if the adjective "good" were definable, ethics could no longer claim autonomy, but would be reducible to those sciences relevant to the terms of the definition. Every subject, according to Moore, must have its own proper postulate, distinct and independent, and "good" as an indefinable, yet objective quality ("object of thought") is the central postulate of ethics.[1] This claim was to some extent weakened by Prichard, who argued[2] that objectivity in ethics follows only from the quality of rightness perceptible in certain actions, *as* actions and quite apart from the question of motive. Far from (as Moore had contended) actions deriving their rightness from their ability to produce the greatest amount of good, the perception of the rightness of an action is immediate, and statements about rightness yield no entailments about 'good'. If we say, Prichard maintained, that an action should be done because it will produce good, then we have to make a link of the kind 'what is good ought to be', for example. But we do not in fact need arguments of any kind to convince us, or to justify our perception, that what we see as obligatory really is so; we see a certain action as what we ought to do in a certain situation, and there is no more to be said.

The link that Prichard found superfluous, and to lie outside the moral experience, was developed by A. C. Ewing[3] as an alternative to Moore's account of 'good' as the main concept of ethics. Ewing argued that if "good" means 'what ought to be done', then "good" must be indefinable in any but a formal

[1] *Principia Ethica*, para. 15.
[2] 'Does Moral Philosophy rest upon a mistake?' in *Mind* (1912).
[3] *Op. cit.* p. 2, n. 2, above.

sense, and rightness gains a sense in terms of good without rely-ing upon utilitarian—that is, consequential—grounds. Where Prichard held that motive is irrelevant to rightness, Ewing maintained that a man could determine his motive at the time of acting since, even if he has a bad motive for the action, he need not accept it as a reason for acting.

Within the time span of these publications, and limited in scope to their contents, there had developed a series of detailed controversies about the meaning of "right", "good", and "obliga-tion". At this time the terminology of moral theory was still domi-nated by that of Bradley and Green,[1] but gradually there came to be a new demand for precision in ethical discourse, together with a growing uneasiness about the possibility of its achievement.

With academic ethics divided in this way, and positivism still a remote, 'overseas' product, the denial of meaning to ethical concepts, especially when presented with the inimitable clarity of Ayer's writing,[2] seemed catastrophic. Philosophers who supported positivist or near-positivist doctrines contented themselves with abandoning ethical discussion, perhaps assum-ing that some naturalistic account of the moral sense would soon emerge from psychology. Some moral philosophers, for instance W. D. Ross and A. C. Ewing, satisfied themselves that arguments against positivism were at least as potent as argu-ments in its favour, and subsequently disregarded it. Others, occupied as they already were in the effort to disown natural-istic ethics, and save themselves from the supposed disap-proval of Moore, either continued to throw discredit upon naturalistic ethics, or turned to the possibilities of analysing the moral judgment according to its latent purposes. Little attempt was made to bring the positivist theses into ethics as providing criteria of method. This is perhaps surprising, for since there are social rules, there must be problems about obeying them. No reasoning, however brilliant, can eliminate matters of fact, and even in the acceptance of positivist prin-ciples there could be little danger of a final disappearance of philosophical ethics. Nor could the allegation of lack of literal significance in words standing for ethical concepts remove the complexities and personal variations of the moral problem.

[1] In which words like "consciousness", "motive", "intention", "moral", etc. are assumed to refer to states of mind familiar to all.
[2] *Language, Truth and Logic* (1936).

We should look briefly at two examples of the argument that ethical concepts are pseudo-concepts, and that ethical sentences express pseudo-propositions. The attitudes of Wittgenstein and Ayer will serve our purpose very well, but we can here only take a cursory glance which will scarcely do justice to their views.

First we should remind ourselves of certain necessary conditions of values: for they presuppose juxtaposition, being relational. If there are objective values, they still have to be perceived as such. Now to assess assumes at least two distinct objects, the viewer and the assessed; at this simple level, the object of assessment must be assessed relatively to the assessor, and even if the value did result from some further existence, it could not be distinguished as such. Given at least three objects, however, and one being the viewer, then the other two may be assessed in relation to each other, on the basis of some common qualities, even if only those of space or position; this standard is necessarily fixed by the assessor. It may be intensity of colour, or of significance—its urgency; and this could be measured in terms of money, or, if the assessment concerned action, as 'good', 'better', 'best', etc. Since it is a necessary condition of valuing that something is perceived, it follows that when the perceiver is unaware of himself and does not perceive that he is perceiving, then he cannot value one object alone, he can only identify himself with it. He can value two or more comparable objects, but he will regard their values as matters of fact, he will see the values as pertaining to the objects, as part of them, intrinsic to them.

These requirements of value and valuing lie behind Wittgenstein's remarks in paragraph 6.4 of the *Tractatus*: 'In the world everything is as it is and happens as it does happen. *In* it there is no value—and if there were, it would be of no value. If there is a value which is of value . . . it must lie outside the world'. "The world" was used somewhat ambiguously by Wittgenstein here to mean (i) what is, what can or could be discovered and seen, and (ii) what anyone has as his idea of the world. It is in sense (ii) that it was used to speak of the different worlds of the happy and unhappy, and of the world that ceases at death. But it is in sense (i) that he denied the world the value of value, and, unless I have mistaken his views, it is in *both* senses that he declared ethics to be transcendental. Ethical values are part of the perceiver's apparatus of perception, they influence the way he sees the world. Thus they are not part of the world as the world, and so they cannot be expressed, since the only true or false propositions are about the world, and only propositions are expressed as statements of fact. If we contain in ourselves the conditions, or the possibility—as Kant said—of experiencing objects, we cannot assume that any quality we perceive as pertaining to these objects does in fact belong to them. But we can, by comparing our experience with that of others, and in observing an object in many different ways, give some account of what is given us from outside ourselves and what is not. That which stands the test of common observation is regarded as "the world"; that which does not survive the test is subjective. Wittgenstein admitted the subjective elements, but refused to allow that they can be described or spoken of since they cannot be distinguished as objectively 'there'. They can be shown in perceptual activity, including discussion, but they cannot be pointed to.

If Wittgenstein intended to deny that anything can be said about our values because they are that part of the structure of the world we apprehend which comes from ourselves, then it is easy enough to agree that they can only be shown, that our values appear in our judgments and other behaviour, which must be described in certain conventional, that is, recognisable, ways. But his views went further than this, for he denied that any value could be objective, and maintained that when value appears to be objective, it is only because it has been supposed to be so, and valuational terms have been given some meaning which is then reflected back in the uses we make of them. So far as value is concerned, a human being, as a person, is isolated. Wittgenstein seems to have gone a step beyond mere isolation, and questioned whether there was anything, anybody, to be isolated: for in paragraph 5.54 of the *Tractatus*, he denied any unity of soul, as sentience, in a person on the ground that, as subject, a man and his thoughts, or experiences, constitute a unity. To say: A thinks, or believes, that p, is to say: There is an A such that A-believing-p. No plurality of such propositions can be said to produce a unity or the continuity of A, or of A's soul. The experiences of A are disparate, discontinuous, different in kind, and logically independent. A may have as many souls as he has experiences of this nature.

Before leaving Wittgenstein for the present, we should also note that in *Philosophical Investigations* 74–7, he attempted a demonstration by analogy of ethical and aesthetic concepts; he supposed a "picture" of blurred colours, which we desire to convert into sharp outlines. Decisions have to be made as to what sort of outlines should be drawn, for, considered as shapes, it does not matter what kind of outlines are chosen. 'Decision' is the operative concept here: for, providing all the picture is covered, the precise nature of the outlines is not so important, though it must approximate to the changes in colour on the surface. What clearer analogy of the task of the theorist could there be than this. But we must bear in mind that Wittgenstein did not remove the blurred picture from the world either in its blurred or in its sharpened version. It is merely excluded from relevance to concrete, that is, clearly defined, things; and in paragraph 76 he remarked that the similarity between the blurred and the clear pictures is as undeniable as the differences which result from the drawing of contours. Perhaps he meant to say that what you see and what I see as relevant to ethics or aesthetics may be very similar in some sense, yet the way we see it, or the way we describe it to ourselves, may vary. There is room here for both subjective and objective theories: a pseudo-concept must have its origin, since it has occurred as someone's thought.

Ayer's account of ethics is rather more prosaic. He agrees that ethical sentences say nothing since they do not fall within what is *logically* available for empirical verification, and holds such sentences to be metaphysical. Given meaning by a moral system, ethical sentences can give rise to discussion only as a logical exercise, yielding tautologies, or analytic truths, which are in effect statements of linguistic conventions. We should note what is at stake here: for we can agree, certainly, that elucidation within a conceptual scheme is mathematical in character, without also conceding that it is solely concerned with the use of words. It is true that, if a word like "good" is given a meaning, the analysis of allied concepts will in effect be an analysis of the original definition of "good". A good definition, Ayer admits, may lead us to discover new truths, but that they have not previously been recognised is due to the limits of our perception and skill in reasoning rather than to any mystical quality of concepts.

In refusing a sense to normative ethical concepts, Ayer does not dismiss them as rubbish; if they are nonsensical, it is as non-sense, non-sensible. Ethical concepts are unanalysable, and Ayer makes no attempt to account for the respect accorded by common sense to words like "good", "right", etc. Instead he shows that the purposes of making moral judgments may vary widely, and that these variations are important in distinguishing the judgment as a judgment of value and not merely one of fact. In 'On the Analysis of Moral Judgments',[1] he suggests that since moral judgments occur, and people make them meaningfully, they may have a logic of their own which has different criteria of validity from those applied to verifiable statements. That "statement" should be reserved for empirically verifiable propositions he lays down as a convention, as a decision about the use of language: and we should note that, although convention may determine how a contingent 'given' is dealt with, convention cannot of itself in any way alter that 'given'.

This being so, Ayer has still to account for the fact of the moral judgment. In *Language, Truth and Logic*, chapter 6, he distinguishes between (i) ethics proper, the giving of definitions to ethical terms, and the criticism of the adequacy of those definitions; (ii) descriptions of moral experience, belonging to psychology or sociology; (iii) exhortations to moral virtue, the domain of the moralist as distinct from the moral philosopher; and (iv) the moral judgment. He remarks that moral philosophers commonly disregard these distinctions, with the result that it is hard to be sure what it is they are discussing. Now a moral judgment refers to an action, or kind of action, and thus contains descriptive language; but it also pronounces upon what is described, and no detailed elaboration of the descriptive element will suffice to explain away the pronouncement that the action is good or bad. When all that can be said about the action which provides reasons for its preferment has been said, it must still appear that sentences which say that an action is of a certain kind and sentences which say that actions of that kind are good or bad are not linguistically the same. This being so, some account is required of the difference between them. Ayer favours an emotive explanation or analysis: that moral judgments are expressions of feelings, part of emotional

[1] *Philosophical Essays* (1954); first published in *Horizon* (1949).

behaviour; and he distinguishes this view carefully from the subjectivist account of the moral judgment as an assertion of feeling, which in effect makes ethical sentences empirical and synthetic. On Ayer's view, to say 'It is wrong' is to show, not to say, that the speaker feels some kind of aversion towards an action, and in his later essay (page 238), he extends this view by regarding the moral judgment as expressing an attitude rather than mere feeling. This is tantamount to saying that such judgments issue from some enduring or structural facet of the personality rather than from some transient state. 'The fact is rather that what may be described as moral attitudes consist in certain patterns of behaviour, and that the expression of a moral judgment is an element in the pattern.'

Ayer's method of dealing with the moral judgment is to clarify it by exposing ambiguities in respect of purpose and of linguistic form; but in the various non-propositional accounts of the moral judgment that arose partly as a result of his first book there is little evidence either of system or of method. Sometimes the moral judgment is considered to be a form of words, sometimes an expression of intention or purpose. In the former case, meaning is given to the component words and expressions which make up the sentence expressing the judgment regardless of the fact that when they do occur in such sentences, the sentences are particular and in a context. In the latter, on the other hand, the whole personality of an imaginary speaker may pass in review, under the vague phrase 'contextual implications'. The curious tendency of the philosopher to regard anything that can be included in one class as capable of one explanation or definition is nowhere so frustrating as here: for why should there be some one prototype of moral judgments?

Thus with the attempted elimination of the metaphysical grounds of ethical statements, and the assignment of the critical examination of such statements to logic rather than to ethics, moral philosophers seem to have been left with two alternatives: they could proceed with ethical questions as hitherto, trusting that logical positivism would fade away, or they could attempt to devise non-propositional accounts of the moral judgment which would meet the criticisms at least of Wittgenstein and Ayer. But however interesting and productive these experiments in analysis may be, the average thoughtful citizen wants an answer to the challenges made to moral philosophy: he is not impressed either by vehement repudiation or skilful sidetracking. Is any inquiry into ethical concepts an exercise of logic within a theoretical 'given', or is it an examination of 'moral', as a sub-class of 'human', behaviour?

As the third, and perhaps the most straightforward, of the three trends that threaten ethics, there is the question of responsibility. Doubts are widely felt as to the legitimacy of praising or blaming a man if he is part of a causal process, if he does what he does because he is what he is, and he is what he is because of an inexorable combination of birth and social conditioning. Once start nibbling at the notion of man as a source of free activity, and where is one to stop? 'To be *im*pelled' becomes, albeit imperceptibly, 'to be *com*pelled'. The advance of science into the very stronghold of a man's personality is a weighty argument against his claim to autonomy.

Responsibility and freedom to act—at its simplest that there is a choice between doing action X and not doing it—are usually considered to be two sides of the same thing. Kant wrote of 'the freedom which must be the foundation of all moral laws and the consequent responsibility'.[1] In jurisdiction, responsibility is a rebuttable assumption,[2] analytically related to agency, but as such it is ill suited to morals, since there is no agreed concept of man to support it. Law is based upon the general assumption that the citizen is, as agent, answerable for what he does; law itself is built up by and for the citizen, and legal processes rely upon the concept of a citizen as a member of a state. Morals makes and includes no corresponding assumption about a man. It may be that all men are not properly to be described as "moral beings", merely because they are 'human beings'. That morality is a fact of social life is not refuted by an assertion that certain persons cannot be said to be moral beings; as, for instance, the statement that horse racing is a national sport is not refuted by the statement that many citizens have nothing to do with it. But if legal responsibility were subject to these doubts, law would fall to the ground: law must postulate a legally responsible man.

[1]*Critique of Practical Reason* (Longmans, 1954), p. 190.

[2] I do not propose to use Hart's term "defeasible" for the analytical association of responsibility and action in morals. If a concept is imported into morals from law, it should come in under its own colours. See 'The Ascription of Responsibility and Rights' in *Proc. Ar. Soc.* (1948–9).

It seems to follow from these remarks that if an assumption of responsibility is made in ethics, it is assumed as a metaphysical theory and is thus open to the objections that can be made to any metaphysical statement. The increasing tendency to make use of legal analogies in ethical discussion without troubling to examine the validity of this procedure is perhaps a symptom of the insecurity felt by many moral philosophers in respect of their subject. Moral philosophy, or ethical discussion, is not a subsidiary, or an imitation, of law: to treat it as if it were is not only to ignore the historical origins of law but also to abandon the very core of moral theory, which is the question of what principles should be adopted, and not, as in law, the question of what principles are already contained within the law, or indicated by its previous administration. To say, for instance, that the English system of Common Law is largely based upon precedent rather than upon authority is not to justify a view that ethics is a mere affair of convention; and that, since moral responsibility is a traditional ascription by society to its members, there is no need to look into the grounds of that ascription. It is true that Kant was content to assume an analytic connection between morality and freedom, contending that it would make nonsense of the former to deny the latter, whereas no one could deny the fact of morality: 'The moral law is the condition under which we can first *become conscious* of freedom'.[1] We do have what appear to be alternative possibilities of action, and this in itself could be said to be a sufficient condition of having a choice. Bradley, however, insisted that those alternatives must be before the mind at one and the same time if choice was to be actual[2]. That a man should deliberate between two courses of action, and require criteria of moral worth, was enough for Kant; but Bradley, who had the advantage of growing up with the new scientific approach of psychology, was not so easily satisfied.

For the moment such matters do not concern us. What we have to answer is the question whether, on a theory that the empirical sciences can, or could, logically, account for all events as occurring in a continuous, unbroken process, it makes sense to speak of free will, and to consider those who displease us as deserving of censure. In the third antinomy, Kant showed

---

[1] *Op. cit.* note to p. 88.
[2] *Ethical Studies*, 2nd edn., pp. 298–9.

that inquiries into empirical grounds of freedom must be abortive, since the arguments on one side are as strong as those on the other, and yet are incompatible. But the same kind of demonstration could be made when logic is applied to any form of life: for life has always two aspects; on the one hand, those habitual ways by which we speak of it as a 'world', recognise it, identify it, together with the phenomena into which our conventions, our training in perception, lead us to divide it in order that we can control and order it; and on the other, the processes by which science accounts for the emergence of these. The line between cause and effect is, as Bradley called it, an ideal line: things become causes or effects according to the position assigned them in a process.[1] They are, as it were, arbitrary limits, using "arbitrary" in an extended sense. That reasons can be made to look equally convincing for an account of freedom and for its denial follows from the fact that reason assumes, by attempting a comprehensive account at all, that it, whatever it is, transcends the material it is presenting. This assumption is the condition of the major premiss on either side of the antinomy, and thus the two major premisses cannot be compared: they have equal validity, and equal lack of it.

Such an answer as that given by Kant to the question of freedom will not satisfy us today. We feel uneasy in our attitude towards social offenders, diffident in calling our friends to account, confused on the subject of sanctions and half-ashamed of our prisons. Our disquiet is not allayed by theories that freedom or responsibility are ways of describing the world, or ourselves, or that they are 'dimensions' in which actions occur. Such attempts at elucidation only confirm our nascent recognition that we do not in fact know what they are, nor are we so sure as we would like to be how and when the concepts should be applied. It may be that a great deal of our perplexity is due to a suspicion that the word "empiricism" has in some way changed its reference, with, for example, the discovery of what is called "subception". We have to admit that what we do is greatly influenced by what we do not consciously notice in what is presented to us. But we might take comfort from the fact that philosophers have long made use of the word "intuition" as a cover term for processes of assimilation and response

[1] *Principles of Logic,* 2nd edn., p. 539n.

of which we are unaware. There is no logical objection to the use of "intuition" for a communication from a group of perceptions with no direct access to those parts of the brain concerned with conscious thought and deliberate action. Such an account would tally with Nietzsche's distinction between the 'big wisdom' of the organism as a whole and the 'little wisdom' of consciousness, or those rational processes consciousness enables us to survey.[1] To agree with the positivists that such remarks constitute a misuse of language is not to suggest that Nietzsche had nothing of importance to say, but rather that he failed to say it in the appropriate language, that is, that of physiology. For if it is a condition of the acceptance of sentences as meaningful that they are empirically verifiable, logically so, then there is an important sub-class of such sentences asserting hypotheses that mark time and make do in the interval between the logical and contingent possibility of verification. That intuition is, as Bradley seems to have supposed,[2] dependent upon sense-experience, that it is reducible to perception, is in principle a verifiable proposition. We only wait for the proper experiments to be devised.

This gap between the 'could be known' and the 'is known' is of the utmost importance. It is a feature common to the philosophy of Hume and of Bradley that both were willing to admit a difference between what we experience and what we knowingly perceive and can substantiate which is 'felt'. Hume found himself unable to account for self-identity, and had to content himself with saying that we feel 'a connection or determination of the thought to pass from one object to another',[3] while Bradley's whole philosophical position, especially in respect of logic, relies upon a 'felt whole' from which we abstract what we perceive and know and can indicate.[4] It is precisely because we do have such feelings, or experience, and because science has not developed sufficiently to be able to account for these, that we are in the quandary we are in about freedom and responsibility. It is as a person knowing himself as a source of his actions and supposing this knowledge in others, that a man speaks of responsibility and is said to have rights.

---

[1] *Thus Spake Zarathustra*, IV.
[2] See, for example, *Ethical Studies,* note to p. 194.
[3] *A Treatise on Human Nature,* Appendix.
[4] See *Appearance and Reality,* ch. 19, & *passim.*

This third question, that of responsibility, is not merely of theoretical importance in the minds of many men; for the suspicion that a complete empirical account of human be- haviour, falling within the relevant sciences, would entail acceptance of the philosophical doctrine of determinism, gives significance to the curious suggestion that there may be nothing to be gained in trying to do what is right. Why argue, then, about ultimate or less remote grounds of goodness and of right- ness? It is true that a set of propositions giving a complete account of empirical conditions could not entail an assertion of determinism, since contingent truths, or truths of nature, cannot attain logical certainty. But this academic nicety will not suffice to save responsibility: for what concerns the justifica- tion of effort towards a moral end is not so much the logical possibility of responsibility as the contingent fact of freedom. If no one can be said to act freely, then responsibility, so it appears, is a chimera.

These three sets of arguments cannot be disregarded: they must be met, must be conceded if found to be irrefutable, and it would then be for moral philosophy to demonstrate its ability to absorb and transcend the concessions it had made in fair combat. Now if there is to be a combat, there must be a place, a territory, where the combatants meet; some common ground is needed, some occasion for display. We should look at the three main questions we have posed, and see whether any of them offers that occasion.

The first deals with the scope of philosophy, whether there is a place in philosophy for moral disputation; the second con- cerns the material of moral philosophy, the meaning of the terms most intimately bound up with the subject; and the third asks whether there can be a subject at all. To inquire whether philosophy can properly discuss ethics is to ask if ethics can be presented in such a way that a critical philosophy can cope with it, that is, whether the material of ethics is accessible to critical treatment. If, for instance, Wittgenstein has said all that there is to say in saying that ethics is trans- cendental, we should find it hard to justify any further philo- sophical probing. Ayer too has written that 'ethical philosophy consists simply in saying that ethical concepts are pseudo- concepts and therefore unanalysable'.[1] But before we can

[1] *Language, Truth and Logic*, ch. 6.

decide whether there is in morals suitable material for philosophical criticism, we must know something of that material.
We cannot, accordingly, take our second question as providing
the material which is to be properly presented, since it is that
very material whose existence is in doubt. It may be illusory,
the familiar masquerading under false colours of strangeness,
the factual posing as valuational. If we are not certain what our
material is, we can hardly discuss its presentation. Thus we are
left with responsibility, the ground of ethics, the responsibility
for our actions which rests upon freedom of choice and of
character-building. Responsibility it is that must form the basis
of our attempt to show that philosophy has an account to settle
with ethics. We must ask whether philosophy is competent to
answer questions such as why it is that we tend to regard men
as responsible for what they do, and upon what kind of ground
we do this; and again, we will want to know why we think we
are justified in ascribing responsibility in the various spheres of
morality, politics, law, etc. If we inquire thus of philosophy, we
shall at least expect some opinion or conclusion about the
nature of these questions, whether they are the kind of questions
to which it is sensible to look for answers. Again, even if
philosophy denies that such questions have sense, we can offer
the evidence that man's use of "good", "right", etc., seem to
have some influence upon his conduct, especially in making
choices, if he can be said to make choices. For if their use should
be causally connected with conduct it can hardly be maintained
that they have no claim to literal significance. The logical
status of such influence would be a further topic for discussion.

It could be objected that there is a confusion here of epistemological questions with those of ethics. But we are not, at this
stage, sure what ethical questions are. It is true that to challenge the use of "good" "right", etc., in ethical sentences is to
raise an epistemological issue, but since the criterion of verifiability, in both its stronger and weaker forms, is itself a formulation in or of epistemology, the objection loses its force. For it is
the epistemological threat to ethics that has given rise to the
current emphasis on non-propositional theories of the moral
judgment, and it is nonsense to suggest, in the face of this fact,
that epistemological considerations are irrelevant to moral
theory. The strongest evidence for ghosts is, after all, the fear of
ghosts, which must be founded on the belief that ghosts exist

in some way, or, should we say, that some kind of ghost exists. It is, in my opinion, the bare refusal to entertain epistemological questions implicitly present in ethical problems that has discredited much of academic ethics in the eyes of the man of practical intelligence.

We said that it would be for philosophy to say in what way a problem should be presented; and it is always for a science to determine its methods of research and inquiry. But before considering how philosophy will proceed with regard to responsibility, we should be warned about the inevitable metaphysical assumptions that lurk within the conventions of language. In asking questions, for instance, we may be presupposing the nature of our answers. It has been neatly said by C. A. Hamblin[1] that a question is 'a statement with a blank in it'. The form of the answer is preordained by the form of the question. So we should look critically at our questions. It can be said, for example, that since words are signs, the use of any material object word assumes the existence of the world as we know it, and the possibility and validity of referring to things. Ryle has revealed many of the pitfalls that beset those who do not look closely at the kinds of words they use—for example, in composing subject-predicate sentences.[2] But theoretical knowledge is not necessarily linked with correct practice, and we should look again and again at our arguments to see if, perchance, presuppositions have crept in that we would not wish to make, and which, moreover, would prejudice the relevance of any conclusion we might reach if we were not aware of their origin and could make allowance for them in a final analysis.

When confronted with a word like "responsibility" it is easy to suppose it has some definable sense, that it is used to signify one kind of thing. Reflection, however, soon discovers it to be a generic term under which sub-classes—of political, social, legal, moral responsibility—should be brought. It then appears as a category-word, and we cannot ask what responsibility is, over and above the specific questions as to what legal, moral, etc. responsibility is. Nor can we assume that a casual alignment of sub-classes is scientifically justified: for who is going to say what differentiates social from political responsibility, or family from social, or social from legal or moral? It is sometimes thought

[1] *Australasian Journal of Philosophy* (1958).
[2] 'Systematically Misleading Expressions', in *Proc. Ar. Soc.* (1931–2).

that moral responsibility is prior—logically—to any other kind, on the ground that if a man is responsible for his actions, he is responsible for them in any of the spheres in which they occur. But this is by no means apparent. What does seem to be the case here is that we are not so much considering responsibility as those particular responsibilities a man may have. And 'may have' is not 'has'.

We encounter a parallel difficulty if we look at the world and try to discern instances of responsibility. The world we look at is the world of social relations, and our evidence would be documentary and phenomenological. We would soon be forced to admit we were investigating instances of responsible behaviour in its various aspects; and our empirical researches would come to an abrupt halt if we were asked how we knew where to look for those instances. We could not know how to classify the instances until we decided upon criteria for the purpose, and it would soon be obvious that current distinctions between the political, legal and other contexts of responsibility overlap and are ambiguous. How should we, for example, know whether to call summoning the fire brigade for a neighbour's blazing chimney an exercise of social, legal, moral responsibility, or simple neighbourliness? In some cases the law will, either as civil or as criminal code, require services which more properly class as friendship. Wilful neglect is a highly adaptable legal concept: it marks as it were the legal limits of selfish withdrawal.

We might then be forced to admit we were in effect collecting instances of certain kinds of duties, where these could be called 'responsibilities' of the average member of society. And to do this is to come near to defining responsibility in terms of obligation, as a system of claims. But we would not say that, for instance, if Mr A was responsible for staff appointments, any one particular appointment was obligatory upon him.

It seems, in short, that before embarking upon such an inquiry, there must be a prearranged plan. In collecting and classifying plants, the botanist—let us suppose the present science to be non-existent—can describe the specimens he finds, and at some point similarities in structure will become apparent. His preliminary classification will be subject to constant amendment, until his scheme of arranging has reached a certain degree of maturity. But he will have known what he meant by a plant from the start, and certain features would accordingly be recognised as essential, or intrinsic, for the correct inclusion of any specimen.

In seeking recorded instances of the application of 'responsibility' we cannot assume that occurrences of the *word* cover all instances, unless we presuppose that no other words or expressions could convey the same sense. This is probably not the case. And since our search is an empirical one, let us recognise that it could not be exhaustive. This 'could' is not only contingent but also logical: for documentary uses would include records of particular cases as well as prohibitions and rules, general in character. A rule is a different kind of fact from a living instance brought under it, so that we should have one classificatory system for actual instances, and one for normative instances. There would be Mr A's contract, what he was to be responsible for, and there would be his interpretation of it in practice. Accordingly we should have two meanings of "responsibility", one proceeding from practice, and one a norm of social agreement, hypothetical in character. We should, moreover, have no grounds for supposing that either was correct in isolation from the other. To say for example, that Mr A was responsible for *xyz*, or that Mr A is a 'responsible man' as a man having responsibilities, is not to say that Mr A has a 'sense of responsibility': he might be bullied into doing his work by his boss or his wife.

It is on account of difficulties of this kind that the elucidation of concepts such as those which govern the use of "responsibility" becomes a matter for philosophy. For philosophy is concerned with the way we describe the world, and thus with the way we express our thoughts, since the expression of our thoughts is part of the world. But do not let us fall into the trap of supposing we are in this investigating *language*. Man is logically prior to the words he uses.

II

A SEARCH FOR EVIDENCE

I. PHILOSOPHY AND KNOWLEDGE

Philosophy is generally held to be the love, and hence the pursuit, of knowledge, springing from the desire to know why and how what we perceive comes to be what it is. If we are to have knowledge about anything, we must (i) know what we mean, formally, by "knowledge", and (ii) know how our information is obtained. We require at least some definitions and a specific method if we are properly to speak of our conclusions as knowledge.

Knowledge is the reproduction of what is perceived as true in communicable, that is, in meaningful, form. It is important to be clear on this point, for it is sometimes overlooked that knowledge is something that can be recorded and made use of, and that the only means of such preservation is verbal formulation, assertion.[1] The tape recorder can preserve only what we might perceive, not what we have perceived, and a camera only records what is there to be seen; such equipment is in effect the extension of our sense organs, it enables extension of our perceptions, but it does not in itself imply perception.

Emotional or aesthetic experience may be repeated, re-established, or re-lived, but this remains a repetition, an occurrence. Revived experiences may occur spontaneously as a result of features common to them and to present perceptions, but they cannot be deliberately produced. If we deliberately recall some feature of an earlier experience, that experience may be revived, or it may not. On the other hand, our decisions about, explanations and descriptions of, such earlier experiences can be deliberately recalled, because they are part of what we have done, part of our reflection, our verbalising; they took place in time, in the long process of our 'doing'. We can say that we fixated our experience in words, and we can either recall the words, the formulation, or try to recapture

---

[1] I propose to regard what is called "knowledge by acquaintance" as a stage in the processes of perception.

their experiential context in order to revise the account.[1] To say that the sentences, or statements, we remember are meaningful is to say that we receive what they were intended to convey: for in memory we communicate with ourselves over the years, and that communication is technically the same as our communication with others. 'I remember saying . . .; but now I wonder what I meant,' is a remark we have to make to ourselves from time to time. The meaning of sentences is the intention that guided their formulation.[2]

These statements are contingent, and concern the subject-matter of psychology. There are, however, two objections that could be made to this account of knowledge on philosophical grounds. (i) It is fairly widely held that to use "know" correctly involves the truth of what is said to be "known". Against this I maintain that it is impracticable to assume an analytic relation between knowledge and truth, because while such a relation, and the attainment of both, is plainly the ideal of philosophy, we do not realise our ideals by merely supposing them in our efforts at realisation. To attempt to use "know" only when what is known is true would mean that most of us had to substitute "think we know" for "know", which would be both dreary and inelegant—although this can hardly be called an argument against the use. Stronger is the argument that, since science advances by discarding one hypothesis in favour of another, and tends to embrace several schools of thought even in the one subject, we would, if we accepted the use, have to say that science students have no knowledge. This seems to be absurd; for science is getting to know, and if it is a fact that sciences grow and extend, then something must be known *en route*. Thus I take "know" to signify having evidence upon which to base an opinion, and being able to quote other

---

[1] We may experience something in the sense of catching a glimpse of it, of being aware that something 'occurs' to us, and we may attempt to recapture that something, to experience or be aware of it clearly. It is the use of "clearly" here that indicates what I intend by fixating in words, for the 'something' must be objectified sufficiently as a distinguishable something for a descriptive account to be made. Often words and sentences 'occur' but we cannot reproduce them. We do not 'know' what they were.

[2] This must stand for the moment, and is preferable to saying that sentences are "used" to make statements, which suggests sentences are hovering about somewhere waiting for a cue. To suppose a language consists of all the sentences that could be correctly said is surely an academic hypostasis. But these matters must be tackled squarely later.

opinions. This leads to the second objection. (ii) On this account of knowledge it could be said that knowledge is reduced to that which satisfies us. If a man has in his view sufficient reason to believe 'that p', then on my view here he can say he knows 'that p'. I would reject this argument as invalid, because I find a conceptual difference between believing and knowing: the two notions are not interchangeable. If a man says he knows, it does mean that he is satisfied, and if he argues wrongly on some occasion from 'I know that p' to 'p is true' then I accept that he is mistaken, and that others can assist him to find the error in his reasoning. It is one of our practical problems to know when we should accept the pronouncements of authority and when we should not, and learning to deal with this problem is in fact learning when to speak of knowledge and when to use "believe".

As against both these objections it can be said that if "knowledge" is taken to signify true knowledge, we would either have to disallow a man's ability to make use of and accept the conclusions of science as 'his knowledge', or as 'having knowledge'; or accept public decisions as the source of true knowledge. For our purposes here it seems to me preferable to say that what a man can reproduce, support, demonstrate, is what he knows; what is ultimately knowable or true is a question for metaphysics. If we find that we are in difficulties over the epistemological question of 'getting to know', we can deal with it when we come to it.

What is necessarily true is that we cannot recall an event which did not occur: to re-glimpse what is past through some detail, such as a scent, or the mention of a name, is not to recall an event, for it is analytic that an event is seen or perceived as a whole. It is part of some series, it is a logical construction, an isolable part of experience. We do not perceive as if we were looking out of a rear window of a moving car: but in the sequence of sights and sounds we perceive significantly, objects and events emerge as meaningful configurations in the melting pot of sense. Thus it is necessary for recall that events and objects are perceived through recognition of what they are, and recognition involves naming. If an object has not been identified, then we do not remember it as what it was, but merely as 'some object', 'something'. We may perceive that an event appears significant, we may say 'it strikes me that . . .', without understanding why this should be so; but unless we do later succeed in relating it significantly to some interest or purpose, we assume we were mistaken, that it did not mean anything.

It is not necessary that recognition should be correct, so far as remembering is concerned. To seem to recognise an object, to forget the 'seem' and assume the object was there because we remember the name, is common. To recall incorrectly is to recall faulty perceptions, not to make mistakes of recollection; to make mistakes in remembering is to fail to recall, to have forgotten, to substitute imagination, rationalisation or falsehood, for recollection.

These distinctions are of paramount importance for philosophy, since philosophy has to deal with statements, with meaningful sentences. Those who obtain hypotheses, recollections, answers to practical problems, as 'intuitions' still have to have them in words, as sentences, before they can be aware of them as occurrences. A sentence or form of words which occurs 'as a whole' in 'the head' is still a sentence. It has to be thought as such, or said, before it can be made use of, even in thought. It may be 'read off' on appearance in 'the head', and thus become a statement, a sentence which is meaningful. So-called intuitions of knowledge can be looked at, criticised, supported, rejected, disowned as unworthy, welcomed as guidance, but they must be statements; they must be capable of being said, and thus of repetition. If a hallucination, for example what Freud calls *a* symbol and Jung calls *the* symbol, is to have any significance, if it is to *be* a symbol, it derives that significance from the description or explanation given of it; for itself, it is nothing without interpretation, even if only in terms of "like . . .". Something, a proposition, is made available, is there to be 'known'.

To recall may be prompted by need, as the need to supply information or to maintain a conversation, but it is prompted. Where memory just occurs, it is not proper to speak of recall, but of reverie, musing on the past or future, autistic thinking, day-dreaming, all these phenomena are commonly distinguished today. Such memories may not be in the form of events, but of the stuff of events, the sensory sub-stratum of experience, partially interpreted. It is incorrect to speak of knowledge with regard to this, since what presents itself in this way is rather the material of knowledge, that which we can have knowledge of or about. To say that memories arising or occurring with reference to some event constitute evidence for or against its significance would be a gross assumption: we should first have to establish an account of those memories before we could criticise them as evidence of anything beyond their present occurrence. And such a process takes time, it is not an affair of instantaneous intuition, but a complicated business of sifting and comparing: to recapture a process of thought in such a way that it can be called a train of thought is to produce a series of statements in time, something which is actual in a way that the sequence of a reverie is not, though the reverie itself may be. If we want to have the stuff of a reverie as real, as actual, we have first to reduce it to statements, and to do this is usually to dispel the reverie.

Thus it is not correct to speak of knowledge except in respect of statements. The question as to what a statement is can be left for a later chapter. What I know is what I can state, just as, to take Ryle's account, what I know how to do is what I can do.[1] But even with this latter, this 'knowing how', before I can call it knowledge I must produce statements of it, although to do so involves describing what I do from watching myself. Can I say I 'know' where all the typewriter keys are, just because I can type without looking at them? I do as a matter of fact know that I cannot write them out correctly. So I suppose I have forgotten where they are, even though my fingers seem to 'remember'. But with my fingers it is surely merely a question of touch, of relational, patterned, movement.

What I have been saying in these last few pages has two aspects: from the one, I have been laying down the sense in which I mean to use the words "know" and "knowledge". And in so doing I have had to relate it to other words, such as recall, memory, statement. But it could just as plausibly be said that I have been giving a phenomenological account of thinking and speaking. If the latter is taken as my purpose, then what I have said belongs to psychology; if the former, I have, according to the late J. L. Austin, been 'legislating', choosing the language I propose to use. In other words, I have been adopting some technical terms, some conventions. Neither of these processes is properly speaking philosophical; but philo-

[1] *The Concept of Mind*, ch. 2.

sophical inquiry cannot dispense with this kind of preliminary unless it is content to lose itself in a maze of criss-crossing usages. Whether we say we are theorising about facts or adopting conventions of language is a matter of preference: for if a word is not given a meaning there is no point in using it, and if the meaning is not actual in the sense of being capable of being indicated, then we would not have a word for it.

2. THE PROBLEM OF METHOD

Austin conceived of philosophy as the general field of man's inquiries, from which the sciences are one by one distinguished, and set up on their own.[1] Mathematical logic is, he thought, the most recent of the sciences to be separated out, and he believed in the possibility of a science of language as the next. Since the terminologies of science are agreed definitions, it seemed to him that philosophers could reach agreement as to the reference of ordinary language with regard to ethical problems. Yet he also fully appreciated that there is an evolutionary movement of language, of the kind which is demonstrated in C. S. Lewis' fascinating *Studies in Words*.

It would be hard to set any limits to philosophy; for it can surely concern itself, directly or indirectly, with any kind of knowledge, and where phenomena have not been brought under any system of explanation, philosophy can ask why. It has thus to look at the phenomena with a view to deciding what kind of system they should fall under. Assertions suitable for philosophical investigation represent their objects, they do not present them, or point to them: and it is on account of this requirement that philosophers say that their investigations do not increase factual knowledge, that they are clarificatory. And, as remarked above, Wittgenstein made his somewhat ill-fated statement that philosophy leaves the world as it is. What we have already said about the use of "knowledge" and of "recall" and "memory" is consistent with these views: for if we are given a description either of what has been or what may be seen, or remembered, we cannot question its accuracy. We can question its consistency, and raise doubts about its limits, but to apply any practical test we would have to compare it with

[1] 'Ifs and Cans', in *Proc. Brit. Academy* (1956).

another account, another description purporting to deal with
the same facts. These accounts could differ in respect of the
classificatory systems they applied, but once a practical problem has been raised, philosophy can only say what science
should try to solve it; for science deals with the world of fact,
and solutions are sought in fact. Philosophy cannot offer
solutions, but by elucidation of the problem, philosophy can
indicate where solutions might be found.

If philosophy is to investigate 'responsibility', it must
accordingly have some statements about responsibility as subject-matter. So far we have only one statement that appears to
be a statement about responsibility, and that is the assertion
that responsibility is a principle upon which ethics relies, that
if we cannot speak meaningfully of responsibility then we also
cannot speak of morality. But if we look again at this assertion,
we see that it is in fact not about responsibility at all, but about
morality, and about morality as a phenomenon. Again, we
must not assume that to make a moral judgment, as most of us
do, presupposes that he who makes it or he to whom it is
applied is responsible for his actions; for to say that he is would
not be to assert an analytic relation between morality and
responsibility, but to conceal the significance of the word
"moral" by placing it on either side of an equation, viz: A is
morally judged (or judging) $= A$ is morally responsible. Here
we merely assert an analytic relation between responsibility and
judgment, where judgment is not necessarily confined to the
field of morals. Even so the relation is one of theory only: for
since the assumption 'that S is a moral judgment' is one that
we cannot make in practice, being beyond our terms of reference, our given, we can hardly go on to argue that because we
have an instance of morality, we also have an instance of
responsibility; or that, having an instance of judgment, again
we can suppose responsibility in some sense, for 'judgment'
with or without the 'moral' quality, is merely an assertion of
fact or of opinion. It can be taken as evident, by the most
cursory glance over society, that there is no necessary connection between utterances, as opinions, and responsibility.
When we speak of responsibility we do not just mean that a
man can talk. Whatever method we find to guide our investigation, we must insist upon one which does not assume precisely what we set out to establish. Method, however, we must

have, and we will review in turn the ways in which we could attempt to find statements about responsibility.

A. Collecting utterances

This we have already eliminated in chapter 1, as it was so obvious a method that we resorted to it at once. The method is inductive, and we found the utterances would divide into two groups: (a) those in everyday conversations, and (b) those in recorded decisions, codes of law, contracts, and so on. To attempt any comprehensive survey of all of these would be out of the question, and philosophy cannot escape the practical difficulties by high-handed talk about 'what could be found'. For no science could be based upon a supposal that its basic postulates might or could be found—as instance the difficulties semantics now finds itself in. However, a most interesting survey of utterances, taken as typical instances, has been attempted by N. Haines in *The Concept of Responsibility and the Theory of Democracy*.[1] He has classified the instances according to their contexts, or situations, and to some extent also by syncategorematics. Then he has analysed these groups into the factors immediately related with the use of "responsibility". But his analysis is governed by an ideological bias in political theory: that the role of the individual is being or should be increasingly recognised. Thus the whole inquiry is discursive rather than objective, and the account of responsibility appears as if designed to support certain supposed sociological trends. On account of this, there cannot be said to be any necessary connection between the evidence and the final result. To search for a definition is inevitably to presuppose some kind of definition with reference to which the data is selected. But this work can be recommended with confidence to those who accept the validity of what Austin said he would like to call 'linguistic phenomenology' if it were not 'rather a mouthful'.[2]

B. The Paradigm Case

How are we to start, what are we to look for, in our attempt to find sentences or statements about 'responsibility'? 'A word has

[1] Thesis for the degree of Ph.D., University of London (1958).
[2] 'A Plea for Excuses', in *Proc. Ar. Soc.* (1956–7).

the meaning someone has given to it', wrote Wittgenstein,[1] and pointed out that while some words have clearly defined meanings which can easily be tabulated, others are used 'in a thousand different ways which gradually merge into one another'. Even if we had instances of the uses of "responsibility", what should we do with them? Could we take the context of the utterances, and try to locate the empirical grounds of responsibility? There are two serious objections to such a procedure. (i) It would fall within psychology, and we would have to use the techniques of the empirical sciences, which would prejudice the emergence of a principle, and (ii) when we had acquainted ourselves with the data upon which the responsibility relied, we should still have particular instances, and could not assume that what we found in these would apply in other situations. For if an instance is universalised by including enough details to enable the description to be applied to another instance, it is unlikely that such another instance will be found; while, on the other hand, if those details only are included which will permit of the finding of similar instances, then the similarity is not sufficiently precise. The same argument applies when several particular instances are taken. This twofold difficulty defeats the Paradigm Case argument, as, for example, it is given by Flew to demonstrate the expression "of his own free will".[2] Any necessity there is in such an account comes from the adoption of the instance as a paradigm: that is, it is a matter of convention, and, as such, may be challenged by the simple device of following another convention.

C. Austin's proposed method

Since if we talk about words, we have to do so in sentences, we should consider applying the method advocated by Austin for dealing with excuses.[3] This article is perhaps the most comprehensive statement available of the possibilities that lie in approaching the practical situation through, or by means of, words. That we are to approach it, and not content ourselves with verbal forms, is made clear: 'When we examine what we should say when, what words we should use in what situations,

---

[1] *Blue Book* (edn. of 1958), p. 28.
[2] A. Flew, 'Philosophy and Language', in *Essays in Conceptual Analysis*.
[3] 'A Plea for Excuses', in *Proc. Ar. Soc.* (1956-57).

we are looking again not *merely* at words (or "meanings",
whatever they may be) but also at the realities we use the
words to talk about: we are using a sharpened awareness of
words to sharpen our perception of, though not as the final
arbiter of, the phenomena'. For the study of excuses, Austin
suggests three source-books: the dictionary, legal cases, and
psychology. In addition, he reminds us we need imagination.
From the dictionary we are to narrow down the field of inter-
related words, from law we are to take our practical situation,
and through the observations of psychologists we are to widen
our view of the issues involved in any consideration of human
conduct—for example, by comparison with that of animals.
The presence of the concrete situation, the words, and the
comprehension and classification of behaviour lead to recognition of the source of confusion and muddle in moral discourse:
the concept of action. Austin appears to have believed that
some order could be introduced here, that we could relinquish
the easy, slipshod, loose use of "action" for every phase and
aspect of behaviour, and reduce actions to what they in fact are.[1]
He does not specifically lay down that we *could* find concrete
concepts of action, but the approximation he advocates of word
or descriptive expression to 'stretches' of action, the careful
distinction of model and reality, gives sense to a supposal that
we could adopt, in ethics, those names for actions that are on
the level of ostensive definition.

It appears from Austin's article that he found, presumably in
his practical experience, that a number of persons discussing a
real situation, even if only a recorded legal process, will, as
their knowledge of the facts widens and becomes more detailed, tend to make use of the same descriptive and explanatory
expressions. If they do not, the difference may lie in a conceptual disparity rather than in a different perception and
assessment of the facts. That is, what A calls or subsumes to X,
B will call or subsume to Y, or to XY. Such differences can be
argued out. But it seems plain that this method of Austin's
would have to be followed by everyone if it were to yield any
permanent fruit: for surely what he really wanted to do was to

---

[1] It should be noted here that Kant's account of the application of the
Categorical Imperative makes no sense unless a real action is envisaged in an
actual situation by a real agent. The action, as an action, could be non-moral. See
H. J. Paton, *The Categorical Imperative:* e.g. VI. 5, VII. 3–5, VIII. 7–8.

establish concepts, to order the application of words. He does admit to the aim of defining as many words as possible, but in effect the results of this method would be not so much to lay down definitions for all to use, as to produce conceptual schemes in the minds of those participating, as a tutor has to instil concepts into the minds of students when starting on a new subject, before he can talk about the subject at all. Thus Austin's method appears pedagogic in character, rather than experimental.

There are two very striking suggestions in Austin's proposals for investigating excuses. (i) The consideration of legal cases, of which he has given a detailed example in his article, leads us to ask why we should not consider the moral rather than the legal situation. To my mind there is no doubt but that the great moral thinkers of the past always kept their eyes upon the situations of their actual experience; they were not content to build some sort of theoretical edifice out of conventional or standardised descriptions. Consequently, if a practical situation—for legal cases are certainly both actual and practical—is needed, why prefer the legal?

(ii) The other constructive suggestion that I want to dwell upon is the production of a set of related words. Austin has given two ways of finding these, the first to start from scratch with the obviously relevant word or words and proceed to follow up all those other words the dictionary uses to explain the original one. The second is arbitrarily to select certain words seen to be closely related, and follow these up in the dictionary. The net results will be the same, a number of words all concerned with the same subject, linked in their ability to express a certain kind of idea, in this case that of excusing oneself, or escaping liability. But what do we do with this set of words when we have it? I intend to leave this question for a later section, and meanwhile to try out another method of obtaining the words that are found to be associated with "responsibility".

D. A method of verbal substitution

In method *A* we found we have no means of recognising instances of responsibility unless we begin with some sort of definition, and this has to be ruled out because it is to be our end, not our beginning. On the other hand, when we tried method *B*, we had instances but no way of deriving from them criteria for finding others. We have thus a failure to co-ordinate theory and fact. Now if we assume that in a natural language we can usually find alternative expressions for the same sense, we might be able to compromise between theory and fact by taking various uses of the word "responsibility" and, with some regard for the supposed context, by trying to express the same sense without using that particular word.

Let us take fifty sentences in which the word "responsibility" occurs, each sentence referring to a different state of affairs. We can make use of Roget's *Thesaurus* to widen the uses of "responsibility" that we cover. We can now go through the sentences one by one, re-writing them to express the same sense, but without using the word "responsibility". When we have finished this task, we have a large variety of substitute expressions for "responsibility".

There is inevitably much overlapping in the substitute expressions, and we have to find a way of classifying them. The method I have used on the fifty sentences in the Appendix to this chapter is as follows. In sentence 1 the substitute expression is "answerable", or "accountable", and I marked it 'A'. The second seems to indicate a trait of character, and also some effort which is not restricted to prescribed duties or functions. I have marked it 'C' for character, and also 'P' for a positive use of responsibility. Sentence 3 is again answerability, 4 and 5 deal with character, while 6 seems to indicate actual duties, and I have marked it 'D'. Sentence 7 suggests risk-taking, and is marked 'R'. Number 8 is an instance of both answerability and risk-taking, and 9 can be similarly marked, with a third element of positive or subjective responsibility. With 10 we come to a promise, or some kind of undertaking, and, as 'P' is used for positive responsibility, I have marked it 'U'. Number 11 is plainly only concerned with agency, and we should not assume that answerability is implied. I have marked it 'Agency', and we find that in 15 we have another instance of agency, but this time with the notion of accountability. Sentences 12, 13 and 14 are all concerned with ability, sense, being capable and reliable, and are marked 'S'. Thus we can proceed through the fifty. Probably the set of sentences would be interpreted differently by others, and I have accordingly left a space for readers to mark it for themselves if they wish.

The result of the classification is:

Answerability or accountability, which includes agency	15
Positive uses of "responsibility"	13
Descriptions of character	8
Fulfilment of duties	7
Risk-taking	7
Undertakings, or promises	3
Sense, as ability, reliability, etc.	12
Agency without accountability	1
	—
Total number of markings	66

In addition, there are the sentences that received more than one classification. Their markings are included in the general list, but here are the details:

AR	3	SD	1
ARP	1	PD	2
AP	2	PC	1
AS	1	PR	1
RC	1	UD	1

As a result of this experiment, which must be looked at critically below, we have a cluster of concepts, rather than the cluster of words Austin would have gleaned by using the dictionary. But since "responsibility" is a word with several meanings, we are more interested in a cluster, or constellation, of those meanings, than in a number of words which would, if brought under the category-word "responsibility", only be there in virtue of a common meaning. If, that is, we found words like "duty", "initiative", "reliability", "answerability" to be closely related to "responsibility", we would not know how to set about determining that relationship, to eliminate overlapping, for instance, between "answerability" and "duty". For though all these words could be used as stand-ins for "responsibility" they could also be used in instances when it was not correct to speak of responsibility. And we would not be able to differentiate between such cases except with the help of a definition of responsibility which we have not yet obtained, and which, if we had obtained it, would leave no room for this inquiry.

If we look briefly at our list of concepts, we see at once that there is an objective element, that of accountability, of being responsible to someone for something, and that of agency which is implicit in every instance. Responsibility is being responsible for what one does, it is not a latent state. But there is also the subjective side of it, for what is done by the agent is, when he is said to be responsible, describable as risky, foolish, competent, and so on. Responsibility then, as represented by our cluster of concepts, would involve a descriptive account of a man's agency, his actions, and the applicability to him of the concepts of risk-taking, fulfilling duties, as such, exerting personal influence in virtue of his character, making, and understanding his making of, promises. Thus to discern instances of responsibility, we should need an empirical account of action and of a man's personality in order to be able to decide that we could correctly call him responsible. And these we are not going to derive from a set of concepts. For concepts are the way we apply or use words, of themselves they are nothing.

However, we can note certain weaknesses in our method, and then consider whether our set of concepts and the set of words that Austin's method would supply can be made use of in some way. If we find we cannot justify the method, we can at least try to determine why it has failed.

(i) One strong objection to this method of substituting words as exemplified here is that all the sentences originated in one brain. Even Roget's help was accepted by the same brain that provided the rest of the instances. Also the first set of sentences as well as the second, substituted set owed their formulation to the prompting of the same conceptual scheme. It might be said in defence of the enterprise that no linguistic analysis can escape from the linguistic larder of the analyst, but I fear that this defence only casts doubts upon linguistic analysis in general. In using the dictionary, Austin committed himself to the terminological implications stored there, and would have to make use of his own mental machinery and experience in the ordering of it.

(ii) Fifty sentences, it can be objected, and admitted, are a mere drop in the ocean of usage. What means have we of assuring that they are representative in any way of the full uses of "responsibility"? All we can say about this is that fifty sentences are better than forty for our purpose, and forty than thirty. And nothing prevents us from looking again at ordinary usage as we proceed to investigate the results of our small selection.

(iii) The third objection is the most formidable. For when we speak of a 'cluster' of concepts revolving around and within that of 'responsibility', we have no hope of plotting their orbits. We have seen that the uses overlap: *how* they overlap could hardly be determined. How much, if anything, of them is essential to 'responsibility'? Such a question cannot sensibly be asked unless we adopt the naive view that one word has one sense, and this is not what we know of language. That we have so many applications of 'responsibility' that contain more than one of the concepts might indicate that responsibility results from what C. A. Mace has called 'alternative conjunctions',[1] But since we have no way of showing that the classification by which we obtained our concepts is sound, we could not even assume those concepts to be distinct with regard to responsibility. For instance, it could be argued that the class of duties fell within that of accountability; and anyone who holds that the maxim 'Promises should be kept' is self-evident would include category 'U' within both 'A' and 'D'.

Would Austin's cluster of words escape this final objection? He pointed out that no group of terms could be expected to fall into some neatly delineated scheme of reference and meaning; and since we must use words in any conceptual discussion, it may be that the same sort of difficulties must occur whether words or concepts are taken as the starting point. Austin expressly mentioned differences in conceptual systems as a source of confusion in communication. That words overlap is plain, and follows from the richness of a natural language, especially one which, like English, has at least three sources. Where two or more words are suitable expressions for something we want to say, we may first satisfy ourselves that they are equally suitable, then make a choice on a point of style— the balance of the words in a sentence, or the sound of the word, its emphasis, etc. That words overlap does not imply that concepts do, or indeed that they could do. In translating sentences from one language into another—and certainly in translating into languages such as Greek which have different grammatical changes from our own—the words seem to cover different associations of ideas, of sense. A word may be the only one we can use in our translation, yet it may have some element

---

[1] 'Causal Laws in Psychology', *Ar. Soc. Suppl. Vol.* (1949). He is speaking of Sir Cyril Burt's findings on the causes of juvenile delinquency.

of meaning that we do not wish to include. Or it may mean something that we would have to say in several words, and here we would have to suppose, not a cohesion of concepts, but a failure to distinguish them. Most of us tend to regard concepts as somehow distinct, and as units of sense they would of course be distinct by definition. Further credence is given to this last point by the researches of Professor C. E. Osgood, which so far seem to indicate that similar concepts are acquired by persons regardless of country and language, although of course the similarity is in respect of their formal limits: given that the conditions of acquiring certain concepts are there, they will be acquired as similar concepts.

(iv) There is another fundamental difficulty about making use of a method such as the one advocated by Austin in order to investigate responsibility, and it is important to see it for what it is. If we should make use of any of the recommendations we have considered in this chapter—for instance, an inquiry into the moral as distinct from the legal situation—we must bear this difficulty in mind, as a precaution against deceiving ourselves into believing we are achieving any genuine results. This difficulty is that, with regard to responsibility, the method of inquiry would give us no point of contact between a set of words or ideas and the actual world. Austin was very well aware of the danger of talking round a subject without getting to grips with it. He said that ethics might get off to a fresh start *if* we examined the uses of the expression 'doing an action' by studying the ways in which actions may fail to be done. This, he thought, could throw light on the more precise and proper uses of "the" action, "an" action, etc. It is hard to say whether Austin believed that ethical terminology could be made sufficiently precise to claim to be 'ostensively' defined, and to refer. Yet, even if Austin's hopes were realised, it would not help us with responsibility, which falls outside ethics. The use of action names must either beg the question of responsibility by assuming that "action" means the same as "free-action", or it must leave the question of freedom completely aside. By whatever method of inquiry we proceeded we would, in producing a cluster of words or of concepts, be producing merely one more deliberately organised, theoretical account of a general term, of whose reference we were never sure. And this is precisely what the traditional metaphysicans did, and did very well, and is accordingly precisely what they are now condemned as mere speculators in ideas for having done.

We may take any set of concepts and apply them to a concrete situation, but that application remains arbitrary: there is no guarantee that in any recognisable feature it corresponds to actuality, to any existence. Or we may have the words that should describe a matter of fact, and yet in our use of them we have somehow to avoid misleading ourselves about that matter of fact. We must not make distinctions in the world of things because we have words which seem to indicate such distinctions. Our dilemma is this: we cannot make any progress in a linguistic inquiry without bringing in the world of things; and we cannot find a terminological definition (as distinct from an ostensive one) without producing a group of concepts of which the agreed inter-relations may be misleading in practice. To put forward a system or scheme of concepts with doubtful relevance to actuality is to drop the 'curtain of words' before the 'fairest tree of knowledge', to use Berkeley's expressions,[1] and this curtain he believed to be woven of abstract ideas and what would now be called emotive meaning. That some schemes seem more appropriate than others is of no philosophical, that is methodological, importance: they are all open to the same logical objection, and the newer practices are all the more dangerous in that they purport to avoid the pitfalls of the older, and yet re-introduce them in a more subtle way. Our problem is to find an account of responsibility which will enable us to locate instances. It is not enough to reach a formula to be applied by a psychologist. H. J. Eysenck, in *Dimensions of Personality*, has shown how a scale of neurosis might be used to excuse responsibility, but to make it excusable in this way only presupposes it. Also to prove that psychological criteria of this sort are applicable to such a problem would fall outside psychology. What Eysenck purports to excuse may be culpability, and we do not know that there is a necessary connection between culpability and responsibility; for they may have a different logic. We must beware of assuming that only those concepts apply to responsibility which would in effect make the concept of responsibility a formal concept, a construct, a sociological fiction.

---

[1] *Human Knowledge*, introduction, 24, paras. 19–20.

E. *The criticism of existing theories*

We have found that from a set of words or concepts, relevant though they may be, we cannot establish their relations in such a way as to form a theory. But we have still to find statements about responsibility. And we want statements that occur in practical situations. We could, indeed, take some such statements from a well-known theorist, and proceed to analyse them. But here we have to decide what shall count as a statement. And in order to be sure that the sentences we selected really said what we took them to say would involve a thorough examination of their author's use of words. What we would in fact find ourselves doing would be a trial and error perusal of philosophical systems to see if we could find one which seemed to suit our purpose and meet our criteria, once we had decided on these. We should not be particularly pleased to be caught engaged on such a project if Spinoza or Hegel were to call unexpectedly upon us. It would merely be a logical exercise, occurring within the confines of our own knowledge and ability, of a meditative rather than a scientific kind.

Yet we might throw some light upon our problem if we took a comprehensive, or allegedly comprehensive, account and criticised it from the point of view of its applicability to the facts as we know them. If a theory is properly constructed, we should expect it to allow for all contingencies. And surely, so far as the contingencies are concerned, we have them all before us: for what is more familiar than our daily problems and our deliberations as to what we should do. If a theory—that of Bradley in *Ethical Studies* springs first to mind—of responsibility is complete, it should lead us to the relevant facts; and if it is not, then, by its omissions we should be able to find the missing facts. But what if there are no facts which are relevant to responsibility; suppose it is a name for a relation, or suppose it to be an ideal? What, in any case, *do* we mean by fact? For, if we are not sure, we can hardly make fact the basis of any criticism.

3. AN AMBIGUITY IN THE PERCEPTION OF FACT

We have said that philosophy does not consider the facts but accounts of those facts. Philosophy must, however, consider the relation of the accounts to the facts in order to determine what kind of account is presented. And such a consideration might lead to another way of providing an account. It is possible that the difficulty of finding statements about responsibility stems, not from the lack of criteria of selection, but from the absence of facts about which such statements could be made. There may be no facts to describe, none to provide the grounds of theory. To say that a man is responsible for doing X may merely mean that A and B have decided to praise or blame him for doing X. The facts relevant to this instance of responsibility are facts about A and B and not about the man who did X, except as the-man-who-did-X. Responsibility would then consist in its ascription. Human nature being as it is, anyone with a fair experience of the world would recoil from an account of responsibility as mere ascription by decision in this way: for what easier than to make a decision to hold someone responsible for what he has not done, provided he is not in a position to prove his innocence? By such an account, he would then not only be held responsible, but, if ascription is *all* that responsibility *is*, he *is* responsible for X. We might even extend this to say that, *if* a man is held responsible for an act, and he is praised or blamed for it, then that in itself means that he *was* actually the agent. This is not the kind of account we wish to have.

But we should pay attention to the use of language here: for to say a man is responsible for an act X does not indicate whether he is causally concerned in X, whether he has been observed to perform the act X, or whether it has been decided on circumstantial evidence that he must have done X. A 'statement' that he was responsible for X could be accepted by three different people in three different senses. Some would accept it on the third interpretation for the psychological reason that they liked to think they had the power to make the world conform to whatever pattern they thought it should have. It is a matter of common observation that many people continue to protest their innocence of an accusation after it has become clear to everyone concerned that they are in fact guilty, and the motive for this persistence is probably to persuade themselves they are not in fact guilty. Refusal to accept the obvious is by no means a rarity in daily life; and that speech-acts have far-reaching, and one might almost say immortal, effects is a matter of conviction with many people.

'Liberty of conscience' clauses, and the like, in constitutions, and the remarkable lengths to which men will go to withhold consent, or to maintain their beliefs, is strong evidence on this point.

Have we then no access to facts in respect of responsibility? Can we ask what facts might be relevant? Or are we, in these practical matters, to accept its application as being at the mercy of personal decision, or public decision, with all the attendant dangers, with but the thin guard of precedent against abuse and injustice?

If philosophy is to admit appeals to fact, it must regard fact as the ultimately knowable and yet permit the restriction of the factual to that which is so far perceived and rationalised. In the first of these two uses, fact is the correlate of true propositions, that which makes a statement true or false; while in the second, it provides the meaning and reference of our discourse. In the first we should, to be strictly correct, only speak of 'fact'; in the second we may describe, reason about, argue from 'the facts'. In distinguishing in this way between 'fact' and 'the facts', I am not recapitulating Bradley's notions of 'reality' and 'appearance': what I am trying to do is to express in some simple way the difference between what could logically be completely known and what we do know, between what could be perceived and what is or has been perceived, between the contingent in principle and what we are satisfied is the case. For when we appeal to facts, we appeal to what can be found to be the case if we look, we are in some situation to which certain facts are relevant; but there are, even in such situations, certain matters of fact that cannot be ascertained, merely because nobody paid attention to them, or because physical changes occurred which were not observed or understood, but which may have had important results in altering the nature or effects of someone's action. When we come across such matters of fact, we can use disjunctive sentences, and say that 'this' or 'that' is or is not true. Thus we fill the gaps in our knowledge.

What we are doing here is to say that statements of fact are statements that can be true or false. We do not say they can be verified, but that we should be able to give the conditions of their verification, we should know what would count as evidence, if it were available. Sentences or statements for which we can do this we call contingent. But in accordance with this we must be careful how we use 'fact'. That Richard III either did or did not murder the princes in the Tower is a fact, but 'Richard murdering the princes' is speculation about facts, it is theory. 'Richard III murdered the princes' is not a statement of fact, it is conjecture. 'That Richard III either did or did not murder the princes in the Tower' is, however, necessarily true on these grounds: statements of fact or sentences about facts are statements that can be true or false; if a statement is a statement of fact it is necessarily true that it is true or false; 'that Richard III either did or did not murder the princes in the Tower' is a statement of fact, therefore it is necessarily true. But that 'Richard III murdered the princes' is not a statement *of fact*.

Practical philosophy is concerned—one might say in its practical aspect exclusively concerned—with this distinction. Distinctions between matters of fact as such and opinions about matters of fact are not only the essentials of clear thinking, but the necessary conditions of wise acting. In a universe where, so far as is known, the only constant feature in the physical world is the speed of light, and the attempts that have been made to measure variations in personal achievement also yield a constant,[1] we have to accept that fact is in some way formally relative to our powers of observation. We have no evidence to support a view that if we discount the conditions of perceiving from what we do perceive we should have anything left at all.

However, what has happened, what has been, is, or will be a matter of fact, must, we believe, be the basis of true statements. We must give a sense to "change". On a principle (not the theory) of evolution, what now is would not be as it is if what had been had not been as it was. Thus the world would not now be knowable as it is if the statement that Richard III murdered the princes in the Tower were not in fact either true or false. Without becoming involved in the terminology of absolutes, of ultimate reality, of objective truth, etc. we can at least agree that we often give an account of the facts that later proves to have been inaccurate.

These considerations are certainly the concern of philosophy; for if philosophy does not offer or provide information beyond

[1] S. J. F. Philpott, Presidential Address, British Psychological Society, 1950. In *Quarterly Bulletin*, B. P. S., Jan. 1950, pp. 264-80.

what is presented to it for critical examination, it must surely give reasons for regarding some statements about facts or of fact as more reliable than others, and it can hardly give those reasons without reference to the nature of fact. The theoretical criteria of truth which philosophy, as normative, lays down, are not necessarily either applicable or significant for practical philosophy.

We should look more carefully into the use of "fact" through a substitute expression. Let us say that 'fact' is 'what is the case'. This expression is two-sided: it refers to whatever is the case, and it points in this reference to an account which is beyond further question, to 'what really happened'. And what exactly *is* the case? Is it the case that, for example, George was late home for tea, or that he had intended to buy Susan a birthday present and forgot? Or is it the case that George did not know tea was to be earlier, so that he perhaps could not be said to be "late"? Or that he thought of buying Susan a birthday present, but changed his mind? In a case of dispute we say: 'Look at the facts'; but what do we take as fact and how should we look at it?

It could be said that George knows the facts. But does he? How could we decide whether as a rule people retain some kind of unchangeable picture of what happened, some indestructible record, or whether their verbal formulations, their thoughts, their accounts, their justifications, and so on, constitute 'the facts'? We cannot be sure that an account of events does not become 'the events' in memory and in purpose. Decisions about what to say may become decisions as to 'the facts'. They may be the brush strokes with which a man paints his self-portrait, the record of his experience. To one person, what is the case may be the panorama over which he can look again and again, revising his account if he wishes; to another, the immediate interpretation of, the significance of, what occurs *is* the panorama. In the former case, a man distinguishes himself from what he sees, or perceives, though he may perceive himself objectively as well; in the second he does not, he is what he sees, and any questioning by others of what he says he sees appears to him as an attack upon himself and his good faith.

In both cases, the sense of "what is the case" remains the same, but the reference does not: for in the first mode of perception 'the facts' are static, external, an objective part of the world, while in the second 'the facts' already contain some rudimentary judgment, some interpretation in terms of convention. To be able to see 'the facts' as distinct from any account of them is to retain them pictorially, as imagery, rather than verbally, and is to admit that experience falls outside and beyond the expression we are able to give to it. When some philosophers try to allow for this discrepancy by speaking of 'reality' and 'ultimate truth' they may be told by others that they are misusing language; yet it might be more correct to say that, so far from misusing language, they find language inadequate, and this inadequacy gives rise to the adaptation of verbal symbols to meet it which is the evolutionary surge by which a natural language develops. On the other hand, it is certainly improper to condemn theories which take their origin in the second mode of perception as subjective, on the ground that men perceiving in this way describe phenomena and establish values in terms of their personal experience, failing to distinguish between feeling and the forms they use as expressions. For those very forms are social rather than personal, and the phenomena described through them have the same claim to objectivity as those issuing from an inner experience where there is always a margin of incommunicability. Philosophers have no divine right to judge the one mode as proper and the other as unworthy. The main import for philosophy is that the one kind of perception admits of doubts and revisions, whereas the other does not: nothing is so absolute as the incontrovertibly relative.

There is, then, some justification for two definitions of 'fact', the one giving it as distinct from any account, the other as account. The former involves defining fact as that which makes statements true or false, the latter requires to define fact as the correlate of true statements. In the first, 'fact' is assumed to be prior to an account, to the statement; in the second, the 'true statement' is an assumption. Between them, these two definitions mark the ambiguity of 'what is the case'. If we say that George really intended to buy a birthday present for Susan, then we shall have to say that it was a fact that George had intended to buy a birthday present for Susan. But if we say, on the second account, that 'George was late' is true, then we are also saying it was a fact, or it is a fact, that George was late. It is interesting to note that Tarski's theory of truth, which would require saying 'The sentence "George was late" is true if and only if George was late',[1] appears to compromise; but, against the background of the ambiguity pointed out here, it must be admitted that it does not so much as touch the problem it purports to solve.

If philosophy is held to be necessarily normative, it escapes the ambiguity in 'what is the case' by postulating that there *might* be, if contingently possible, a true version of what is the case, and that this is what we mean when we speak of true statements of fact. It then defines a proposition as what might be true or false, since it is what we think or say about facts. But if we allow that philosophy may be only contingently normative, that it can criticise from a viewpoint of present knowledge and technique, as well as from a sophisticated viewpoint of what would constitute perfect knowledge, this circular dependence of truth and fact is unsatisfactory. It looks like linguistic convention, a way of making an assumption without which philosophy cannot proceed. If we admit this account, we would, in investigating statements about responsibility, be building our inquiry upon a presumption of the status of 'fact'. If we believe responsibility is itself the basis for an ethical life, we make the same assumption about our ethical discussions. For to accept facts as appearances of a 'real' and unattainable subject of our judgments, as for example, Bradley did, is to accept them as supposed correlates of the judgment. The alternative is to accept the statements and the concepts they yield as real, which is what Plato did, and which many rationalists do, although they might not be willing to admit it. But for myself, I am not content to let the matter rest.

A consequence of the ambiguity in the perception of fact is to throw doubts upon the possibility of a verification principle. For we can conceive of, say, five hundred observers agreeing about 'the facts' as distinct from any one account of them, and another five hundred merely attempting to co-ordinate their several accounts. It might be said that such an attempt is fairly certain to be accurate, but 'fairly certain' is not 'logically certain'. It could be said that the first group discuss the facts, while the second discuss accounts of facts. In practice, it would not be necessary for the second group to have any direct or

---

[1] 'The Semantic Conception of Truth', in *Readings in Philosophical Analysis*, ed. Feigl and Sellars.

renewed experience of the facts, and they could even pass on their accounts to someone else for purposes of sorting out. The first inquiry would then be an empirical inquiry while the second would not. The first would be an attempt to reach a consistent and agreed account, but the second would be an attempt to find a common denominator. The first inquiry would end with a decision about the facts, and the second might appear to do so, except that it could be said that the whole inquiry is second-order, so that the facts are never in question. Linguistically, the distinction is so sharp that it evades, in the conventions of ordinary language, detection in our everyday discourse; but it is there, and it is probably to blame for many bitter arguments and feuds not only in philosophy but also in every sphere of social life: for members of the one group tend to regard the members of the other as obstinate and prejudiced, and *vice versa*. To speak vaguely of a principle of verification as the possibility of testing correspondence between statement and fact is to override the ambiguities of perception, and in that overriding dwells an unseen barrier between philosophy and truth.

If the verification principle, in any form it takes, can be said to rest upon a decision as to the facts, rather than upon facts themselves, there is no need to limit the application of the verification principle to material object sentences. For it is just as applicable to the pronouncements of opinion as it is to the properties of tangible objects. We could not with consistency deny a statement to the effect that an opinion is a tangible, or visible, or audible, property of a person and accept a statement that blue is a tangible property of the sky. A man's statement that he feels himself to be responsible for what he does must then become a statement about a tangible property.

The doubts raised about 'fact' here are of great importance. For, although we are not now concerned with the status of ethical concepts, we cannot but observe that, if 'fact' is a somewhat evanescent notion, we can hardly deny meaning to ethical terms on the ground that they do not refer to fact. If we do not know what we mean by "fact" then the use becomes innocuous, futile. Nor could we deny meaning to "responsibility" on the ground that it did not refer to concrete fact. Again, if we cannot be sure of facts, neither can we admit any claim of empirical science to explain human conduct without reference to responsibility and morality. These are perhaps negative considerations, but they are strong and demand some answer. That there is a general recognition of these kinds of difficulty with regard to fact and verification is shown by the many attempts which have been made to establish the relations of fact and statement as conditions of truth. To some of these we should now turn. For we have yet to discover what we are to accept as a statement if we are to obtain statements about responsibility.

APPENDIX TO CHAPTER II

The following sentences, 1—50, were all written before any substitutions were made. Then the substituted sentences, 1a—50a, were written as far as possible on an objective interpretation of the originals. In some cases, where the meaning seemed difficult to express shortly, two sentences, or a reply, were used. No attempt was made in the substitution to vary the senses: this was assumed to have occurred in the original fifty.

	Reader's mark	Author's mark
1. He is responsible to *A* for the efficient running of the office.		
1a. He is answerable to *A* for the efficient running of the office.		A
2. He is largely responsible for the pleasant atmosphere here.		
2a. It is mainly due to his influence that the atmosphere is pleasant.		PC
3. Don't let me down: I am responsible for seeing it is done.		
3a. Don't let me down: I am accountable to someone for seeing it is done.		A
4. Some responsible person? One who can be relied upon.		
4a. Someone who can be relied upon to be honest and fulfil his duties.		C
5. He has patches of irresponsibility.		
5a. Sometimes he is foolish and unpredictable.		C
6. I am going to cut down my responsibilities.		
6a. I am going to contract out of some of my duties.		D
7. It is too great a responsibility to shoulder.		
7a. It is too exacting and risky a burden.		R
8. Do that: I will take the responsibility for it.		
8a. Do that: I will be answerable, and take the risk.		AR
9. He did it on his own responsibility.		
9a. He did it on his own initiative, he was prepared to take the risk of having to account for it.		ARP
10. Who will be responsible for this?		
10a. Who will undertake to do this?		U
11. Who is responsible for this?		
11a. Who has done this?		Agency
12. Give it to his younger brother: he is more responsible.		
12a. He has more sense, is more reliable.		S
13. He is afraid of responsibility.		
13a. He is afraid he will not come up to scratch.		S

Reader's mark Author's mark

14. He will soon get confidence if you gradually give him responsibility.

14a. He will find out he can be relied upon.   S

15. Wait till I find out who was responsible!

15a. Wait till I find out who did it, whose fault it is!   A

16. On whose responsibility did you do that?

16a. On whose authority did you do that? Your own?   A

17. All right, but I take no responsibility for the outcome.

17a. I will not be praised or blamed for what happens.   AR

18. He can't be expected to see to everything. Someone else should share the responsibility.

18a. Someone else should undertake certain duties or offices.   DP

19. It's a responsibility he has taken on himself . . .

19a. . . . to provide us with vegetables from the garden. He offered to . . . .   P

20. We asked him whether he would be responsible for them.

20a. He said 'yes'; he promised to provide them.   U

21. Haven't you *any* sense of responsibility?

21a. Can't you be relied upon to do *any*thing? To see to this, to help him, to live up to your position?   P

22. You should have done it: it's your responsibility, not mine.

22a. It's one of your duties.   D

23. I cannot take the responsibility of going against his orders.

23a. I could not take such a risk.   PR

24. Don't try to evade your responsibilities.

24a. Don't try to get out of your liabilities. You know you ought to do it.   UD

25. Don't you feel responsible for it?

25a. Doesn't your conscience urge you to do something about it?   P

26. It's your responsibility!

26a. On your head be it!   P

27. His behaviour is my responsibility.

27a. I am bound to answer for him.   A

28. I do not want to take responsibility for him.

28a. I am afraid I shall expose myself to censure.   AR

29. I cannot help feeling responsible. It was my idea.

29a. I couldn't exempt myself from blame if anything went wrong.   A

30. He has far too much responsibility for his age.

30a. He has taken on too many duties; he has to make too many decisions; he cannot be expected to live up to such a position of trust.   SD

31. He has a strong sense of responsibility.

31a. He won't shirk his duties; you can be sure he will do it; he won't try to wriggle out of it; he will do everything expected of him.   C

32. It is too responsible a post for him.

32a. He isn't really able to cope with all that the job involves. It isn't fair to give him such a job: it will wear him out trying to live up to it.   S

33. Such dangerous work is a heavy responsibility.

33a. He is very level-headed, but it gets him down sometimes.   RC

34. They should appoint someone more accustomed to assuming responsibility.

34a. You can't really blame him; he does his best.   S

35. With my indifferent health, I dare not be responsible for a wife and family.

35a. I might not be able to support them.   P

36. He did everything he could to get out of the responsibility.

36a. He tried to put his duties on somebody else.   D

37. You will never pin the responsibility on to him for all the losses: he is far too self-righteous.

37a. He is sure to get himself out of being blamed.   CA

38. You can't get out of your responsibilities to the firm just by not co-operating over this.

38a. The firm will hold you accountable along with the rest of us.   AP

39. I am responsible for his welfare.

39a. I am bound to try and put him on his feet.   PD

40. If you repudiate your responsibility for their conduct, you will be thought quite heartless and very mean.

40a. You should face up to the position properly.   C

41. A. I can take no responsibility for my own incompetence.

41a. B. Your indifference is staggering!   S

42. Don't blame him, he can't help what he does, and he does not understand how others look at it: he's hardly responsible.

42a. He may be legally accountable, but he can't help himself.   S

43. He is not responsible for his actions.

43a. Poor fellow, he does not know what he is doing.   S

44. I will make the decision and see that it suits him; better not to leave the responsibility with him.

44a. He doesn't think things out properly.   S

45. I hold you largely responsible; you should have had more sense.

45a. I think you are partly to blame.   AS

46. I will make him responsible while I am away, then I can be sure things will go smoothly.

46a. I can predict with certainty that he will behave with tact and discretion.   C

47. You will be generally responsible for the selling side.

47a. You will have to use your initiative to build up sales.   PA

Reader's mark   Author's mark

48. I am responsible to no one but God, and to my
conscience.
48*a*. I shall answer for it to God.   A
49. You are a fool to accept responsibility, you knew
nothing about it.
49*a*. But I should have known.   A
50. We all have some responsibility for the less able.
50*a*. We ought to help those less fortunate than our-
selves.   S

Results

A	Answerable	15
P	Positive	13
C	Character	8
D	Duties	7
R	Risk	7
U	Undertaking, promise	3
S	Sense, ability etc.	12
	Mere Agency	1

No. of markings   66

Composite analysis (included in above)

AR	3	SD	1
ARP	1	PC	1
AP	2	PD	2
AS	1	PR	1
RC	1	UD	1

III

THE KIND OF EVIDENCE:
WORDS, OBJECTS AND FACTS

Truth may be said to be attained when we make an utterance which is in accordance with fact, when we assert what is the case. It is a relation between language and fact or, some metaphysicians would prefer to say, it is an aspect of reality. Given the world, and given that men describe it, and talk about it, then, when the descriptions are correct, we have truth, or true statements. If facts are stated correctly and accurately, then the statement of fact is true; if they are not stated correctly or accurately, the statements are false. It follows analytically from this that if we do not know what counts as fact, we also cannot know when a statement is true and when it is false; indeed we may not know when to speak of a statement at all.

However, since we have to discuss these topics in sentences, we are constantly making statements which appear to be successful, in that they enable us to manipulate the world we are in and so deal with our practical problems. Consequently we can approach the question of truth from two angles: (i) How is it possible for us to make statements of fact? What conditions must be observed? (ii) How are we to know when these statements are true and when they are false?

Because we must use words to think and speak, we have to start with words, then turn to the objects they stand for, and thus arrive at some account of fact. We cannot proceed directly to discuss fact, for, as we have seen in the previous chapter, there is a fundamental difficulty in speaking of fact, due to its perception either as a given in sensibility or as a given in verbal expression. Those who are limited to the latter are so because they are unaware of themselves as perceiving, and the processes of sense-perception, the sensory images, occur perhaps below the level of their awareness. Only when their perceptions have reached a verbal form do they reach consciousness, or awareness—in other words, are they noticed. Plainly these differences occur in varying degrees, some people being

aware of both modes of perception as alternatives, some knowing them as stages in the one process of perception, some again
with a power of choice as to what shall be retained as sense
imagery, and what consigned to words. All that concerns us
here is to note that there are such differences, and that they
give rise to different theories of fact and truth.[1]

Of those theories I propose to take four: the account of fact
and its relation to language given respectively by Bradley,
Carnap, Wittgenstein and Austin. I shall take them in this
order, because, although Wittgenstein's earlier theory preceded that of Carnap, Wittgenstein's theory both resembles
and differs from that of Austin, while there are certain features
common to those of Bradley and Carnap. Questions arising
out of the theories may thus the more easily be arranged to
prevent overlapping and reference forward.

I. BRADLEY

Bradley held that since words are general, and are applicable
to kinds of things as names of qualities, relations, etc., no
sentence can express fact, facts being particular, unique. The
wholeness of a particular thing can never be reached by a
description in words; for, words being general, the account
given can logically always be applicable to some other particular thing as well. Accordingly, to speak of judgments of
fact[2] is inaccurate: judgment can only refer indirectly to fact,
and fact cannot be given in the judgment, it cannot be stated.[3]

The word "fact" is used in Bradley's writings to indicate any
kind of thing that we can talk about, and thus that we can
objectify for purposes of talking about it. An idea when it
occurs is a psychological fact in that it occurs—it has duration,

---

[1] In saying that differences in the perceptive processes are partly the source of
differences of theory, I must add that it would be entirely outside our terms of
reference to attempt to locate these. To do so is the task of psychology: what concerns us here is the account of fact, not its dispositional ground.

[2] For Bradley, to make a statement of fact is to perform an act of judgment:
'judgment' may be taken as equivalent to 'statement'. See below, ch. iv, p. 92.

[3] *Principles of Logic*, p, 46. 'But can we reach self-existence and individual
character by manipulating adjectives and putting universals together? If not, the
fact is not given *directly* in any truth whatsoever. It can never be stated categorically.
And yet, because adjectives depend upon substantives, the substantive is implied.
Truth will then refer to fact *indirectly*.'

quality, intensity—but the content of the idea, what it is *as
idea*, is a generalised feature, or generalised features, of other
ideas which have occurred previously as psychical facts.

Perhaps the easiest way to understand why Bradley believed
that description must always fail to present particular facts is to
take his notion of the concrete universal. He held that abstract
generalities, such as 'red', 'shiny', are figments of the imagination, that there could not be such things as redness in abstraction. If the reader will pause and attempt to imagine an
abstraction of this kind, he will find that it tends to particula-
rise itself. Thus Bradley argued that it is only by refusing to
accept any features of these particularisations that we can have
a negative idea of an abstract universal: it is a 'mental creation'.[1] For himself, he posited concrete universals, universals
that only consist in their actual instances. We see, he said, not
whiteness, but a particular whiteness; and, in looking at it, we
see *the same fact* that we see when looking at another instance of
whiteness. We are not seeing two instances of the same thing,
we are seeing the same thing twice, and what we see is the
universal.[2] It is of course conditioned as to size, shape, etc. by
the other qualities or universals present in the particular thing.
In our account of it we can only list all the universals and their
relations by names, we cannot catch them in their specific
character as inherent in one particular thing. We can never get
our account specific enough and thus the particular eludes us.

We might illustrate this point by saying that if a designer
produces a blueprint for the manufacture of an article, there is
no logical limit to the number which could be manufactured
to that specification; for if it was desired to produce unique
objects, he would have to add some different feature to each
article over and above those in the specification. Bradley's
argument is that a description, however detailed, could logically always fit some other object because, since it *is* in general
terms, it cannot also include that which makes the object
unique and so particular. 'Mere analysis of sense', he wrote on
page 61 of the *Logic*, 'could never suggest that limiting relation
which gives it uniqueness'; and again, on page 64: 'The given

[1] *Op. cit.* pp. 119 and 189.

[2] See H. B. Acton, 'The Theory of Concrete Universals', in *Mind* (1936-7).
Also I am greatly indebted to Professor Blanshard's demonstration of this point
during a discussion on 'partial identity' at the Royal Institute of Philosophy,
following C. D. Broad's lecture 'The Philosophy of Bradley' on 28 Nov. 1958.

... is unique, not because it has a certain element, but because it *is given*.'

It can be seen from this account that, since facts never enter as such into our language, it is a matter of indifference what is taken as fact. For we have always to take it as a supposal: *if* this *is* so, if this *is* fact, then it is hard, red, etc. In describing, what we do is to apply a number of descriptive words to a supposed feature of what is—if we could get at it—real. The supposed feature is what we take as fact, and what we say in the judgment, both in the grammatical subject and the grammatical predicate, is an adjectival content that we ascribe to the selected feature. Thus this feature acts as the subject of the whole judgment which is a predication of it. The real subject of the judgment is the actuality of which we speak.

What might truly be said to *be* fact could only be known if the whole of reality were known; and this, by definition, could not be described, because in Bradley's system, the ultimate reality is experience, which transcends description and truth itself. Consequently we must learn to select our facts in such a way that we can bring them into coherent systems of thought. To Bradley, knowledge is always comprehending, never a mere collection of facts. We should beware of allowing a discordant fact to upset any carefully constructed view of the world we may have, for the fact might prove to be illusory, and apparent contradictions in our evidence of reality could be resolved in a wider synthesis.

Bradley's account of judgments of sense presupposes an ultimately real with which we come into contact only in experience, as feeling. This our perceptions are unable to reduce to rational knowledge. In our attempts to obtain knowledge, we take some feature of it, leaving the rest as a background, a 'felt whole'. Of the selected feature we predicate qualities and relations that we perceive as contained in it. Thus the remote particular (because unified) real is the ultimate subject of our judgments, while the selected feature, perceived by our senses, is at best appearance: the way in which the real appears to us. Our judgment being a predication of a feature of the real it cannot in itself contain that feature as fact. What we see and hear, we suppose to be fact, and of this supposal we predicate what we can. Fact itself is concealed behind the supposal.

2. CARNAP

At first sight Carnap's account of fact might seem to be the direct opposite of that of Bradley: for he tries to give meaning to expressions by labelling with a word the simplest forms of sensation and feeling. He thus aims at basing language upon a direct encounter with the given in sense experience, since it is this encounter that provides ostensive definitions of the words we learn to use. Sentences asserting these ostensive definitions might be of the type "Blue, now", "Joy, now", "Here, red". Carnap has tried to give such words as usually describe our experiences a meaning or reference which everyone can recognise, and which can consequently act as a reliable basis for communication. If 'blue' cannot be described, when it occurs as an experience, without demonstration, then at least those who can speak of 'blue' would locate it in the same place on a shade card when given the word "blue"; they would then agree about the nature of their experience. Any deviations from an identity of sense experience would pass unnoticed, covered by the conventional mantle of words. What you call "blue" and what I call "blue" may differ, it is conceivable that they do; but *that* they do is not only beyond proof or demonstration, it is also beyond our ability to question.

But we are not to suppose that Carnap intends these basic sentences or statements to be a matching of language and fact: for the two are different in kind and cannot be compared. The sentences (*Sätze*), called observation or protocol sentences, are not to express the simple sense experiences out of which we build the world we see; they are rather the irreducible elements of knowledge into which our sentences and statements about the world can be analysed.

An object is given to us in sense and we describe it. In our experience of it are all the various kinds of ways in which it is sensed, the way it is given in touch, in sight, in hearing, etc. We cannot distinguish these, but nonetheless they are logically distinguishable as they are different, and because we have different words for the perceptions through different sense organs. Thus when we speak of a material object, the material object is a logical construction out of what is given discretely in sense, and our statements about it are reducible to protocol statements about its component qualities and relations. To be meaningful, to have sense, all sentences must be—formally—reducible to sentences of this type.

If, however, basic or protocol sentences represent ultimate units given in sense, 'fact' and 'what is the case' are in danger not, as with Bradley, of being merely supposed for purposes of talking at all about anything, but of disappearing altogether. If the things we talk about are only real when our sentences about them are correct, and if, by definition, their correctness relies upon a reduction which is in practice impossible, then we may indeed ask what it is we do talk about, if anything.

Words being as it were hooked on to sense experience in this way, it becomes impossible to discuss the nature of the objects we see about us. For if we cannot reduce our sentences to something tangible, we cannot discuss things as if they were tangible. So what we do in order to increase our knowledge is to discuss the language in which we talk about the world. Carnap distinguished between object language, the way one actually speaks in practical situations, and metalanguage, the way one discusses the correctness of, and the construction of, sentences in the object language. Now if it is laid down that an object language must be in the form of sentences reducible to protocol sentences, we are in effect laying down rules for that object language. If we wish to make true statements, or sentences, we must, when we speak, keep the formation rules of the language we are using. Language I, the object language, will accordingly be a system of rules, and it follows that what is said in it will be analysable only within that system of rules. Language II, the metalanguage, which examines the syntax of language I, determines the rules, and can also be used to discuss what kind of words and expressions and sentences are being used in language I. Accordingly, metaphysical questions arising in the object language can be excluded from it if the rules do not allow for them, while the metalanguage disposes of them by transforming them into questions as to whether there should or should not be certain rules. An object language may speak of tables as objects used in certain contexts; but the metalanguage has to decide that "table" is a thing-word, and it does not need to proceed beyond this to ask whether tables, as objects, or things, do really exist. The question of existence is lost in the rule that the word can be used. 'To accept the thing-world',

Carnap wrote in 'Empiricism, Semantics, and Ontology',[1] 'means nothing more than to accept a certain form of language. . . .' We could express it thus: we have to decide *what* we *can* talk about, what entities shall be accepted as 'arguments', as values for the variables in the propositional function. The rules for the discussion of the nature of those entities and hence the correctness of the terms used, will be extra-systematic, falling in language II, and again excluded, if desired, by the adoption of some rule.

According to Carnap and Neurath, all sentences purporting to describe facts could be translated into the language of physics; thus it is possible to unify all the sciences, since they aim at knowledge of the world, by translating the sentences of all of them into those of physics. And to say this is equivalent to saying that their sentences could be reduced to protocol sentences. Fact as we know it does not, we can see, figure at all in Carnap's system. What, then, is his criterion of truth? Or is truth ousted by the notion of correct usage? If I choose my language carefully, make all the rules, then what I say in that language must, necessarily must, be correct; and if words are correctly linked to facts, it must also be true. But what do I say? Why speak at all? For I am creating the world in accordance with my rules for speaking of it, and if I do this, can I be said to be seeking information about or understanding of that world? Carnap waves these questions aside: for him, if I follow the rules, I can only say what has sense, and if I understand what I am saying according to the rules of the language, then I know, and know adequately, what I am talking about.

Is it possible, we may ask, to decide that we can criticise language without looking also at the world? As Bradley said, in discussing 'this', we logically distinguish the 'this' from that which we do not select for discussion, but which is present in experience. What is taken indicates in some way what is not taken. So that if we elect to criticise certain expressions occurring in a material mode of speech, are we not treating that speech as part of the world? As fact? Even in the objectification of the sentences under discussion, we are using another material mode of speech: for who could say that sentences, words, linguistic rules, are not objects, and material ones at that? We are reminded of Bradley's contention that all ideas, when they

[1] *Revue Internationale de Philosophie* (1950); reprinted in *Meaning & Necessity*.

occur, besides being 'sense' and ideal content, are also, *in that* they occur, psychical facts. It seems that when Carnap argued for the 'logical syntax of language', he took language as the fact, given as sense, its existence. To speak of syntax, of formation rules, is merely an alternative to speaking of other facts; that we talk about language and not about tables and other features of the world is a contingent, and not a necessary, condition of philosophical discourse. And it is interesting to note that, on this view, Carnap was right in saying that the language of physics could express its own syntactical rules; for any discussion of the language of physics would make of that language a material object.

Finally, we should note that if we cannot compare statements or sentences with facts, we cannot choose between statements on the ground of their agreement or non-agreement with facts, nor can we use arguments against theories of language which are based on appeals to facts. Carnap's choice of the language of physics as the prototype of scientific languages, and thus as the language of truth, rests upon an assumption that a coherent, scientific account of the world is the nearest we can hope to approach to a true account of what is real, as fact. Truth and reality here reduce to what is coherently presented and could be sensed. Language, we see, only serves indirectly to make statements that are true or false: for language does not, on this view, deal directly with facts, does not *state* facts, but supplies the observational material out of which facts emerge. Thus we see that Carnap's method of approaching truth, like Bradley's, rests on a rejection of the facts as we know them in our everyday world.

But whereas on Bradley's view we can, by applying logical criteria to what is presented to us by sense, attain a deeper insight into the nature of reality, on that of Carnap we can only reach out to truth by a rigid curtailment of the content of perception. Carnap seems to regard 'perception' as a highly stylised notion, as an ideal or perfect instrument of knowledge. In his *Logical Syntax of Language*, on page 317, he says: 'The statement of the protocol-sentences is the affair of the physicist who is observing and making protocols'. With the assumption that what we perceive is to be prescribed we can hardly agree. And again, it is one thing to say that, in perceiving, we either perceive or we do not, that degrees of perception are inconceivable; and quite another to suppose that when we perceive something, we immediately perceive it in its completeness. It is the latter fallacy to which the notion of protocol sentences tends to give rise.

3. WITTGENSTEIN

As a remarkable attempt to match words and things, we should try to understand Wittgenstein's early theory, that put forward in the *Tractatus*. It is no argument against the excellence of this theory as theory that Wittgenstein became critical of it in later years. The thought of a man evolves as his experience grows, and Wittgenstein became more and more concerned with the practical difficulties of philosophical inquiry, and less interested in producing a neat and intelligible system out of his perceptions.

I can only give the essentials of his theory, as relevant to 'fact'. Thinking and speaking take place by means of language, we think and speak about the world. To think and speak about the world we must think and speak about what we see of it, and we always see, or perceive, it as a collection of distinguishable objects in relation to each other. If we did not, there would be nothing we could perceive or say. If we could see an object by itself there would be nothing to say about it; but we could not perceive it as itself and by itself, we must see it as part of a configuration.

When we assert a configuration of objects that we perceive we have a proposition that mirrors a fact. For what we are aware of when we look at the world we call facts; and in thinking and speaking of facts, our thoughts and utterances are propositions. The proposition is the form of our thought as the fact is the form of our perception of the world. Thus the form, the structure, of the proposition and of the fact is the same: the one form corresponds to the other.

Objects may be material objects, or relations between objects, whatever can be singled out *as* an object; and, as such, as object, it is single. Since objects are primary in our perception—logically primary—they are the substance of the world, and the configurations in which we become aware of them are the facts we perceive. Facts, can, according to Wittgenstein, be reduced to elemental facts which are fundamental, irreducible, and independent. These fundamental, or atomic, facts are such that one can exist without another, nor does it make any difference to any one of them that others exist or do not exist. The world is the totality of such facts. We must understand that 'the world' does not contain the facts as parts of a system: the facts are, and the world is merely the miscellany of them. The negative fact is included in this miscellany as the necessary condition of the false proposition. For the thought, or the picture, that we have of facts is made up of propositions, and it is the proposition, not the fact, that is expressed in the sentences we use when we speak truly. Since propositions correspond to facts, it follows that if anything can be thought it is also possible as fact.

Those who identify fact with their own account of the world must find it difficult, if not impossible, to appreciate Wittgenstein's notion of 'fact': for his account requires that we can retain our sense perception as such, so that we can give a sense to "facts" without already falling into language. If we are once committed to language, we have propositions, but not facts, before us; in the proposition, we are correlated with facts, and they themselves are beyond our thought and speech. Thus it cannot be denied that Wittgenstein's theory of atomic facts, and of the correspondence of propositions and facts in respect of structure comes within metaphysics: for no scientific language could deal with it.

We should perhaps take an example. Let one horizontal line *be—not represent*—the mat and one vertical line *be* the cat. Then $\perp$ is the fact which is the *meaning*, the *sense* of the sentence 'The cat is on the mat'. We can leave out the ambiguous "is" and say 'Cat-on-the-mat'; and we have thereby narrowed the proposition, and, in consequence, narrowed the fact which supplies its meaning. But we cannot say we have reached an atomic fact, for an atomic fact remains an affair of theory—it is by definition the final set of configurations into which facts can be analysed. The word "atomic" is used metaphorically, as indeed it used to be in early physics; and in the requirement that an atomic proposition would correspond to an atomic fact we have the assertion of a necessary relation between fact and proposition.

In the proposition 'The cat on the mat is drinking milk,' the 'Cat on the mat' proposition is part of the wider proposition, corresponding to a wider fact. It is only 'a' proposition when it is taken by itself, as above. This is made clear in 5.54, where Wittgenstein shows that the combination of words and expressions in what we say reflects the combination of facts. If a man is aware of a proposition, he is aware of it as true or false, he can consider it against the evidence of facts. But if we say of a man that he believes a proposition to be true, then we are saying that he accepts the facts that correspond to the proposition, and when we say this, we express a proposition to this effect. The proposition that '*A* believes *p*' corresponds to the fact '*A*-believing-*p*' which is a discernible configuration in the world. That it can be reduced to elemental or atomic propositions corresponding to elements of fact does nothing to disrupt the unity of the fact as the meaning or sense of the proposition: for to say that facts and propositions are reducible to atomic facts and propositions is not to say that those facts and propositions which can be reduced are composite. They are facts and propositions because we perceive and speak of some objects in the world juxtaposed in that way.

'Fact' plainly is, in Wittgenstein's use, a category-word for any kind of configuration given in perception, for whatever occurs. It acts as equally valid for what each of us sees or perceives when we look at the world in different ways. Thus it successfully avoids any awkward questions about ultimate truth, or about what the world might *really* be. To these questions, however, Wittgenstein does have an answer: for in saying that the world is the totality of atomic facts, he supposed a common substratum to which every perceived fact would reduce, and thus, even though 'fact' remained what anyone or everyone perceived as such, we would not have to postulate countless worlds. He reconciled the privacy of perception and the objective world in a highly plausible, simple way.

Before leaving Wittgenstein, we should note his uses of "sign", "symbol" and "sense". Words and sentences, as verbal forms, represent objects, which are named. Names are simple signs, and the name *means* the object, the object *is* the meaning of the name. Suppose I ask someone to pass me a book, and the reply is "Which one do you mean?" The objects which are named are represented in the proposition by simple signs, and a name may be said to be a simple sign because it is unanalysable. 'In propositions', wrote Wittgenstein, in paragraph 3.2, 'thoughts can be so expressed that to the objects of the thoughts correspond the elements of the propositional sign. These elements I call "simple signs" and the proposition "completely analysed".' Wittgenstein spoke of "a symbol" when a proposition characterises its sense; and any proposition, or any part of a proposition, which does characterise its sense, he called "an expression". By characterising its sense we are to understand predication as distinct from naming: thus "an expression" says something about the objects named. The sign in, for instance, 'Socrates is mortal' is what we see or hear or think; while we should regard as the symbol 'Socrates—mortal', which characterises the object named by the sign "Socrates". The whole proposition 'Socrates is mortal' is an expression, and is also a symbol, since it characterises the sense, i.e. what is there in the world to be sensed. It is important to understand that Wittgenstein distinguished between "sense" (*der Sinn*) and "meaning" (*die Bedeutung*): by "meaning" he indicated or referred to what is named, and thus, if only objects can be named, meaning only concerns objects. It is an extensional term, roughly approximating to "denotes". On the other hand, "sense", in Wittgenstein's use, refers to what is the case, what can be found in the world, that which is real. As we do not sense single objects, or objects in isolation, but always in some configuration, sense only pertains to the proposition which mirrors that configuration. And since the proposition alone has sense, a name only has meaning in the context of a proposition. As we saw above, objects can only be perceived in configurations, so that names for objects only have meaning, only are names for objects, in a proposition; for without the proposition we would not be able to find them, they would not be available in a sensible (*sinnlich*) way.

4. AUSTIN

Carnap and Wittgenstein have concerned themselves with laying down the rules, the conditions of a language which, if used correctly, would result in statements that were certainly true. Their accounts of this language are theoretical, and reach beyond the scope of our ordinary experience to corroborate and determine. In contrast, Austin was content to analyse our actual use of language, and to describe the processes by which we attain meaningful speech. By observation, Austin thought rules could be found which, if we then deliberately adopt and apply them, would ensure that our discourse would be accurate and our statements true. He assumed the world as reality, and described the conventional links between words and world— or things—which could yield truth as a faithful statement of what is the case. In 'Truth'[1] he went so far as to suggest that the expression "is true" may be a description of the relation between words and the world: to assert 'p' would then differ from asserting " 'p' is true" in that 'p' would be a sentence purporting to make a statement, while " 'p' is true" would assert that the sentence does in fact make a statement and that the statement is true, truth being correspondence between sentence and fact. To assert 'p' might be said to be unsupported assertion, while to say " 'p' is true" or "p is true" expresses an acceptance of 'p' as adequately supported. It could, for example, indicate the adequacy of 'p' as a basis for further argument, or experiment.

Austin regarded all language as convention. When certain rules are found to hold within language, and when such rules are deliberately adopted and adhered to, we have what he called legislation. In contemporary writings and discussions the ambiguities arising out of variations in the use of "convention" and "rule" are very numerous, and in pursuit of clarity, I shall attempt to regularise my own use of these two expressions. By "convention" Austin meant the habitual uses—social habits—of language that occur without any especial notice being paid to them: we all talk, and so, since we learn all that we do by imitation and precedent, we talk in certain ways and not in others, we use certain expressions in certain contexts, and we disregard, either through ignorance or choice, other expressions that other people might use in the same contexts. When we come to examine ordinary language, we find a variation of expression in what appears to be a similar context. By studying these variations, we should be able to arrive at an accurate account of the application of words to those contexts, for the variations will be found to bear out rather than to conceal the similarities of the contexts ('A Plea for Excuses'). In other words, differences in the expressions used will lead us to distinctions in the world of fact.

[1] *Ar. Soc. Suppl. Vol.* (1950).

However, once we begin to question these variations and uses, we begin to see the conventions which give rise to them as sets of rules between which we can choose. It is important to remember that the choice only occurs because we become aware of the conventions *as* conventions. This distinction applies to any kind of activity: for we may be so accustomed to doing a certain task in a certain way, that we are somewhat taken aback on seeing it done in another way, until we reflect upon both of them, and perhaps decide the second way is better. The adoption of one of these ways as a rule is what Austin meant by "legislation". For myself, I propose to use "rule" as "recognised as a rule", and thus having some background of authority, however slight.

Austin believed that the sorting out of conventions in language, and the consequent deliberate adoption of some of them as rules, could be applied as a method in moral philosophy. I am very doubtful about the soundness of this belief, since it turns philosophy into science by the expedient of adopting technical terms. Nor am I particularly sympathetic with the assumption, essential to his project, that choices made by an individual or a small group can be applied by analogy to society in general. For "legislation" is not a word that is normally used to refer to personal decisions, and the very fact that there are varying uses to investigate must lead us to expect that when choices are made between them, and rules are adopted, there is great variation in the choice and selection of conventions as rules. It seems to follow that where there are varying conventions the results of legislation will also be varied; and, further, if, as Carnap admits,[1] natural languages have too complicated a structure to be reduced altogether to systems of rules, then when legislation does occur, it can only occur within a range of conventions arbitrarily assembled. And this we must regard as valid for ethics as for any other subject, for it was particularly in connection with ethics that Austin hoped his method of legislation would prove effective.

We look through or past words to the world, and since, according to Austin, the words we use are the tools of implicit convention, they never, in his view, determine the things to which they refer, nor do things determine language. We are limited, however, by the resources of language, and we may

[1] Carnap, *The Logical Syntax of Language*, introduction, p. 2.

find ourselves in a situation which we cannot properly describe for want of words. It may then be of some help—presumably Austin meant for purposes of successful communication—if words, as sounds, do reflect or mirror in some way the reality they serve to indicate, as, for instance, is more usual in poetry; yet he dismissed altogether the notion that there must be any common structure between language and facts. Since we use language in order to communicate about things—the world—we have certain agreed words to signify them: we may either take the thing, or the situation, and fit words to it, or we may take words and sentences and find things to exemplify their use. Austin neutralised 'words' by speaking of 'vocables', the sounds we make when uttering words. We can pinpoint this distinction by saying that a vocable, a verbal form, to become a word, must have a use in the language. "Selag" is a vocable in the English alphabet, but not a word, though it looks like one and is easy to pronounce.

I do not doubt that Austin thought language could be as it were sorted out. In 'A Plea for Excuses' he said that ordinary language was certainly the *first* word, but certainly not the *last* word. 'In principle', he wrote, 'it can everywhere be supplemented and improved upon and superseded.' He saw also that whenever a decision is made to use a word in a slightly unusual sense, or for a slightly unusual purpose, the decision creates a precedent, and influences the development of language. In view of these concessions, it is very difficult to see what would be gained by the 'sorting-out' of language: for there seems to be no third alternative to creating a system of technical terms and keeping to it, or leaving personal decisions to create precedent in any direction they will. Yet in his essay on Excuses Austin did, I think, commit himself to the view that if we are confronted by the same situation in sufficient detail we will in fact say the same things about it. Here we find him assuming an objectivity in perception that can overcome even the difficulties of linguistic duplication.

In his paper 'How to Talk—Some simple ways',[1] Austin outlined his practical notion of legislation. He called things—stones, etc.—"items", and distinguished between applying a vocable to an item, that is, fitting the vocable, as word, to the object, and starting with the word and indicating the object to

[1] *Proc. Ar. Soc.* (1952–3).

which it refers. In the latter, we may say '*This* is a stone,' meaning 'This is the sort of thing we mean when we use the word "stone";' while in the former we merely say 'This is a *stone*'. There is thus always some emphasis in what he called the 'speech-situation', so that sentences cannot always be understood fully apart from their speech-situation. The same considerations lead to differences of direction in, for example, 'All A's are B' and 'Some B's are A's' which are not accommodated in the traditional logical forms of immediate inference. Austin also rejected the interpretation of 'All A's are B's' as 'If anything is an A, it is B'. All these variations in expression he regarded as reflecting differences in the speech-situation, and his purpose in analysing linguistic forms was to throw light upon the practical or actual situation, not merely to argue from the linguistic forms to the speech-situation. We should look again at the facts, at the actual situation, he believed, in the light of the differences we have become aware of by studying forms of expression.

Plainly one could not argue in this way without making the assumption that the world we perceive is in fact what it appears to be. Austin had little sympathy with the view that what we perceive is unreliable, and that accordingly we should advocate coherence as the criterion of true statements; for this view postulates some basic stratum or level of fact which could be accurately described, leaving all other accounts to be presumed as only partially true. If we look carefully at the speech-situation, and are meticulous about the way we apply words to things, then it seemed to Austin that there is no objection to saying that our statements about things are true. 'A statement is said to be true', he wrote in 'Truth', 'when the historic state of affairs to which it is correlated by the demonstrative conventions (the one to which it "refers") is of a type with which the sentence used in making it is correlated by the descriptive conventions.'

Austin raised a battery of questions as to what we ordinarily mean by "statement", "proposition", and "fact". Of speech-acts he said in effect that our purpose in speaking influences or forms part of the meaning of the words we use. If we are trying to find instances of a type of thing, we may be exemplifying or instancing, and it is typical of his method that he drew a distinction between these, as acts. If we give examples, we show the multiformity in the pattern, while if we give instances, we 'neglect the full specificity of the item'—for we give only a certain view of it ('How to Talk'). If philosophers include all speech-acts under the word "statement", he remarked, how can one differentiate between "sentence" and "statement"? A statement is often said to be true or false, but a statement must be made by someone in a situation, a statement is not some detached expression of a proposition, independent of context. The statement is what is asserted, but it cannot be severed from its context if we are to be sure what *is* being asserted. What Austin meant on this point is, I am satisfied, that since statements must be made in words, it is not possible from the words by themselves, to determine *what* statements are being made. Words are themselves a refinement of gesture, and where they begin and end are other signs, which communicate in other ways. To take the vocables alone may be to miss some essential element in what is being communicated. The facts that words refer to, the reference to the historic situation, is the sense of the sentence: for conventions of sense, demonstratives, associate the vocables that are chosen as words for types with certain kinds of things. And in describing a historic situation as being of a certain kind, certain features of it are asserted in a certain way. In a sentence, what Austin called the assertive link, the link between the name of the item and the type-word must be matched by a natural link between the item, as object referred to, and the objects attached to the type-word as its agreed sense. Although Austin rejected the notion of language as showing the same structure as that of facts, it is hard to see much difference between the correspondence he required and that laid down by Wittgenstein: for what is this 'assertive link' but the showing of the relation between linguistic representatives of elements in the historic situation? Although both names of things and descriptive words, type-words, are determined by convention, the association of one with the other is a matter of inspection—of seeing that it holds *in fact*, if it is to be true.

Austin used "type-word" where "predicate" is more common; and we must be sure of the grounds upon which he did so. If item and vocable are to be associated by convention, then there can be no way of breaking up this association in order to provide 'sense' as 'idea'. It becomes impossible to indicate meaning except by indicating things. So if it is desired to say that a certain item, for example, Felstead, is a horse, we are not to be understood as predicating certain characteristics of Felstead in virtue of which he is a horse; but rather we are saying that of all the items referred to by the type-word "horse" Felstead is one, he is included. Again we are not saying that he is in a certain 'class', for Austin would have agreed with Bradley that to go looking for classes is to chase chimeras; but we classify, and to classify is a kind of speech-act. Austin's method of classifying is to assert of an item the extension of an item/type, and thus, by inference, to assign to it the characteristics common to those included in that extension, while also permitting the possibility of countless features—specificity—which are not common to the individuals, but which occur among them. These distinctions are easier to maintain as descriptions of acting or procedure than as uses of language.

Between statement and fact, according to Wittgenstein and Austin, there must be a correspondence, the assertion of which is truth and the denial of which is falsity. What is stated to be the case is only contingently true or false, but that what is stated is a matter of fact is a necessary condition of stating. Austin's only modification of this position is that "stating" is a word for putting together item and type in various ways, for, that is, different speech-acts. These two philosophers, however, seem to differ as to the kind of correspondence there should be between statement and fact: for Wittgenstein supposed a mirroring of structure, a reflection of configuration, while Austin was content with a system of labelling objects, events, and types of objects, events, etc. The whole transaction for him was extensional, referential. Uniqueness of reference—he described it thus: '*demonstrative* conventions correlating the words (= statements) with the *historic* situations' ('Truth')—is the hinge of Austin's system, as precise correspondence between atomic fact and proposition is the hinge of Wittgenstein's early theory. Yet if we say that the items Austin 'named' fulfil the function of the objects Wittgenstein regarded as the substance of the world, the prerequisite of speaking of the world, of speaking about anything at all, then there hardly seems to be much difference between them. For, as pointed out immediately above, Austin required, for the making of a statement, that the assertive linguistic link be matched in fact, while the 'fact' for Wittgenstein was already a complex or configuration of linked objects.

For Austin, items could be demonstratively accepted as 'there'; for Wittgenstein, 'an' object was unthinkable.

Both to Wittgenstein and Austin, philosophy was an activity, but while to Austin it was partly legislation and partly reference back to fact, and thus a series of attempts to fit language to sense, for Wittgenstein it was a development of thought through the successive stages of perception. Wittgenstein theorised as he went; he pictured the world, then compared the picture with reality, revised it with the new experience of facts, and so on.[1] In comparing his picture with the world, the propositions involved in the comparison, those by which the comparison was achieved, he called philosophical, corresponding to no fact in themselves. When they have occurred and have enabled us to correct our picture, then they have already become superfluous, they are the rungs of the ladder which must be cast away. For once we have seen that some part of the world has features that we did not notice previously, or that we failed to understand, then we cannot see that part of the world any more as we used to see it. Any propositions purporting to bridge the gap between our present and our past perception of that part would be nonsensical. Elucidation, or the examination of one thing in the light of our knowledge of other things, is a procedure which gives rise to philosophical propositions: but these all disappear into the tautological once the elucidation is completed.

It is interesting that both Wittgenstein and Austin tended to move away from their earlier positions as a result of their preoccupation with the facts, which brought them under the compelling influence of the contexts of the facts they observed so carefully. Wittgenstein devised his theory of language-games, which almost turns context into a special kind of world, and Austin drew his meticulous distinctions between calling, describing, and other kinds of speech-act, on the ground that we could only be sure of the nature of that act by studying the speech-situation. A result of this kind of distinction was his distrust of the use by moral philosophers of 'action' for any act regardless of its situation.

Out of the contrasts of these four theories of 'fact' we can at least find material for reflection and comment. 'Fact', it seems, is what reconciles reality or existence with our experience of it.

---

[1] 4.031: 'In the proposition a state of affairs is, as it were, put together for the sake of experiment.'

If we did not speak about the world—and we can only speak about the world within our experience of it—we would not have a word like "fact" at all. We can also see that to say that statements of fact are those statements that can be found to be true or false by referring to the relevant facts does not tell us anything at all, for what are the relevant facts? Carnap would require that the statement we wished to prove, or verify, be translated into statements which could be reduced to protocol statements, statements of the meeting of expressions and sense experience. Then the statement would be treated as an explanatory hypothesis in physics. Wittgenstein would have first judged it a statement having meaning, referring to objects in the world, and then he would have inquired whether the linguistic structure matched the structure of the fact asserted in the statement. Austin would have examined the links between word and item, making sure each component expression in the statement referred; then he would have examined the assertive links between the expressions, the item and item-type words, and finally compared these links with the juxtaposition in the world of the items named or referred to. He might have decided the statement was true, or only partially true. Against these procedures, we can set that of Bradley, who would have commended Austin's reference back to the world of sense on the ground that we must beware of drawing distinctions in thought where there are none in fact; but, the statement then accepted as probable, he would have continued his inquiry as an ideal one, to find out if the statement could be made to form part of a coherent theory of the nature of the world. He would have endeavoured to reconcile it with the conceptual system he had within himself, analysing its content to detect any latent contradictions.

The difficulties involved in applying the notion of 'fact' mainly occur because philosophers attempt to deal with it within language itself, and yet are unwilling to apply to it the kind of logic it demands. We may take Austin's advice here and regard statements as speech-acts rather than as complete and self-explanatory, as they would have to be if they were to be found true or false. When I say: 'I see a table', I am *not* saying:

(i) that I am seeing something others can see,
(ii) that the table is or is not ultimately real,
(iii) that the table is perceptible in certain ways,

(iv) or that the statement 'I see a table' can be translated into
      an infinite number of hypothetical statements about
      sense-data.

What I am saying is that in 'my' line of vision there is some
object 'I' can act upon in certain ways. In other words, it is a
hypothesis upon which I can base a number of physical experiments. This number is not infinite, because it is necessarily
limited by what I am able to devise. I can place a tray on the
table, I can thump on it, I can turn it upside down, etc. And
I know in advance, and can to some extent predict accurately,
what kind of perceptions I shall have when I do these things.

At first sight it might seem a quibble to say that (a) 'the
pragmatic statement "I see a table" means that I can predict
the result of many experiments with it', is different from (b),
'the phenomenalist statement "I see a table" is reducible to an
infinite number of hypothetical statements about sense-data'.
For (i) if I do carry out experiments, I shall have more and
more sense-data and there seems no reason why I should not
describe the object as the occasion of all these possible sense-
data; and (ii) if I am only able to sense the table by means of
or in terms of sense-data, then I am only able to sense it in this
same way during any experiments I make with it.

But if we look at (b) and at (i) again, we see there is something wrong about them. If, after reading (i) we return to (b),
we find we have left out an essential feature: for if we say, in
(b), that the object I see is the occasion of the possible sense-
data, we do not fully allow for the occurrence of sense-data at
all. Sense-data must occur as modifications, or as the causes of
modifications, or as the end-products of modifications, of
persons as material objects. So we need not only a material
object such as a table, but also another as a person if we are to
speak of the occurrence of sense-data. It makes no difference if
we lay it down that sense-data are merely what is presented to
sense, for were the senses not there, nothing would be presented.
In fact, to speak of sense-data in respect of a material object
makes it analytic that the material object is in relation with a
person, while if we speak of a material object the presence of a
person is only contingent. Thus if I predict future, or hypothetical, sense-data, I also predict a person. And this amounts
to saying that 'A-thumping-table' is reducible to A having or
sensing certain sense-data. We should now return to (b).

We have to restate (*b*) as follows: 'The statement "I see a table", which is about material objects, is reducible to an infinite number of hypothetical statements about sense-data occurring in one of them.' I do not specify in which one they occur. The *existence* of both objects stands or falls together. If I find the table illusory, a trick of light perhaps, then I have experimented, and the experiment has failed. Thus I retract my statement that I see a table, or I declare it to be false.

My point is that when I make a statement such as 'I see a table', that statement may be true or false. I have to verify it. I have to confirm or disprove that the table I see is what we commonly mean by a table. There is no need for me to go beyond my own experience. If I believed my experiment to be successful when in fact it was not, I would deceive myself, and if I refused to make any experiments to verify the statement, then I could be said either to be already sure, or to be interested in maintaining an illusion. But in this situation I myself, as concerned in the prediction of future sense-data, would also be illusory. Since 'fact' is dependent both upon the world and upon the perceiver, the observer, to doubt 'fact' as fact does not make sense. What we can doubt is the extent of our perceptions; we can give up the absurd notion that we have only to open our eyes to see what is there, that knowledge is two dimensional, like a picture on a canvas. Once we admit that 'fact' has depth as well as surface, we find that Bradley, Wittgenstein and Austin meet in the endeavour to plumb those depths, to refuse to be satisfied with anything that offends our powers of comprehension.

We also find, I think, that Carnap is right in saying that existence is a question which falls outside material object language, but wrong in supposing that it can be disposed of as a matter of decision about language. We do not decide to use material object language, we use it willy-nilly, even if we discuss another language. When a man says he sees a table, he asserts himself as seeing the table. He is not beyond the limits of the world, but in it. When we doubt the existence of material objects, when we ask ourselves if the whole world of our perceptions is illusory, we echo in our thoughts the long process of the physical evolution of the sense organs out of the primeval sentience of the simplest forms of life. Beauty, we might say, came into being with the eye, but we do not despise it or try to explain it away. We see, hear, and feel things as we do because our sense organs are what they are; but if the world were not as it is, our sense organs would not have adapted themselves to it in the way that they have. And if knowledge of what is ultimately true were possible without sense organs as we know them, we should never have come to cast doubts on our sense-experience: for we would have regarded it as irrelevant to knowledge from the start. Anything more absurd than this can scarcely be conceived.

Before leaving this chapter, there are certain comments that should be made on its contents, since they are inevitably concerned in any inquiry. These deal with the logic of statements of perception, the relevance of qualities, the logically and contingently possible, and objections to the notion of a 'public check'.[1]

(i) If we consider what kind of things we think of when someone throws doubts upon a statement of fact that we have made, I think we must agree that those things would come under the heading of experiment; that is, they deal with the ways we would test our own observation, and would reach a conclusion as to whether we had made a mistake or not. Arguments of this kind are conducted in statements of fact, and their validity is tested by material implication. In practical philosophy the distinction between material—or formal—implication and entailment is of great importance. With regard to perception, it is incorrect to say that a statement that X is a material object *entails* the statement that there is a certain set of hypothetical statements about sense-data; for the inference requires the premiss that material objects are only known through sense-data. This assumed statement, however, is itself contingent, and the implication thus becomes material. Further, if we say that the assumption forms part of the concept of a material object, then the statement that a statement about material objects entails sets of hypothetical statements about sense-data is a mere tautology. It is noteworthy that Ayer[2] has argued that theories of perception are arguments about what language we should use, about the adoption of

---

[1] Some of the questions I raise here, and many others, especially those connected with 'verification', have been ably discussed by W. H. F. Barnes in *The Philosopical Predicament*, which to my regret I had not read when writing this book.

[2] *Foundations of Empirical Knowledge*, pp. 1–57.

certain linguistic rules, rather than about what is the case. For only thus could we correctly speak of entailment.

(ii) This brings us to the relevance of qualities: for it is argued that, since the appearance, for example, of a rose, differs in kind from the chemical and electrical changes which occur in our sense organs when confronted by the rose, the appearance of an object is something that can never be explained, and qualities are philosophically but not empirically interesting. Yet if we say that the names of qualities are the names we give to the object as known to us through sense there does not seem to be any room for mystery: for if "green" is the name we give when we have a certain sensation, we can either say the object we perceive is green or that we have sensations of green. To say that "green" is a name for a quality is to apply the distinctions we are able to make in our sense experiences to the objects we suppose to give rise to them.

(iii) If we say that statements of perception are related by material or formal implication, and that they can be verified, not by public agreement, but by experiment, we must distinguish between statements that can be verified in principle, and those that we can actually verify. Epistemology avoids such questions by postulating statements that no one would ever make, and disregarding most, if not all, the statements of perception that we do in fact make. It is no solution to say we merely have to make a decision about the language we will use. If we have to act, and act now, we have to have some method of dealing with many kinds of statement, some of fact. We must know how to distinguish between the logically possible and the contingently possible, or, on the evidence before us, we might attempt to act upon all sorts of vague possibilities. It is not enough to say that a statement is a statement of fact if we can give the conditions of its verification, even though to realise those conditions is contingently impossible.[1] What is needed in a practical situation is some method of distinguishing between statements of fact and statements which purport to be of fact, but which are theories about facts, just as material object statements in one aspect can be said to be theories about our sense experiences. Austin's method of returning to look at the facts, at the world, suggests that practical criteria for weeding

[1] For the difficulties in 'possible', see for example von Wright, *An Essay in Modal Logic*, pp. 31–2.

out spurious propositions from genuine first-order statements of perception might be found. What is contingently possible would seem to relate in some way to our knowledge of the world, while talk of the logically possible is only limited by what is thinkable. Yet it is true that we do apply a consistency test in our practical thinking, and that, whereas our knowledge of the world tends to confine us to what we have previously experienced, it is the unexpected, but the conceivable, which more often intervenes in actual fact.

(iv) From what has been said on pages 45-6 and 73 above, it appears that in principle the notion of a public check is both untenable and unnecessary. I want now very briefly to bring five arguments against this notion.

(*a*) We are mistaken in supposing that the language in which we speak of our own perceptions and that in which we speak of those of others is the same. We cannot quote the perceptions of others in support of our own, though we can, if we wish, use the perceptions of others in experiments to prove the reliability of our own. When an observer, say B, notes that a light is shining into A's eyes, he can state with a fair degree of probability that A is having visual sensations, or sense-data, but he cannot say with any degree of certainty what it is that A is perceiving. Again, A is aware of his perceptions, and his analysis of them into sense-data is postperceptual. Thus we have the anomaly that to B, observing A, the language of sense-data is logically prior, while to A the language of material objects is logically prior, for to speak of 'a bright light shining' is to use material object language. The two languages may be alternative languages, but they are not alternative ways of describing the same phenomena, unless we rule that perception should only be applied to the person having sense-data. In the first case the material object is an inference, in the second it is a logical construction. It is clear these considerations have an important bearing on the question of a public check, for when we suppose others to be observing something, it is we who are in the position of B, and they who take the place of A. Thus the basic difficulty remains untouched.[1]

[1] For the further difficulty that the notion of a public check requires inferences from private experiences to objective fact, see A. Phillips Griffiths: 'Ayer on Perception', in *Mind* (1960). I am not concerned with the sceptical argument here, except that I would not admit merely from A's statement that he saw an object, that he really was seeing it. See ch. v, p. 129, below.

(*b*) The validity of a public check requires that observers tell the truth, and thus we have as a convention that to 'say' is to 'say truthfully'. This provision is on a par with the assumption that when we look at the same thing, we all see the same thing, subject to different angles of vision. This is an assumption that should not be made in philosophy. Similarity of syntactical form does not imply logical symmetry, and while such assumptions may be convenient for the provision of a perfect language, they do not conform to the facts of everyday discourse. In philosophy they defeat their own purpose, for what philosophers try to do is to establish the grounds of truth, not to assume them. It is because words fail to correspond to or to mirror fact, or to communicate infallibly, that philosophers trouble to examine them, and that there is a problem of truth at all.

(*c*) There is no agreed usage in the case of a public check, except in the sense that we could probably make our perceptions agree if we tried, but that everyone would say the same thing under the same circumstances is a risky assumption. Because they have different experiences, men have different criteria for their perceptions, for using words—for instance, who decides the difference between a tree, a bush and a shrub; or between a house, a cottage and a hut? The fact is there is no decision about these apart from a context, what is subject to public check is not statements, but things, and in order to agree about things, we must have common meanings for words. So far Carnap's criterion for statements of fact seems to be justified. But it is analytic that if we first agree about words, and then about the things we use them to refer to, we are merely arguing in a closed circle: without using any words at all we could simply find out that something was the case, and leave truth and the public check out of it. For as soon as we use an agreed terminology, we are in effect using scientific method.

(*d*) When we speak of a public check, we assume that a person has only to look at 'the facts' to see for himself what they are. This account leaves no room for deficiencies of perception, for personal bias and for variations of comprehension. Why should we restrict truth to statements about those things which almost everyone can agree about? For that is what the 'public check' in fact achieves. In matters of opinion we can resort to sampling and questionnaires, but we rarely find that the results give a 'verdict' that is clear-cut. What a 'public check' does is to reduce what can be said about a thing to its minimum, as a basis for reference and communication, and it looks like a device for projecting a definition. The difference between the look of a palaeolithic worked flake lying in loose soil to an archaeologist, to a child wanting to throw stones at a bottle, and to picnic parties needing to prevent paper bags from blowing away is a timely reminder that, in trying to equate our experiences in order to find a common denominator of truth, we may so prune our range of truth that truth itself loses its significance for us. As indeed if we seek to find the answers to our thoughts in the phrases of ordinary language, we may only succeed in ensuring that our thoughts are as ordinary as our passing conversations in bus and train.

(e) Finally, we return to the question of verification briefly dealt with above; for the notion that matters of fact are in principle verifiable is closely related to that of a public check. A matter of fact is also in principle observable by anyone who happens to be in the right position. But what if nobody could be in such a position? Can we know that, in a matter of fact, there could be no observer? Could we formulate a statement purporting to be of fact, yet unobservable? We can put the point more stringently: if there is to be something observed, there must be an observer, and this is a necessary, not a contingent condition. Does it make sense, then, to speak of a fact being in principle verifiable, or observable, if it is the case that there is and can be no observer?[1]

Verification has been used as a criterion to discredit judgments of value and speculations about the ultimate nature of the world and the destinies of human beings. If the findings of depth psychology are to be allowed, even as the findings of something unspecified, then we must admit that perceptions tend to form themselves into some coherent world-picture. Here Wittgenstein's account of fact is at its most plausible: for we take our picture back to the reality in perception, and make corrections. And we find in this unified background to our thought a simple explanation of the way the unusual or the unexpected seems to seize upon our attention and produce an alertness that no deliberate effort could attain or simulate. We

---

[1] I am aware that this question may be nonsensical, since it could be argued that we could not speak of such a fact as we could not have an idea of it. But what of past events?

carry on with our daily tasks and amusements, while all round us others carry on with theirs; when suddenly some feature of their behaviour, some result of our actions, strikes us as odd, it refuses to fall into place as part of the pattern of formal implication we always have ready to absorb the events of the day. So we start to puzzle the matter out, and as we do so, more and more of that background to our thought becomes the foreground, and we find out just how much we do know about the world. We may have to revise our estimates of the possibilities of human behaviour, we may have to part with some prejudice, but in the end we usually discover that the significance of the discordant fact lay in its ability to prevent us from making a foolish adjustment, from behaving unsuitably. Sometimes a very small discordance may lead to a discovery of serious default in those we trust. The value of the discordance, the significance, may seem out of all proportion to the triviality of the fact which is discordant. It is a question of an unexplained emphasis in our perceptions of our surroundings. Thus are the small discrepancies of everyday righted, and thus are the great discoveries of science achieved. Yet when such emphasis occurs it is not an observable fact, it is an intensification of certain judgments of perception which could, as an intensification, never be subjected to a public check. Nor could it ever be observed, since it is a quality of observation itself.

IV

DEALING WITH EVIDENCE: LANGUAGE AND LOGIC

The brief reviews of theories of 'fact' in the previous chapter have served to show that we are not at all sure what we mean when we use the word. This is hardly the occasion upon which to make a decision, but if we are to continue our attempt to find statements about responsibility, and if we at least agree that a statement must state something, we shall have to adopt some conventional criterion of 'statement'. For if we cannot decide what we mean when we say a statement must state facts, we shall have to inquire whether we can lay it down that a sentence is to be meaningful, or significant, that it must refer, if it is to provide us with a statement.

Referring again to the four philosophers who furnished us with accounts of 'fact', we can ask what guidance they can offer. Bradley regarded the judgment as the attribution of an ideal content to a subject beyond it. The whole judgment is a predication, and, as such, it is one idea—the grammatical subject and the grammatical predicate are ideally combined in the attribution. In this combination we have another version of the configuration required by Wittgenstein as characteristic both of 'fact' and of 'proposition' or 'thought'. Where the configuration is to be found in the world is indicated, for Wittgenstein, by prearranged names for 'objects'. But Bradley predicated the whole content of the judgment, names and adjectives, of a feature of the world which was abstracted as 'this' from the 'felt whole' which is our experience of the world, whatever the world may be. 'Standing-for', or signification, was, for Bradley, at best an approximation, but in Wittgenstein's view we are able to locate the facts and events signified by name, since we do succeed in naming and recognising those objects present to our senses. How this signification is achieved is described minutely in Austin's account of 'legislation'. By definition, Austin's account must be choice between existing rules, though I suspect that many philosophers assume conventions to be rooted in a kind of public legislation. But there seems to be no evidence in support of this either in social anthropology or in philology. Thus we must either choose between what we find or adopt an artificial language.

Carnap, on the other hand, has made a distinction between the logical syntax of language, and semantics. The former is to be separable from linguistic syntax as an object of study. Linguistic syntax, the rules we learn in the grammar book, is not "pure", since the position of words in a natural language depends upon emphasis and conventions of style. But logical syntax is "pure", because it is independent of sense, consisting entirely of rules.[1] It can be said—I hope rightly—that logical syntax concerns all those formal and logical concepts that have to be included in a notation. We would be tempted to say that it includes everything about a sentence that contributes formally to comprehension of the content without giving that content.

Semantics deals with the meaning of the sentence taken altogether, the objects referred to and what is said about them. In this way it comes about that logicians talk about intensional and extensional logic. Carnap has thus not maintained his thesis that syntactical analysis of scientific sentences is all that philosophy demands of logic. He speaks of two tendencies in logic,[2] the one emphasising form, 'the logical structure of sentences and deductions, relations between signs in abstraction from their meaning,' the other emphasising 'just the factors excluded by the first, viz: meaning, interpretation; relations of entailment, compatibility, incompatibility, etc., as based on meaning; the distinction between necessary and contingent truth, etc.' Calling them syntactical and semantical tendencies, Carnap goes on to say: 'Theoretically they are not incompatible, but rather complementary to each other,' and that these tendencies have been ever present in logic, usually combined 'without explicit distinction', though one logician might emphasise one at the expense of the other. What we are asked to accept is that there are two processes, two sides of logic, complementary, of which we could take the following

---

[1] In his *Logical Syntax of Language*, Carnap makes this bare assertion, on p. 9; but in *Meaning and Necessity*, p. 5, he gives these rules as rules of (1) formation, (2) designation, (3) truth and (4) range. The last seems equivalent to 'domain'.
[2] *The Formalisation of Logic* (1943), preface.

illustration: (i) '*A* being a *B*', and 'All *B*'s being *X*', together yield *syntactically*—'*A* is *X*'; and (ii) '*A* is a man' and 'Man is mortal' together *entail* '*A* is mortal'.

The danger in such a contention is that the distinction of two such tendencies, if systematised satisfactorily in language, might come to be believed to correspond to some distinction in fact. If there is a valid distinction to be drawn between words and expressions on the one hand, and meaning or content on the other, it must be based on a distinction within the extension of "sentence", "statement", "proposition", and "fact". If we want to find an actual distinction, then we can treat our search as a practical problem and apply practical methods. What I propose to do now is to try to locate a phenomenological distinction, and then, if we find it, legislate. And it will be legislation in Austin's sense, for most philosophers have adopted rules for distinguishing pairs of words such as "intension, extension", "sentence, statement", "words, things", "sense, reference", and so on. Whatever conclusion we reach, we are almost certain to be in agreement with one of these pairs of defined terms.

On page 70 above, I said that 'fact' reconciles reality or existence with our experience of it. It is a product of our perception of the world. When we look at the world we do so against a background of factual distinctions, or relations of facts—for these are but two sides of the necessity by which we see 'things'. The world is, for each of us, a conglomeration of such distinctions and relations. That there is such and such a distinction to be made, that there is such and such a relation of things, is the form of the proposition. A proposition is the way our perception of fact is presented to us, the way we do perceive fact. It may be presented as imagination, either in visual, auditory, tactile, or verbal imagery, but it is presented as a proposition.

Let us take an example: suppose I am taken round a neighbour's garden, with which I am well acquainted. I remember all the flower beds and what grows in them. I am looking at them, enjoying the pleasant experience of colour and scent, noting how much the plants have grown, and so forth. Then I see a new plant I neither remember nor recognise. By comparison with other plants familiar to me, I try to classify it, and I wonder where it has been obtained. As various possibilities occur to me, I look more closely at the new plant, I accept certain suggestions and reject others. Finally I may ask: 'What is this? A lily?' Now the possibilities that have occurred to me occurred *as* propositions—for example, one or two features noted visually and the word "liliacae". Bradley called these stages in my thought 'levels of reflection'.[1]

As I tried to find a name for a set of visual qualities, it is probable that many of the propositions occurred as visual images, with a few verbal ones here and there; but when I finally put my question, I put it in verbal form. Yet still it contained the same kind of proposition, the same content in a different medium.

We can take it as probable that the dog whose tongue wanders round his teeth, and who has at the same time a fleeting visual image of the tree where he has buried his bone, or a fleeting scent of that bone or that place, is experiencing in the form of the proposition: 'I'll just go and get that bone.' The proposition is the form of our adjustment, the practical use of our perception.

The proposition is neither mental or non-mental, but actual. When we communicate it to others, we make a statement and we make the statement *as* a sentence. We do not make the statement *by means of*, *using*, or *in*, a sentence; we make it simply *as* a sentence. Also in our own reflection, if we wish to continue it, we must fixate the proposition in words, otherwise we cannot recall it, or be sure of retaining it for purposes of criticism. It might, if not verbalised, occur again, it might not. In verbalising it we are in effect communicating with ourselves by means of public language, something that is part of the world, and can be remembered and dealt with as such. But we may act upon the proposition without the intervention of words—and if we do, we have 'no reason' for acting that is not merely an impulsion from our view of the facts.

If we accept this account, then, when we say a sentence has or makes sense, we are saying it makes a statement or expresses a proposition. But 'statement' and 'proposition' are on the same reflective level; the words stand for the same thing,

---

[1] *Principles of Logic*, pp. 114 and 663 especially. Bradley does not of course mean to differentiate on grounds of mere succession; but as we consider something, it is perceived in greater detail, by the application of more and more of our ideas. Thus as reflection on one subject proceeds, our judgments become selective on wider grounds: ' . . . that which is implied in principle need not be before our minds at the start' (p. 663).

except that a statement is a proposition in a sentence, while when we use 'proposition' we do not specify the medium of presentation.

But if we adopt this usage, what are we to say about Wittgenstein's view that objects are the *meanings* of words? We cannot say, in our usage, that facts are the sense of propositions, for we then have a reduplication in 'fact', 'proposition' 'sentence'. But where is the reduplication? We can say: "Sentence '*S*' has sense '*p*' "; or "Sentence '*S*' makes the statement '*p*' "; or "Sentence '*S*' says '*p*' ", but we cannot say "Sentence '*S*' says the fact is that '*p*' ". We seem to be equating "sense '*p*' ", "the fact is '*p*' ", and "'*p*'". The odd one out seems to be "the fact is '*p*' ". "Sentence '*S*' says the fact is that '*p*' " is where the redundancy lies. We cannot say "says the fact is", for on our definition to "say", used of a sentence includes the fact without further addition. We could put it thus: "According to sentence '*S*' the fact is that '*p*' ", since, as Wittgenstein said, 'the fact is' is only a sign for a formal concept. A statement, then, is 'of fact', and a sentence is 'about facts'.

Here '*p*' is notational for statements of the S—P kind, however the words are arranged. It is a propositional sign. The notations in mathematical logic are not *about* but *are* sense. When a proposition in mathematical logic is 'translated' into words, confusions arise: for instance, if '*p*' is used in ordinary language it tends to mislead because it is a formal concept for all propositions, but as soon as it receives values it becomes, not a mere sign, but something that *was* a function, and we find ourselves with, not mere words, but a sentence and a statement. Now it is impossible to distinguish a sentence from a statement unless two alternative expressions of one statement can be given, and what is common to both *sentences* taken as the statement, the proposition. Even so, when we remove the statement, it is hard to say what we have left.

Propositions are sense, we have said, and sense is *our sense*; it is not what is the case, but what we perceive as being the case. Consequently, statements as propositions cannot refer, since a thing cannot be said to refer to itself. If statements are verbal expressions of propositions, statements cannot refer. Since, however, it is indubitably a function of language to refer, it must be the *sentence*, as such, which refers. A sentence refers to objects perceived and distinguished as objects, as things, and makes statements about them, statements of *fact*, which may be true or false. Put it another way: words and phrases refer to objects and things, sentences which are meaningful then refer to the world and make statements about them. It is impossible to conceive of a statement being made in a sentence that does not refer: thus it is the words, the verbal forms, the vocables, which link language and world, and enable something to be said. Signification is a matter of words, meaning is a matter of sense. Sentences are significant if they contain words which refer to things: they are also meaningful if they express propositions. Here I have not used "meaning" in Wittgenstein's sense, for he uses it for "reference". But I propose to keep to "meaning" for "sense".

Suppose we now have a sentence: we can either (*a*) find as many other sentences in the language that follow from this one, that are included in it by the relations of the expressions, or (*b*) we can take the statement it makes and find all the other sentences that can make the same statement. Procedure (*a*) is now legitimatised as linguistic analysis, and concerns the relations of words; (*b*) on the other hand, is known as logical analysis, for it deals with the relations of concepts. Many philosophers persuade themselves that the two procedures amount to the same, they even change over between the two methods in mid-stream, as it were; but, as we shall see, they are mistaken in this. That the two methods do sometimes lead to the same result is a contingent, not a necessary, consequence. In (*a*), knowledge of convention, of the language, is a limiting circumstance, while in (*b*), insight into what is the case, that is empirical knowledge—including philosophical skill—is a limiting condition. Accordingly, linguistic analysis is a sophisticated activity, whereas conceptual analysis need not be, unless a conceptual scheme (a set of definitions) is deliberately adopted for analysis. In (*a*) the meaning is manipulated by manipulating the words; in (*b*) the development of meaning governs the use of the words.[1]

[1] Here we should, I think, bear in mind that many professional philosophers, for instance, Bradley, in his essays on Pragmatism, in *Truth and Reality*, and also in that on Utilitarianism ('Pleasure for Pleasure's Sake' in *Ethical Studies*), do not scruple to take an expression out of its context, give it another sense, and ridicule it as inappropriate or nonsensical. What are they doing but abstracting on the linguistic principle and criticising on the semantical? Such misuse of language is also a most usual source of misunderstanding in everyday life. A man who wishes

If we say that the statement or proposition is the sense of a sentence, and that the sentence, as made up of words and phrases, refers, we can see how easily the fallacy arises that the two can be regarded separately. *It is,* I believe, *this fallacy that is at the root of the current habit of distinguishing linguistic and logical analysis as distinct and separately valid forms of philosophical analysis.* We have seen that the sentence cannot be considered apart from the statement it makes, for the sufficient reason that it cannot be distinguished as such. Even Carnap has to say: 'Provided . . . is known to be a substantive . . .' etc. (See page 65, note 1 above). It might be argued that the sentence could be considered as an example of grammatical convention or rule: but I defy anyone to know whether a word is a noun, verb, or adverb, without being aware of either its significance or its meaning or both.[1] We do not learn grammar before we learn to use words, and in learning a foreign language we learn the grammar by means of examples—that is, we learn to build up sentences grammatically and to do this we have to know some words. As an instance of sense without reference, we can take this verse read by the White Rabbit:

> I gave him one, they gave him two,
>   You gave us three or more;
> They all returned from him to you,
>   Though they were mine before.

The King tried to give it a reference, but failed. It is an irritating composition, because there is sense enough to suggest a puzzle; but the component expressions, taken together, make nonsense, and could not be said of anything.

to 'show off', or defeat an opponent at all costs, distorts the flow of argument for his own purposes, and it is, under such circumstances, impossible to get him to recognise what he has done. It is a form of being at cross purposes, and was employed by the Sophists on occasion—for instance, in Plato's *Euthydemus.* We might perhaps describe it in a literary way as an elaborate form of punning. In contrast, the respectable method of reductio ad absurdum preserves both the expression and its sense in the context, and thus faithfully reveals the incompatibility latent within it. By this method the argument is wholly pursued, in the other it is not: but in philosophical discourse it is often difficult to see where the one ends and the other begins.

[1] Cf. Bradley: 'A sign cannot possibly be destitute of meaning . . . If it did not to some extent get to *mean* the thing, it never could get to *stand* for it at all.' *Principles of Logic,* p. 60.

As we are in search of a method, we must look carefully at both linguistic and logical analysis, but first we should make quite sure of our terms. Once more we should consult what Bradley would have called the 'psychical facts' of perception and judgment, since the only way of deciding between rules of language is by examining the results they will yield in practice. Our present position may be schematised thus:

World	†††		Perception	Verbal forms
**	†††		of sense-data	(words & sentences)
***	– – –	Sense-data – – –	as fact. – – –	of
**				propositions
Objects		Fact	Proposition	Knowledge
(a)		(b)	(c)	(d)

We should note that by sense-data here is meant the given-in-sense, and *not* the given-by-sense which is the philosophical concept. The latter is a device to overcome the difficulty that we only see things from some angle, and cannot logically infer a whole object from part of it. The philosophers's use of "sense-datum" leaves it open whether we can speak of what we do perceive of an object, or whether we can only speak of the end results of our sensations. Probably the confusion over sense-data in philosophy arises because habits of perception, the ways in which we perceive the world, become an integral part of the sensory processes once they are established. Philosophically, perception and sensation remain distinct, empirically they do not. However, what I intend by "sense-datum" in this context is that which actually is a modification of our sense organs and their projections, whether we talk of sensations or not: we name those modifications and their names are names of qualities. Sense-data are always objects in relation, we cannot see or perceive just one quality alone without being overwhelmed by it.

Of (a), (b), (c), and (d), both (a) and (d) belong to the world of things and events, and occur in time. They are actual. The process of verbalisation is roughly like that of a till which shows the appropriate amount of money when the correct keys are pressed. When an object is wrongly identified, the wrong word comes to the lips. Referring expressions are the signs adopted for what can be designated. The expression is arbitrarily used, a matter of convention, of decision, but, once adopted and learnt, the connection is direct in ordinary language and in scientific languages. The long process of discernment, discrimination, and co-ordination continues all through life, and if both (c) and (d) are concerned together in it, the process is rational. The intervention of (c) between (b) and (d) is the part played by experience.

A truly psychological account of these four factors in the cognisance of a human being would, in addition, be required to bridge the gap between sense-data and perception: for we cannot assume that what is given as sense is perceived. Philosophers tend to regard themselves as perceiving everything there to be perceived. It is a necessary condition of perception that we attend in some way, that the organs of sense are directed to objects, which of course also include our own thoughts, verbal or otherwise, which occur as psychical facts. We can look for things and fail to find them, as we can search for words or thoughts and fail to recall them. We look perhaps in the wrong place, or we look in the right place and still fail to perceive 'it'. A thing is lost when we do not know where to look to see it.

Perception is logically prior to sensing, since we cannot perceive what we have not sensed and yet we cannot describe what is sensed until it is perceived. When perception occurs, we cannot assume that there is no difference between what is perceived and what was sensed. If we take it that objects are logical constructions from sense-data, then they have their natural home in a world which is also a logical construction.

The accepting of propositions as true or false and the recording of these verdicts in statements occupies time, and thus we should speak of 'perception' as a process. But to those who regard 'perception' as some sort of achievement, we can concede that what we commonly call "perception" is in fact a series of perceptions. The importance of this cannot be overemphasised: for its neglect gives rise to many philosophical controversies, for instance, that of equality. Bradley found this problem very difficult, and we can thank it for his whole account of inference. On our account of the relation of words, perception, sense and fact, it is plain that inference consists in perceptual analysis, not philosophical analysis. We do not see everything that is given in sense in an instant; we have to look again, to bring relevant ideas and knowledge to bear upon it.

This function of perception in philosophy was recognised by Bradley when he said: 'We can fix no limit to the possible information the word may convey, for we do not know how many attributes in the end may be found to be implied in the quality . . .'.[1] And Waismann has allowed for the same perceptual processes in speaking of the 'open texture' of most of our empirical concepts.[2] With regard to inference and equality, if '$a = a$' and '$a = b$' seem to be irreconcilable, it is because they are taken in the same instant of time: but, since inference depends upon perception, it is a succession of perceptions in verbal form, and thus in time. We start with 'a', but as we reflect upon it, the content broadens to include 'b', and if our understanding, our logical citeria, accepts 'b' as essentially a feature of 'a', then we speak correctly of inference. For from the statement of the fact 'a', we pass to "If 'a', then 'b' ", and thus to " 'a' therefore 'b', for 'a is b' ". But in my opinion '$=$' is out of place in any qualitative distinction: 'is equal to' is a term of mathematical precision which is found in quantitative, but not in qualitative, comparisons. When used by philosophers, it seems to me either (i) to presuppose concepts to have the same hallowed essence as numbers in the Pythagorean systems, or (ii) to be a device to discredit definitions by making it appear ridiculous or incorrect that the defined word equals the words of the definition. The example that springs to mind is Moore's use of equality to discredit naturalistic and metaphysical definitions of 'good'.

We have to accept the fact that making statements takes time either as utterances or thinking, whereas to note several features of an object before our eyes does not take time, but occurs simultaneously. It is part of our account of 'fact' that we do not perceive, and necessarily do not perceive, single qualities. It is the multiplicity that suggests the object. It is perhaps because words refer to objects that there is so strong a prejudice towards regarding the grammatical subject of a sentence as existent. Reference does imply existence, at least in the reduced way that what is referred to is something about which something can be said. A chimera is a name for a recognisable traditional image, and sentences about chimeras would not be nonsensical unless they offended rules of logical type. To say

---

[1] *Principles of Logic,* p.184.

[2] 'Verifiability', in *Logic and Language,* ed. Flew, First Series.

'Chimeras are solid' is nonsensical, since the notion of mass is inapplicable to chimeras; but although to say 'Chimeras are inevitable' may be false, it is meaningful, and thus debatable. But, in practice, nobody utters sentences that have no sense, except by mistake. The purpose of constructing a sentence must fall outside language itself, and it could be said to be self-contradictory to speak of sentences which say nothing: for such sentences are deliberately constructed to act as examples of something that might but does not occur: and in this sort of context they acquire meaning, however hard their author may endeavour to exclude meaning from them.

I want now to argue in support of the assertion that the two current philosophical methods of linguistic and logical analysis assume that sentences can be taken as units of language or as units of sense; that is, that they can be considered either in their aspects as language, grammatically, or as making state-ments, and, further, that each of these aspects, taken separ-ately, provides a valid field for inquiry. It is apparently held that study of the grammatical form, the syntax, of language provides evidence of the nature of the world, on the one hand; and, on the other, that explorations into sense leave the verbal form aside as irrelevant. Explorations into sense result, it is supposed, in the elucidation of concepts. If to have acquired a concept is to be able to use a word correctly, then when we want to know what a word means, or to what it refers, we should inquire into the uses made of it in ordinary language, and we shall then discover how to define it in other words. Its relations with these other words will give us insight into the relations of the things to which they refer. Or we can start with the concept, the idea, the sense, and by examining and deter-mining its relations with other concepts, or ideas, we shall eventually also discover by what words it is to be applied. The difficulty of giving a clear expression to these procedures should warn us against their ready acceptance, and before we commit ourselves to examining statements by either of them, we should scrutinise the distinction made between them. As the distinction rests upon the separation of language and sense, it is this separation that we must attempt to justify. I propose to ap-proach the problem with especial reference to the views of Bradley in this chapter, and Frege in the next. Since these two philosophers make use of the word "meaning" in different ways, I must first clarify these uses and reconcile them with the uses adopted by myself.

The word "meaning" itself I shall avoid using as far as possible. Wittgenstein used "bedeutung" as indicating the objects named in the proposition by words, and he used "sense" for the fact mirrored in the proposition. I propose to use "signify" for the naming of objects, and "sense" for the nature of what is named. In ordinary speech we say 'Which one do you *mean*?' for reference, and 'What do you mean?' or 'What are you saying?' for sense. Bradley, however, used "meaning" for "sense", in our use. 'An idea is symbolic', he wrote on page 168 of his *Logic*, 'and in every symbol we separate what it *means* from that which it stands for'. On the same page again, 'It is better to assume that the meaning is other than the fact of which the meaning is true.' We must remember that Bradley used "fact" for anything that could be spoken of, as Wittgenstein used "object". Bradley then, after the passage quoted, continued by condemning the terms "denotation" and "connotation", this 'slovenly terminology' he called it. To connote, he alleged, is to imply, 'and the meaning of a word is not its implication'. He went on: 'With the names of individuals the meaning may perhaps be said to be "connoted", but with adjectives such as "red", and abstracts such as "redness", what is "connoted" is clearly not at all the attributes but the individual reality'. I think Bradley was saying here that in using "red", "redness", we intend to indicate the red that has been before us, the red that is sensed; for in the following paragraph (para. 4, page 169) we find: 'No word such as "whiteness" stands simply and solely for the abstract quality. It means this directly; but it indirectly points to an implied individual, an actual case of whiteness'. This would be in accordance with his notion of the concrete universal, the universal that is unthinkable except in its instances, its actuality. It is from such instances that part of the meaning is 'taken' and used as idea. Meaning, for Bradley, was roughly equivalent to intension.

Frege avoided ambiguities in the use of "meaning" by distinguishing between 'sense' and 'reference', but he introduced a complication in the ancillary "idea" which must be considered later. He did, however, apply "sense" and "reference" to single words, while Wittgenstein used "meaning" only with names for objects, and "sense" for propositions, not words. Bradley avoided ambiguities in "mean" on the whole by using "extension" and "intension", but on occasion he also used "mean" for both of these.

I must first support a claim that Bradley used "judgment", "extension" and "intension" as I propose to use "statement", "reference" and "sense". It may appear confusing that my use of "reference" and "sense" does not correspond to that of Frege, but as it is my especial purpose to argue that philosophers would do better to follow Bradley's guidance in these matters rather than that of Frege, to keep to these same words will, in the end, prove more illuminating. Very briefly now let us look at Bradley's uses.[1]

(i) *Judgment*. Speaking about utterances of single words, Bradley wrote: 'You may utter a word which conveys to you, and which you know conveys to others also, a statement about fact. Unless then you are deceiving, you must be judging' (page 57). Judgment is an act, something we do: 'Judgment proper is the act which refers an ideal content (recognised as such) to a reality beyond the act' (page 10). The real subject of the judgment, according to Bradley, is always outside it, as part of what can only be indicated, pointed at, by "this", the world, fact. The words in the judgment convey to others what "this", what feature of the world we purport to speak about, but that they refer correctly is always a matter of doubt. As a pattern of the inescapably hypothetical statements we make, we could take: 'If this is a table, then it is brown.' But "this" does not here merely signify the object I am touching, for Bradley's doubts were not so crude as that: what he intended as the judgment was something like the following: 'If it is correct to distinguish this as an object which has a part in reality then I ascribe to it the qualities of being a table and of being brown.' This rigmarole does not prevent "table" and "brown" being considered as names for a certain kind of object and a certain shade of colour. Thus the question of what is ultimately real, and of what can ultimately be correctly said, may be disregarded when taking the judgment *as* a judgment: what matters is that the content, the sense, the 'ideal' content, *is* referred to what is taken as fact.

[1] All the page numbers in the following three paragraphs refer to the *Principles of Logic*, 2nd edn.

(ii) *Extension.* The whole sensible reality, the ultimate, individual subject of the judgment, and the feature of it distinguished *as* some feature of it, or some object, is outside the judgment, outside the act of judging; so it is part of the world as we see it, and as we understand it. In 'This bird is yellow', 'It is the fact distinguished and qualified by "this bird", to which the adjective "yellow" is really attributed. The genuine subject is the thing as perceived, the content of which our analysis has divided into "this bird" and "yellow", and of which we predicate indirectly those ideal elements in their union' (page 58). And 'It is still a part of the presented environment which is actually the subject and the real substantive of which this whole complex is indirectly asserted' (page 59). On page 83, Bradley indicated by a note that: ' . . . taking "*A* is *B*" to mean "the things that are *A* are the things that are *B*" is required by extensional theory'. And again, on page 168, he said of the word "horse", 'If it signifies any other idea which includes "horse"; for example cart-horse or race-horse, it is taken in extension. And again, it is otherwise taken in extension if it is used for individual horses'. Finally, we should note a direct account of reference on page 171: 'If we take extension to mean that number of real individuals of which the meaning is true . . .'

(iii) *Intension.* Extension is what we are speaking about, and intension is what we say about it. Intension is attribution. And since when we apply ideas to things, we apply them, Bradley insisted, *as* ideas, intension is general, universal. It consists of part of what something is, something real and experienced, taken and referred to something else. On his view if we say of a portrait that it is charming, we have acquired the ideal content "charming" from other things, other portraits perhaps, which have charmed us. We are not, for instance, repeating what we have read in the papers. Both intension and extension, according to Bradley, 'are relative to our knowledge'. Kant was wrong in supposing that judgments were always synthetic or analytic (in Kant's sense), for the 'character varies with the knowledge possessed by various persons, and at different times. If the meaning of a word were confined to that attribute or group of attributes with which it set out, we could distinguish those judgments which assert within the whole one part of its contents from those which add an element from outside; and the distinction thus made would remain valid for ever. But in actual practice the meaning itself is enlarged by synthesis. What is added today is implied tomorrow. We may even say that a synthetic judgment, so soon as it is made, is at once analytic' (page 185). Here we have another admission that our perceptions of the world are not absolute, but occur as stages in a process, and the truth which might be sought in statements of fact is at best a partial truth.

We can consider Bradley's views on extension and intension under (a) his explanation of the ground of the distinction between extension and intension, (b) his arguments for the validity of reading judgments either in extension or intension, (c) his arguments against such reading, and (d) the force of his arguments on these last two points, and their application to our own case.

(a) Bradley based the distinction between extension and intension upon the principle of identity. Since identity is a principle of reality, the identity of any subject reaches back to the ultimate, all-embracing identity of the individual Real. Thus it is always correct to take a stand upon the identity of a subject. If we take the judgment from the standpoint of the identity of the subject, we find certain attributes occurring within that subject as diverse. We are starting with the existent thing, and bringing those attributes together in it. In this, we are taking the judgment in extension, naming the attributes we find in the subject. Identity requires diversity as its complement, its opposite: they are two sides of one and the same thing. On the other hand, then, if we start with the diversity of the attributes, the different qualities named in the judgment, we assert the connection of the differences in one subject, and we take the judgment intensionally. 'All judgments', wrote Bradley in Terminal Essay III, 'assert an identity in diversity and a diversity in identity; and either of these aspects can be specially emphasised.'

(b) Bradley seems to have changed his mind about the reading of judgments. In chapter VI, book I of the *Logic* he said: 'I will begin by the assertion that every proposition can be read in whichever of these ways we prefer. I will then show, in the first place, how all can be interpreted in extension, and will prove the same, secondly, with respect to intension.' Lower on the same page—174—he wrote: 'It is not true that every judgment

is *naturally* read in both of these ways. It is true that all judgments can be read correctly in either manner, and read
legitimately.' In Terminal Essay III, on the other hand, we
read this: ' . . . a reading simply in intension can not in the end
be called possible. Can then, on the other side, every judgment
be taken merely in extension? Such a view to my mind is in
principle vicious.' We have now to consider his arguments in
support of these varying views.

An *extensional* reading deals with things: if we take 'Dogs are
mammals' in extension, we assert that where we have a thing
which is a dog, that thing is also a mammal (page 174). We are
not placing a class within a class, since classes, when looked for,
cannot be found. The extension of the predicate is the objects
called mammals. Thus what the judgment taken in extension
asserts is that the objects called dogs and the objects called
mammals all possess the attribute 'mammal'. The relation is
between the objects. Since the objects have a common attribute, what we do is to assert an identity between certain different individuals (page 180).

To read a judgment *intensionally* Bradley had to remove the
individual subject, as a thing, from the judgment altogether.
This he did, as we have seen, by supposing the judgment to be
predicated of a real subject outside the judgment, beyond the
act of judging. Doubt about the proper description, the nature
of this subject, leads to the assumption of it as a mere supposal,
and, in consequence, both subject and predicate in the judge-
ment itself are reduced to attributes, adjectives of the particular
subject which is 'an unspecified condition' of the judgment. In
support of this, Bradley quoted 'some' as an example of unspecified conditions rather than as indicating unspecified
individuals. 'Some trespassers must be prosecuted' he instanced,
on page 182, and 'some' he interpreted as 'under some condition'. This argument makes it easy to see why he said that
judgments were not read *naturally* in both ways! Nor does
number bestow extension: for number is itself an attribute.
Thus we say 'a proposition is read intensionally, when both
subject and predicate are taken as attributes hypothetically
related' (page 185).

(*c*) One may suspect that it was Bradley's long investigation
into the nature of inference that led him to revise his earlier
views about extension and intension. For it is plain that those

views were based on taking a stand upon *either* identity *or* difference, and consequently upon the legitimacy of regarding two
aspects of one and the same thing as each of them independent.
But in his discussion of inference, Bradley was forced to acknowledge that a similar pair of aspects, that of analysis and synthesis, could not be severed, though they might be distinguished and the distinction acted upon a practical way (pages
470–1).

Turning again to *extension*, Bradley conceded in Terminal
Essay III that judgment is an act of saying something about,
and that the 'about' could not be wholly excluded. But 'about'
is intensional. In asserting identity and in denying difference,
or diversity, the denial is meaningless without the assertion of
identity. If the judgment asserts different attributes of the one
thing, these different attributes cannot be kept apart in the
judgment, for the judgment asserts them together as one idea;
it is, accordingly, the identity of the different attributes that
enables them to be held apart in the judgment. Thus, since the
identity, within the judgment, of the attributes is an ideal
identity, it is intension. 'To banish intension from judgment',
Bradley concluded, 'is everywhere to reduce judgment to
nothing.'

His arguments against the possibility of reading judgments
in *intension* only are similar: judgments can be read in intension,
since the real subject falls outside them, but they cannot be
read *merely* in intension. The Reality, of which the judgment
affirms, cannot be said to fall entirely outside the affirmation,
and it cannot 'in the end be taken as a mere system of ideal
content'. Thus although one may take the grammatical subject
and grammatical predicate in extension or in intension, implicit
in our thought and in the words we use lies something of both.

(*d*) In assessing Bradley's argument on extension and intension, I want to deal with the following questions: (i) Are
Bradley's arguments in the Terminal Essay based on necessity
or contingency? (ii) Is it possible to regard polar concepts, if
they are aspects of the same thing, as logically separable?
(iii) Finally, can we find, in Bradley's arguments, any clear
ground for either accepting or refusing to accept a distinction
between linguistic and logical analysis?

(i) With regard to extension, Bradley remarked that to read a
judgment merely in extension is in principle vicious (page 642).

This 'in principle' follows from two premisses which are themselves statements of principle: the first, that the very identity of the subject is meaningless without the diversity in the judgment, and the diversity in turn relies upon an ideal identity; the second, that the judgment is 'about' something, and in speaking about anything we apply sense as description, otherwise we could not say anything about it. Thus it follows from the very nature of judgment itself, from Bradley's account of it, that judgments cannot be read only in extension. Accordingly, it must be said to be necessary.

But with intension Bradley's position is not so clear. He said: 'This Reality can not in the end be taken as a mere system of ideal content', and that if this conclusion holds, 'a reading simply in intension can not in the end be called possible'. Is this 'possible' a matter of principle or of fact? That the reading simply in intension is impossible may be said to rest upon two premisses, and each of these I think must be admitted to be contingent. First, if judging is referring ideal content to an actual thing, as subject, then we cannot in fact get an ideal content without the subject. For how should we? As a psychical fact, a judgment must have its occasion, its context. Unless we think or speak about something, we do not think or speak at all. We can always say our thoughts and our speech-acts are about something, even if we turn some former example of ideal content into a psychical fact because it occurs as the subject of our thoughts. We have here the problem that Carnap tried to solve by speaking of languages and metalanguages. But instead of resorting to this kind of puzzle, we can take Bradley's distinction of the idea as psychical fact from the idea as content. When we try to think of ideas by themselves, we turn them into facts, part of the world, by their very occurrence as the subjects of our thinking. This is a matter of fact, not of principle, for it is conceivable that thoughts think themselves in some way we do not know about. It is in judgment as a speech-act, to use Austin's expression, that the ideal content must attach itself to some fact, some purpose.

Secondly, on Bradley's view that ideal content comes from former instances of matters of fact, that all such content rests upon concrete universals, not abstract ones, it must be agreed that ideas are not static, they change with our experience. If we are to use the word "horse" to describe something we see, then the next time we want to use the word, what we have seen in this instance may modify the content of the idea we apply by using the word. On page 184, Bradley wrote: 'If the intension signifies the meaning of a word, and the extension is the number of actual objects of which the meaning can be truly predicated, then both extension and intension are relative to our knowledge, and naturally fluctuate with altering experience'. We can not have 'floating ideas' since ideas are only possible when sense, knowledge, perception, are applied either to an instance before us, or to past events in reflection. And this again is a matter of fact, contingent.

But, if we accept these arguments, we must also say that it follows *necessarily* from them that propositions of mathematical logic cannot refer. An existential quantifier, for instance, could never indicate an object: all it can say is that an object might be indicated, that reference might occur, never that it does.

(ii) Bradley regarded extension and intension as dependent upon the antithesis identity—diversity. He thought them aspects of one thing, so that to make use of the one in thinking was to invoke or to imply the other. Using 'imply' in the sense of 'connotation', we would say the one was part of the connotation of the other. I do not agree with Bradley that 'connotation' if it means 'implications' is thereby condemned: for when we use a word we do expect that something will be implied by it; if we speak of tables and chairs we imply furniture, and so on. If we speak of a house we imply at least one room. The implication is formal or material since it rests on our knowing what the words indicate, and what the fact indicated is like.

We have already seen that we cannot think of a thing without thinking not only of its identity as a thing but also of the diverse characteristics that are its attributes. We would not see a book on the table without seeing either mass, or colour, or shape, or as a *certain* book, and we have either to see one of these qualities and one belonging to the table, or more than one quality of the book as a minimum requisite of perception.

What then does it mean to speak of 'aspects'? Do aspects necessarily constitute antitheses? To speak of an aspect of something—a situation, an object—is to speak of the whole as actually viewed from some point. But it is viewed from some point, it is not, like the philosophical 'attribute', for example, of

God, a manifestation of the whole. When we think of an object we can imagine the whole of it, inside and outside, back and front, as long as we do not imagine ourselves looking at it, making a picture of it; but if we do look at it, we do not see the whole of it, though we can proceed to do so in stages. It is necessarily true that we cannot start looking from more than one place at once, so that if we have aspects we have something we can only express by means of some sort of disjunction. If we start from the aspect of identity, we cannot at once think of diversity, and *vice versa*. This is where the antithesis lies. The object, its qualities, are constant throughout, but we can approach them from either side. From what we have said previously, the qualities as instanced in the object referred to are not the same—and necessarily not the same—as the ideal content by means of which they are specified, distinguished. For the ideal content, as such, is derived from previous instances whereas the object consists of a new set of instances, present ones. Thus we must say that we pass from the identity of the object to the diversity which is ideal; or else that we pass from the diversity of the attributes to the identity of the object. On this view, then, we must accept Bradley's distinction between things as object-identity, or as attribute-diversity, to be different or alternative ways of describing applied to the same thing. We cannot employ them both at once. Thus identity-diversity appear as polar concepts, neither of which has independent meaning; for it is impossible to give an account of the one without also making use of the other expression. It is the two together which enable us to speak of the world as we can know it.

But it is one thing to draw a logical distinction and another to assume the distinction is also one of fact. To say that a judgment may be read *either* as referring diverse and ideal attributes to an identical subject, *or* as finding in an identical subject certain diverse attributes, may be to say that we can start with diversity and proceed to identity, or that we can start with identity and proceed to diversity. From this the logical conclusion is rightly drawn that we cannot do both at once. But what we cannot do both at once concerns the direction of our procedure, not the identity and the diversity: we cannot argue that the two procedures are independent and yet that their content is the same. Because (*a*) if we start with the

identity of the object we must remain within extension and
posit the content of all our previous experienced instances, and
we assert what Bradley called a 'partial identity' of our present
subject with those previous ones; while (b) if we commence
with the diverse attributes we do not include the instances that
are in the object now before us within them. Thus if we read
judgments in extension and intension severally, we are not
going to reach similar conclusions. And since something of
what is in one conclusion is omitted from the other we cannot
say that either by itself is philosophically, or logically valid.
For the judgment contains *all* its content, or it is not the same
judgment.

(iii) If we cannot take the two concepts 'identity' and 'diversity' as self-subsistent, then how can we distinguish extensional
and intensional investigations of sentences? Sentences refer, and
it is only when a proposition is expressed in some kind of sentence that it becomes part of the world and thus can be said
about something.[1] So what should we say about a method
which proceeds on the assumption that by examining the rules
of speaking, the grammar of language, the relations between
words, we are going to find out the plain truth about the world,
and eliminate muddles in our knowledge of it. Or about a
method which relies on the elucidation of the concepts we use
in speaking to tell us exactly what it is we are saying about the
world?

On Bradley's account it is plain that the one method leads—
if imperceptibly—into the other. For let us suppose we
wish our analysis of language to tell us about the world. By
"language" we should signify 'successful sentences', since there
could be no point, if language is communication, in analysing
unsuccessful ones. But how are we to know which sentences
are successful? Surely, if we have a criterion for saying of a
given sentence that it is meaningful, that is, successful, we also
have the criterion which we required at the beginning of this
chapter, the criterion to tell us what sentences about responsibility we can accept as meaningful.

Suppose we say we know all the conventions of our language,
and that, on these, a certain sentence '*S*' is incorrect. Are we to

---

[1] It is in recognition of this that modern educational theory has come to insist
that children must be able to talk aloud before they can be expected to think
realistically, i.e. sensibly.

go on to say that '*S*' has no meaning, or that if it has, or appears to have, it may be misleading in some way? '*S*' can only be incorrect either (*a*) in mixing up words of different logical type, (*b*) in failing to refer, or (*c*) in being self-contradictory. Of these three, no two can be combined, since all three themselves contain expressions of different logical type. But (*a*) can only be decided by looking at the meaning, (*b*) requires that we look at the world, at our factual knowledge of that world, and (*c*) is a matter of sense. Unless, then, we are directly acquainted with every possible sentence in the language, we cannot say whether a sentence is correct or not just by looking at the symbols, or signs. But if we knew every possible sentence in a language, we would, if language contains the truth of the world, already know all about the world.

If, on the other hand, we rule that our language is only to contain words that do refer, we still have to know the context of a sentence to know whether it is meaningful; for we said above that we cannot know precisely what statement is being made by a sentence apart from its context, and unless we can say *that* the sentence is making the statement it was intended to make in its context we cannot know whether the sentence is "successful" or not.

There are two further objections that can be made to the linguistic or extensional method of analysis: (*a*) If truth is the correct use of language, then one could say that one does not have rules or conventions by oneself. When we have an experience that we cannot fully express, according to the linguistic view, this experience has no part in truth beyond the limits of our shared knowledge of linguistic convention. Even if we agree that what is incommunicable cannot claim to be knowledge, and hence also not true knowledge, we need not agree that, because I do not have any previous experience of the rules or conventions for expressing a certain experience, I do not attempt to describe or express it. For how do linguistic conventions arise unless someone first uses the expressions that become matters of convention? If we say that we can never go beyond what has already been said, then presumably language ceases to develop. But it is a contingent fact that languages do develop. It is a legitimate claim that philosophy is not concerned with anything that has not already been said, but that does not mean it can assume nothing more ever will be said.

(*b*) Again, if truth is dependent upon language, which it must be in some way, since truth is giving a truthful account, and is not ultimate reality in itself, are we going to accept the ruling that truth is relative to language rules? That would mean that if one man had a greater knowledge than another of language rules, he would necessarily have a greater knowledge of truth. But if he had a greater knowledge of truth, it is analytic that he would not be able to communicate it, since no-one else would know the requisite rules, and thus he would not be able to establish those linguistic rules by which his sentences would come to count as conventional expressions. This position seems utterly untenable.

Bradley's explanation of mediation in the use of language, that is, that the referring of ideas to features of the world points back to the particular instances in our experience from which those ideas are derived, taken, has the advantage of avoiding the use of "idea" or "concept" in language as if it stood for an entity. Ayer,[1] in speaking of Price's expression 'familiarity with universals', gives its meaning as the ability to use words correctly. By "correctly" he means adhering to the conventions 'which determine the possibilities of its combination with other words', and being able to apply it to the appropriate situations. If I suppose someone explaining to me what are the appropriate situations in which to apply a word, then I agree that the whole affair is merely a matter of relating one set of symbols to another. But to suppose someone explaining to me is to suppose experience, fact. And this intrusion of fact is admitted by Ayer at the conclusion of his paper: 'We interpret one symbol by another; but it is only because this circle is broken by our actual experiences that any descriptive symbol comes to be understood'. Language itself is not enough, we would not need language if we had nothing to say. It is our common and analogous experience as the basis of the descriptive symbol that permits understanding, communication, the explanation of one set of symbols in terms of another. Beyond our use of words, beyond the network of rules, lies not the objective world, but that world as we know it, lies fact: and fact, our known world, *is sense*.

On the other side, there is the attempt to analyse the concept. This exercise, or method, leads directly into language because

---

[1] *Thinking and Meaning* (1947).

we have to pursue it by means of sentences. The concept is taken as the total use of an expression, or as the notion governing the use of several expressions. It becomes immaterial whether we speak of the meanings of words or of the application of concepts. But it assumes we can deal exclusively with meanings, or ideas, and leave reference and the world aside. Elucidation and application are assumed to be mutually implied. The conceptual world, to lead us to truth, must have something in common with fact. Either it is fact in its own right, concepts or ideas being real by themselves, or since they are the medium in which we acquire knowledge through perception, the medium is common to everyone, and thus the world we each of us know and live in is mediated by the same stock of ideas. In this case we would, of course, never know whether it was the real, or an unreal, world, we should never know when our statements were true and when false.

Logical analysis is, in practice, extended by analysing not only the given sense, a sense which was on some occasion given, but also what might be said to be the sense of the words on *any* occasion. In other words, it requires the assumption that a given statement can be interpreted in as wide a variety of ways as is permitted by *any use* of the expressions within it. Thus logical analysis becomes in effect an inquiry into the scope and application of universals. When a given statement is analysed, it is no longer a given statement, but a miscellany of what Bradley called "ideal content", and what we should here call "sense" without reference. Such 'sense' could, on our view and on that of Bradley, only be personal experience. Whether it is plausible to say that any logically reliable result could be gained by such procedures we must consider later.

For the moment, we must content ourselves with remarking that, since language is what we say and is the means of communication, to consider the form of language alone is to abstract from language *as* language; while to consider only what may be communicated is again to abstract from language as such. As grammatical forms, words and sentences would never be used to say anything, for they can only be chosen for use by their communicative function. We do not choose one word rather than another because it sounds pleasant, or because it comes under a rule, but because it indicates what we wish to say, and *also* sounds more pleasant than other alternatives we happen to know. Linguistic analysis ignores that languages may have more than one word for one thing, while logical or conceptual analysis ignores the personal limitations imposed by knowledge upon meaning. To assert that all these considerations can be covered by saying language is an affair of rules, or even of conventions, or habits, is, as Freud supposed in a famous theory, to see the world in terms of rules, and is, in effect, to suppose rules at once the means and the goal of truth.

APPENDIX TO CHAPTER IV

SENSE AND REFERENCE

In support of the distinction made in this chapter between 'sense' and 'reference', I wish to apply it (*a*) to the name-relation antinomies, and (*b*) to the paradoxes of Zeno.

(*a*) In the name-relation antinomies, an expression which is part of the sense of a sentence is used as a substitute for an expression used as a referring expression in another sentence. Since there are two sentences involved here, and both have sense, to attempt to tamper with the sense and reference leads to absurdity; the most that can be effected is the implicit condensation of a syllogism into one grammatical sentence. In the sentence '9 is necessarily greater than 7', 9 is used to refer to the number nine in the cardinal series. In the sentence 'The number of planets = 9', '9' is part of the sense that there are nine planets. As far as the planets are concerned, as the objects to which reference is made, there is no number as such among them. It is we who add the number when we count them, and by saying 'The number of planets = 9' we add the notion or 'sense' of number to both sides of the equation. An equation is here also quite unsuitable as a mode of expression, and its unsuitability becomes apparent in 'The number of planets is necessarily greater than 7'. This sentence is not, to my mind, false, as Carnap supposes, but nonsensical, unless it is agreed as a matter of convention to use "The number of planets" as synonymous with "9", when the sentence becomes true. For what we have done, in the first instance, is to remove the reference of both sentences and put together part of the sense of both. Another way of describing it is as the fallacy of the ambiguous middle, but this would perhaps be regarded as somewhat old-fashioned. Similar difficulties and confusions occur in Tarski's account of the paradox of the liar.[1]

(*b*) With regard to Zeno's paradoxes, which have been supposed to be paradoxes in objects, but which actually arise out of mistakes in language: in Achilles and the tortoise, the sense of Achilles' running is transferred to and used as the reference of "catching-up". But Achilles is not catching-up, he is running, and at some point in that running he is passing. Achilles would not pass the tortoise if his catching-up consisted of an infinite number of shorter and shorter distances. He would, according to the wording of the paradox, stop each time he caught up the tortoise and then have to catch him up again. The verb "run" then ceases to refer. The same argument can be applied to the flying arrow, which depends upon the reference of "instant", and to the Dichotomy, which confuses the reference of starting and stopping with that of running. That verbs refer is shown most clearly by the existence of the gerund.

[1] See his 'The Semantic Conception of Truth' in Feigl and Sellars, *Readings in Philosophical Analysis*.

V

THE STATUS OF CONCEPTS

We are still unsure how to proceed in order to obtain significant sentences about responsibility, nor are we decided as to a suitable way of dealing with such sentences, if we had them. If we want sentences that refer, we shall have to find a situation in which they occur; while if we take statements that can be referred to imaginary situations, we have to find a way of determining the relations of the ideas associated in those statements with that of 'responsibility'. We have, to return to Wittgenstein's metaphor, to decide how to draw the contours, and, we may ask, is it possible to draw them at all, in the absence of authentic reference?

We have seen that the method called conceptual analysis supposes this to be possible, but we must know upon what grounds this assumption is based. In the last chapter we decided that linguistic analysis requires that the analysis be carried out within sight of the facts, and that the implications of our practical experience should guide our verbal inquiries.[1] In this inquiry we were greatly helped by the arguments of Bradley. In attempting to discover what is involved in "conceptual analysis", we may again remember Bradley's views, but to my mind the two most interesting writers on this subject are Ryle and Frege. Should the method be found to be valid, we can then apply it to elucidate 'responsibility' and its conceptual allies; while, if it does not satisfy us, we can at least follow Wittgenstein's recommendation, and ask how we came to learn to use the word.

The study of ordinary language rests on the assumption that every expression can be ruled to have a determinable meaning. If it is assumed that ordinary language contains what people want to say, that what they want to say is what they perceive, and that what they perceive is true, then it could be logically

---

[1] Cf. Hegel, *Logic*, para. 7: 'In order to accept and believe any fact, we must be in contact with it; or, in more exact terms, that we must find the fact united and combined with the certainty of our own selves.'

concluded that analysis of ordinary language will in the end lead to the truth. But there are three assumptions as premisses to this conclusion. And it does seem to reduce truth to a kind of colossal referendum. It also assumes, as remarked above, that perception is something equally available to all, that all see what is to be seen. And yet it took a man of the stature of Kant to sort out what, in perception, is due to the means of perception, the transcendental, and what is in fact to be objectively perceived. The possibility of perceiving a world is not the perception of that world, as the horizon is not the limit of the sea. We cannot, however, see or perceive the sea without seeing the horizon, just as we cannot see or perceive events without noticing time.

We should beware of speaking of language without being sure what it is we are speaking of. For language is on the one hand a flexible assemblage of words and sentences used to refer to and to state facts; while on a different view or aspect it is a vast network of rules within which truth is to be confined; and these two accounts have little or nothing in common. Science, as it finds new phenomena, adopts new words as names for them, and such terms are only meaningful in that special context, since the phenomena themselves are only perceived by its special procedures. Philosophy does not have a special context, since the phenomena it investigates are commonly accessible to all. It has, on this account, to be careful not to adopt new terms for old friends, as, for instance, "sense-data" for "appearances". It cannot justify itself if, in its zeal to avoid "idealism", it substitutes "sense" for "idea" or "concept", and banishes metaphysics by the doubtful device of excluding the contingent fact in favour of the necessarily true linguistic rule. For what easier than to substitute for 'It is warmer in summer-time' the rule that "warm" is *necessarily* used of "summer", not because it *is* warm in summer-time, but because in the language there is a necessary or analytic relation between the words "summer" and "warm". In the language it could be said that 'summer *ought to be* warm' but a sentence such as this is ambiguous: it appears to be a rule for matters of fact, which is absurd. Yet when we say, in chilly March, 'It ought to get warmer soon', we *are* talking about matters of fact, since it is in accordance with the laws of nature, with *probability*, that certain seasons are warmer than others. The difference between necessity and contingency is here clearly indicated; yet while logical analysis would accept the sentence as one of probability, linguistic analysis would find a rule in the "ought", and since rules are matters of legislation and decision, this would have to be a rule of language. 'As if the world had waited on it to learn how it ought to be, and was not,' said Hegel in paragraph 6 of his *Logic*, speaking about the 'analytic under-standing'. The contrast between the two versions brings out the impossibility, in linguistic analysis, of expressing the contingently possible: for when we surmise, or speculate, as we have to do in everyday life, we take the sense of expressions as our premisses and examine by material implication what might follow from their various combinations. So long as we keep to words that have a clear reference, we remain within the possible. But linguistic analysis excludes this speculation: for one cannot have rules for what is not known, one can only deduce from the rules one already has or knows.

Thus the assumption we are to deal with here is that mean-ings are determinable, that we can take a correct sentence, and, provided it contains a referring expression, that it is not a mere grammatical example, we can find its sense.

Many philosophers today hold that if we can give the conditions of the verification of a statement, or sentence, then we thereby show the sense. Suppose we say: 'The boats were laden with fish'; to verify this we would have to have been looking at the boats at the appropriate time and we would then have observed whether they were laden with fish, or not. Thus the sense of the sentence on this view is our perception of those boats in a certain condition. But this procedure will not serve our purpose with 'responsibility', because our trouble is that we have no statements about responsibility to be true or false. All we have is a set of duplicate sentences which do not refer, since we made them up. But suppose we had not made them up? Suppose we had come across them in concrete situations? We should then have the word "responsibility" given a sense by someone in that situation with reference to the contents, or supposed contents, of that situation. It must have that sense as a proposition, since we cannot use a word in a sense by itself. Only propositions are sense, we agreed (page 84 above); it must accordingly be from propositions that we learn how a word should be used. We do not, however, acquire the sense of a word, as if it were a shadow, with a fixed shape. 'What we want to say' is not something that fits certain words: what we want to say is only part of what directs our choice of words. For we may want to use an elaborate expression, or a simple, naive one, or give a set of alternatives. It depends upon the ease of communication, the understanding we have to reach out to. Yet in some way 'what we want to say' remains constant throughout these formal possibilities of expression.

We have seen that what we want to say is what we have perceived, for only that is "sense". And we should remember that we include among our perceptions what we call "intuitions". In what we perceive there are material objects and there are relations between them; there are also persons and the relations between these. As our perceptions duplicate themselves over and over again, certain features are constant, or recurrent, in them, and these we distinguish in the process of objectification. These acquire their linguistic labels by convention. But we cannot learn a name for what we have not already distinguished. Similarly certain patterns reappear again and again in our perception of personal or social relations: 'he is angry', now because of X, now because of Y, distinguishes the anger from the exciting cause, and both become recognisable. Thus "anger", "angry", acquire meaning apart from X and Y as anger-making. We recognise features of situations, not the situations themselves: the qualities of social relations are acquired in the same way, by the same process, as are the qualities of objects.

Ryle has expressed this as the acquisition of concepts by abstraction from propositions having common features.[1] On page 8 he writes: 'The truth is that what we label 'ideas' or 'concepts' are abstractions from the families of propositions of which they are common factors or features. To speak of a given idea is to speak summarily of the family of propositions resembling each other in respect of this common factor. Statements about ideas are general statements about families of propositions.' On the view that the proposition is the fact as perceived, these families of propositions would be the specific instances of concrete universals that Bradley believed the use of an idea as an idea to point back to. But I am not sure that Ryle would take it in this way. From a passage in 'Systematically Misleading

[1] *Philosophical Arguments* (1945).

Expressions', we see that it is our own perception of things, of the world, that gives rise to concepts. Then we turn from our perception of the world to the relations of the propositions which are our judgments or statements of those perceptions. Ryle is thus referring indirectly to fact when, in *Philosophical Arguments*, he says, on page 9: 'As people's understanding of the propositions that they use is always imperfect, in the sense that they never have realised and never could realise all the logical powers of those propositions, so their grasp of ideas or concepts is necessarily incomplete. The risk always exists that confusion or paradox will arise in the course of any hitherto untried operations with those ideas.' "Logical powers" is the name he gives to the relations which hold between propositions in virtue of their form, for example, compatibility and incompatibility. Since ideas derive from propositions, we can, too, speak of the logical powers of ideas, or concepts, for, always, the idea leads back to the family of propositions upon which it rests. Thus Ryle also argues that, before we can explore the logical powers of ideas, we must be able to apply them in practice, they must have been based upon actual use, and it is their application that provides the material of their differences. On page 11, he reaches a point relevant to our present difficulty over 'responsibility': he says: ' . . . the problem is not to pinpoint separately the locus of this or that single idea but to determine the cross-bearings of all of a galaxy of ideas belonging to the same or contiguous fields. The problem, that is, is not to anatomise the solitary concept, say, of liberty but to extract its logical powers as these bear on those of law, obedience, responsibility . . .' Here we have the same position that is reached by Austin's dictionary method, a number of concepts, or words, that we know are related, together with our desire to establish, to discover, those relations. The only clue Ryle gives us is that when we misapply ideas, the expressions by means of which we do it will be found to contain an absurdity: the idea itself is somehow immune, exempt from distortion, since by definition we imply by "idea" what must be itself and unequivocal, being unexpressed. If we apply 'it' wrongly, the expression we give it, the application of it in language, will reveal our fault. We could put it that there are no wrong ideas, but we apply ideas wrongly, and application involves expression. We can certainly agree with Ryle that if we do know how to apply a concept it is analytic that if we can also explore its logical powers we shall do so correctly; but to say this gives us no reason at all to suppose that (*a*) there is a set of concepts which everyone acquires, or (*b*) that if there were, we should ever be able to track it down, or (*c*) that, if we distinguish between the powers of concepts logically, by, for example, 'type', we are doing anything more than applying concepts derived by a study of logical powers to the distinction of those logical powers, a process necessarily mediated by the use of language. The discovery of logical powers is not a matter of rules, but of the perception of the validity and relevance of certain predicates rather than others. It is what we can do with a concept that constitutes it.

What we are really up against in investigating ideas by means of ordinary language is, and *necessarily* is, that while the perception of entailment may be common to all who are interested in such matters, the perception of material implication depends upon factual knowledge. Material object statements are statements of fact, contingent, the sentences which express them refer. What Carnap and others have tried to do is to turn them into the kind of statements whose relations are necessary. To illustrate this, let us take a sentence that Ryle does *not* use: 'Logical powers are discoverable', and we see that it *entails* that logical powers are somehow there, or existent. But the *material implication* is merely that we could find them if we tried. There is nothing here to prevent us defining "finding" as bringing into existence, determining, by verbalising. The latter would be in accordance with what Ryle himself says, the former would not. On Ryle's account of the acquistion of concepts, we remain within material or formal implication because we remain within actuality, contingency.

What we can assert with confidence is that, for Ryle, the word "expression" is used in the sense of a particular expression. For if expressions, according to him, may be absurd, then it is contingent whether they are absurd or not, and the word applies to concrete instances. This is important, because as with "language", "thought", "word", and any other of the multitudinous words that refer to forms of life, "expression" is ambiguous: it can refer to a particular instance of saying something, or to a habitual mode of saying something. In the former case, "expression" may be said to be adequate, inadequate, clumsy, etc; but in the latter, the assumption is made that something is said, and it is in this latter use that it occurs in linguistic philosophy, when this is conducted as an analysis of any expressions in ordinary language taken *as* expressions in order to extract the logical parallel between the world and language—taken, too, regardless of context. This sophisticated use of "expression" must be sharply distinguished from the everyday use in self-expression of some sort, when communication is of secondary consideration. "Expression" in the use we are concerned with is more convenient than "word", since words by themselves do not succeed in conveying precise sense when used as predicates. For logical purposes, Bradley remarked, it is better to ignore the ideal that 'words should mean what they stand for and stand for what they mean' (*Logic*, page 168). Frege—see note to page 113—also thought that if we had sufficient knowledge of the facts, the reference, we should know at once whether a given sense was correctly ascribed, but that in practice such knowledge was unattainable. Perfection of description can be assumed in a perfect language, but if we are to use logic in the pursuit of truth then it is better to admit the disparity of thought or experience and expression.

In assuming that once we have acquired concepts—by abstraction from propositions—we are able to discuss their relations, Ryle succeeds in compromising between regarding the concept as solely resulting from its instances, and in being a definite unit of meaning which is in some way static. For if we acquire a concept empirically, we acquire it as it is contemporarily; whereas if concepts occur as definable units they would have to transcend variations in fashion and verbal distinction. Bradley, in this, stood on the Aristotelian side, Frege on the Platonic. Bradley, in his *Logic*, page 640, wrote: 'There is not and there can not be any such thing as a *mere* idea, an idea outside any judgment and standing or floating by itself. We have here again not an actual fact but an unreal abstraction. The essence of an idea consists always in the loosening of "what" from "that". But, apart from some transference, some reference elsewhere of the "what", no such loosening is possible.' And 'What in every sense comes first is the concrete whole, and no mere aspect, abstracted from that whole, can in the end exist by itself,' followed by the warning: 'The adoption, however legitimate, of an unreal order, entails . . . the ever-present risk of a real lapse into mistake.'

Frege, however, distinguished between the reference of a word, its sense, and the subjective idea with which it is associated in the individual mind. His account of the difference between reference and sense corresponds to the difference between indication and description; we point verbally to objects, thus referring to the world, and we say what they are, we speak about them. In this Frege made the same distinction that Bradley intended in distinguishing "that" a thing is from "what" a thing is, but he did not go on to make the further distinction by which Bradley clarified the particularity of the "this" with regard to the generality of what could be predicated of it. Consequently he found himself in difficulties as between the idea a person has about something, and the idea which can properly be held by anyone about that same something. Bradley insisted that "sense" (the "what") is only *there* in its occurrence, that it is only obtained from our previous experience *as* needed, as called for in further experience; and thus he believed the process of learning what, in experience, is more probably true to be a process of analysing and synthesising the information we can obtain about the world; Frege, on the other hand, believed that we could distinguish in theory between 'one man's idea' and 'the sign's sense, which may be the common property of many and therefore is not a part of a mode of the individual mind.' 'For', he continued, 'one can hardly deny that mankind has a common store of thoughts which is transmitted from one generation to another'.[1] By the associated idea Frege seemed to mean something dependent on what we called the first mode of perception on pages 43-4 above, the recollection of what has been perceived as imagery. Now as soon as we cease to be confronted by things, our experience of them is limited to what we have perceived of them at the time of confrontation, which remains as images. Images are limited to what we have perceived, no information can be derived from them as such, and any information we do succeed in obtaining with reference to them is due to their assimilation with other images by means of thought, of ideas. Thus for Frege, the associated idea is a man's experience in some respect, the relevant images, including words as verbal images, associated affects, and so on. It is *from* all this that ideas are

[1] The quotations from Frege are all from 'On Sense and Reference', in *Frege*, ed. Geach and Black.

'taken', according to Bradley, to be applied to other concrete experience. But Frege supposed "sense" to be distinct from the personal experience, and, as distinct, to be constant as the meaning of certain expressions. It is interesting to note that, while Bradley denied objective reality to objects as perceived, and projected his doubts on to some remote Real, Frege, his contemporary, in his turn doubted the subjective idea, the personal associations acquired by experience, although he gave no account of how we come to make use of 'objective sense.'

As an attempt to distinguish the truly ideal from the merely perceptual, the solution put forward by Bradley seems unassailable. But if we accept it, we must at the same time admit that to speak of the conceptual, or the logical, analysis of any statement, or set of statements, apart from the context, is utterly misleading and inappropriate as a method of clarifying our judgments of perception.

Let us look more closely at Frege's argument; for it cannot be denied that it is held by many philosophers, and by many of our contemporary analysts who perhaps would not care to admit to it, that access to a common conceptual world is the hall mark of the philosopher.[1] Unless they are prepared either to follow Hegel (*Logic*, paragraph 67), and reduce Platonism to 'reminiscence' mediated by education and experience, a position which has the doubtful merit of being irrefutable, or to accept some sociological account of the origin of the ideas we acquire, for example, that of Pareto, he will have to find some very strong arguments to offset those of Bradley. When Hegel wrote, in paragraph 3 of his *Logic*, that 'It may be roughly said that philosophy puts thoughts, categories, or, in more precise language, adequate *notions*, in the place of the generalised images we ordinarily call ideas,' he did *not* mean that personal experience is somehow transformed into an objective field of common inquiry.

Frege thought the associated idea to be an internal image which varies with different people, resulting in the fact that there are 'a variety of differences in the ideas associated with the same sense'. The sense is the thought, by which, wrote

[1] At one time I was much attracted by such a world, but could not bring myself to rely upon any habit of thought which I could not relate to some empirical origin. Gradually, and perhaps thanks to Bradley's *Logic*, I discovered the source of the illusion

Frege in a note, 'I understand not the subjective performance of thinking but its objective content, which is capable of being the common property of several thinkers'. He distinguished levels of 'difference between words, expressions, or whole sentences'. Where the difference only concerns the idea, one person may see differences which another does not, and this is especially relevant to poetic expression. On the second level the difference may concern the sense, and finally, the difference may affect the reference.

Sentences, according to Frege, only have reference when their component expressions refer, and thus it may be said that they have reference in respect only of their truth-values: for without expressions which refer there cannot be any question of truth or falsity. We are driven, Frege thought, to look for the reference of sentences by our striving for truth. Judgments 'can be regarded as advances from a thought to a truth-value'. Frege is here still in accordance with Bradley, the main difference between them being that Frege accepted the object as such, while Bradley only accepted it as a way of seeing reality 'through a hole' (*Logic*, page 70). This difference belongs to metaphysics, not to logic.

Frege's next step is equivocal: it might seem to be towards Plato, but for myself I believe his intention was otherwise, and I shall return to this point later (see page 130). He supposed that when a subordinate sentence occurred within a main sentence, this subordinate sentence would refer to a "thought". In the development of his argument, he had to insist that every expression must refer, and thus every expression that does refer becomes a logical proper name: for it is made a condition of reference that something is uniquely designated. If it can be said that the reference of, for example, reported speech, "*A* says '*p*' ", is the thought as such, then the reference must be to the occurrence of that thought as the speech in its original form. Bradley would have called this the psychical fact. Frege gave both main and subordinate sentences reference and sense,[1]

---

[1] It may assist in throwing Frege's view into relief if we recall Wittgenstein's treatment of composite sentences in the *Tractatus* 5.54, which we considered in ch. III, p. 62 above. Wittgenstein pointed out that such sentences state facts as a configuration which is a co-ordination of objects. Thus for Wittgenstein these sentences are not composed of main and subordinate statements, though grammatically they appear to be so, but they make one statement, and therefore have

the sense of the latter being the fact that the thought expressed in the subordinate sentence *was* thought or said. 'In this case', he wrote, 'the subordinate clause has for its reference a thought, not a truth value; as sense not a thought, but the sense of the words "the thought, that . . .", which is only a part of the thought in the entire complex sentence.' And again: 'The main clause and the subordinate clause together have as their sense only a single thought, and the truth of the whole includes neither the truth nor the untruth of the subordinate clause.' Since the reference of the subordinate sentence is to a thought, there is an indirect reference also to the kind of thought, the purpose of it—command, request, etc. Again we can say that Frege used "reference" for something real, actual, something that took place, and thus had some form. 'A truth value cannot be a part of a thought, any more than, say, the Sun can, for it is not a sense but an object.' Even though, however, we can see that his distinctions are similar to those of Bradley, he does not describe them in such a way that the analogy is precise. Thus we are justified in supposing that the development of his thought might have taken a different direction.

At least we are clear about the distinction between reference and sense; but what we are not clear about is the distinction between what Frege called "the associated idea" and the objective "sense". If this distinction does correspond to the difference between our images of concrete experience and ideas as ideas, distinct from reference, we should have to condemn the current practice of conceptual or logical analysis; for it is certain, and indeed it *has* to be, that in analysing a given statement, or the sense of a sentence assumed in the absence of a context, we inquire into the possible sense of the expressions used and do not confine ourselves to a sense that was intended. In the case of statements apart from reference, or sentences in imaginary contexts, we can never be sure of catching the sense of the words given us as conveying that sense. For it makes no sense to speak of 'sense' when in fact there is no sense. There

---

one truth-value, that of the main subject-predicate sentence. The question of the truth of the subordinate clause does not arise on his account.

Wittgenstein's notion of the 'co-ordination of objects' is, so far as I can see, similar to Russell's 'complex whole' without the constituent of mind (See *Problems of Philosophy*, ch. XII). It is significant that Russell gives a clear exposition of Wittgenstein's views on this point in his preface to the *Tractatus*.

are usually certain statements to be deduced from any given sentence, but, once these are specified, there is nothing more to be said unless the component expressions are taken as permitting wider implications than have been indicated by the given sentence. Thus we may proceed to consider many allied propositions, but we should not deceive ourselves that we are remaining within those strictly enjoined by the original sentence. If the world is a series of objects in relation, then it is arguable that, provided ideas are linked to things by words, we can pass from the analysis of one idea to that of another, and as long as we keep to *our* ideas, based on *our* experience, we will keep in some kind of touch with reality. But if we do not keep to our ideas, and suppose that what we regard as an 'idea' is objectively valid as a 'sense', then, logically, analysis could proceed for ever, it could have no limit, and would constitute the possibility of the universe, as indeed Hegel believed it to do. In this it is in direct contrast with linguistic analysis: for the linguistic rule argument is a dead end just because it is unanswerable; there is nothing more to be said. It is like the parent who always supports commands by the one 'reason'— '*because* I say so'.

What we must do now is to review the evidence that can be brought in support of an objective sense or meaning of words and expressions. We will consider this evidence under three headings: first, the evidence to be found in language; second, that based on a notion of shared experience; and third, the grounds of the argument that ideas are in some way static and are transmitted by society.

I. LINGUISTIC EVIDENCE

(i) There are, in all natural languages, so far as we know, words for concrete things and their relations, words for feelings, for characteristics, and for actions. Grammatically, all such words can be used as substantives, as if they were names. It can thus be argued that if we have a name and use it to communicate, we must be using it in a way that others understand. The name, accordingly, must stand for something, it must mean something, and when we use it we must be talking about something.

Against this argument, we can say that, although languages

contain such words, there is no guarantee that they can be successfully used in communication: for when language is used, and we communicate by means of it, we must speak, or write in the language, and there is no necessary connection between a statement that someone has used certain words to communicate and a statement that everyone uses those words to communicate. For if, when a person wishes to communicate something, he does not appear to succeed, he changes his words, and makes use of other expressions until he has achieved his end. He has to find those expressions which are significant to others. There can be no argument from grammatical to significant use: for although a word, to be a word, must have a use, must have been used, it does not follow it is used by everyone, or that it could be used by everyone, with the same reference. It is conceivable that a natural language might develop in such a way that only material objects had names, and that everything else that needed to be said had to be said by metaphor or analogy, using the same expressions.

(ii) There is also an argument from 'legislation', which asserts that words must have a definite sense because there is some arrangement, some agreement, by which they have that definite sense. The assumption is made that words have the sense they appear to have because it has been a matter of decision and precedent to use them in certain ways.

Formally, we can attack this argument for its attempt to pass back from what we have to what produced what we have, and thus for treating the necessary condition of language, that is, that words must have a sense, as if it were sufficient for decisions on sense. As a premiss, this argument requires the further assumption that what is a matter of convention is also a matter of rule, and that what is a matter of rule is necessarily a matter of decision.

Materially, on the other hand, the argument breaks down on the practical question of reference. It is true that we can define words and arrange those definitions to cover all that we know of the world. Providing the definitions are not contradictory among themselves, they may appear to be comprehensive. But suppose we start from a factual detail, and ask under what word it should fall? We can have no means of determining this: for words can only apply to distinctions we have made already, and if we proceed to make new distinctions, we need new

words, or at least new arrangements of the old. This requirement led Waismann to his theory of 'porous concepts' (see
page 89 above). What is likely to happen if we remain bound
to the former set of words is that the new distinction has to be
brought under one or other of them, and may be shifted from
one to the other because there is no way of redistributing the
verbal descriptions of fact in order to accommodate the new
one. An example of this would be the difficulty of adapting the
notion of a 'public check' to cover a case where it is contingently
impossible for there to be an observer (see page 78 above).
Would we change the account of 'fact' or of 'observable'?

2. IDEAS AND SOCIAL EXPERIENCE

The evidence based on our experience as social beings falls into
two parts. The one consists of an assumption that, since we do
have common experience in many ways, shared experience, we
are able to acquire identical ideas. The other is the notion of a
common conceptual world to which we all have access, in
which we all, to some extent, live.

A. *The case for shared, or common, experience*

Since we do communicate, there must, it could be said, be a
common fund of reference, or we would not succeed in making
ourselves understood. And if there is a common fund it must
extend beyond the concrete, material world, for it is a fact that
we do make ourselves understood and clear to each other on
many matters besides events in the external, physical world.
For the purposes of this argument, we could agree that communication is established in fact, or in practice, if, when we
have told someone something, he replies, including inferences
from what we have said in that reply, or if he then asks a question
which is relevant to what we have said.

We must admit that this argument from the apparent
universality of our experience is very plausible, and it is supported by psychological evidence that all human beings,
irrespective of country and language, tend to make the same
conceptual distinctions, however differently words and expressions may be distributed among these distinctions.

Communication is of two kinds, and social experience must be said to be of two kinds, whether shared or not. For we ordinarily communicate by means of language, yet where there is a strong antipathy between two persons, it may be impossible for them to communicate by language, for there is no access to the same field of reference, however much they may have in common according to training and experience generally. For communication there must be coincidence of factual knowledge, and also some coincidence of feeling. These we must take in turn.

We have already seen that communication is only a matter of degree, and that misunderstandings are common. When there are differences of opinion, we do not change those opinions by sheer force of expression, we have to consider further evidence. For opinions are formed upon the evidence a man has in support of them, unless they are accepted upon authority, in which case they refer indirectly to evidence held by someone else. But if we say this, we accept the principle that all opinions, all use of general terms, refer back to the particulars which condition them, upon which they are based. The concept, on this view, is an intermediary, and only in so far as we share evidence, do we have similar conceptual schemes. That we do form similar opinions, that we do have similar concepts, remains contingent, not necessary.

With regard to feeling, it can be said that, in communication, there is another level of understanding besides that of sharing the reference of words. We may, when we are told about, or when we witness, events, become aware of the effect those events produce on the feelings of those concerned. This is sometimes called imagination, but there seems to be no ground for distinguishing between words and pictures as regards 'sense' or ideas generally. The factual evidence upon which we base our inferences from the content of what we are told is widened by the inclusion of knowledge of states of mind, but this is not what I mean by 'communication' of feeling. We can know what kind of feelings a certain man will have on hearing a certain piece of news, but we need not have any feelings ourselves. It is when we do have the same feelings, or suitable feelings, as those undergoing certain experiences that we might speak of communication or 'empathy'. We can be mistaken in inferring a man's feelings, but we cannot be mistaken in the fact of our own, even if we wrongly attribute them, or wrongly describe them when they occur.

But this argument leads nowhere, since, if we know a person well enough to say how he will feel about this or that, then we are personally involved in what involves him. Those we know well, who are more or less intimately concerned in our own lives, whose gains and losses, joys and sorrows, produce effects upon ourselves, form part of the world as we know it and provide part of that which significant sentences refer to. Our feelings may mislead us, we may be sure a friend will be affected in a certain way, and then discover that some other event, unknown to us, has, in conjunction with what we do know, led him to feel differently.

All we can say, then, on the subject of shared experience, is that, so far as experience is shared, we may have the same field of reference. This in itself does not permit us to say that, on the basis of that shared experience, we do in fact acquire the same ideas. For some loyalty may colour the whole of our experience, and affect all our inferences. And if any man can be said to adhere only to one loyalty, then we might be able to 'share' his ideas; but in fact, a man is a man mainly because he contains many loyalties engendered within him by his varying social experiences.[1] It cannot be assumed that, when communication occurs, the means by which it occurs is anything more than an approximation of reference which is achieved through practical discussion, comparison, and mutual interest.

B. A common conceptual world

There are two arguments in support of this notion: (1) the rationalist view that knowledge of ideas is intuitive, that ideas are 'given' to us, not acquired empirically, and (2) that, although empirically acquired, concepts are such that their relations are necessary.

(1) It cannot be argued that, since reason is common to all, the contents of the rational consciousness, that is, ideas, are also common to all. For when we speak of reason as being common, we mean to refer to the powers of reasoning, the ability to infer

---

[1] The reader may be interested in what T. H. Green has to say about what he calls "common consciousness". See his *Lectures on the Principles of Political Obligation,* H, esp. paras. 139–40.

and distinguish the valid from the invalid argument. If it is asserted that, our reasoning powers being common as are our perceptive powers generally, our ideas tend to fall into common patterns, then we are not arguing for common concepts, but we are, in effect, adding a footnote to Kant's transcendental aesthetic. Even so, we could only establish the fact that those concepts, or patterns of concepts, do coincide by an empirical investigation, as, for instance, the tests for colour blindness. And when we had finished examining each other, the probable outcome would be that we were left with, as a highest common factor, some list of categories, such as that to be found at the beginning of Roget's *Thesaurus*.

Austin pointed out that there is a tendency in philosophy to ask the same questions as to "origins" about concepts that have been fruitlessly asked about sensa.[1] And it is an empirical fact that we cannot ask ourselves anything about an idea as such, without asking ourselves about something that is not an idea. For instance, if I ask myself what kind of concepts, or what ideas I have about penicillin, utopia, railways or democracy, the sentences in which my questions are asked refer, not to my ideas, but to my knowledge of these various subjects. My knowledge, in its turn, is constituted by what I have learned, what I have observed, what I have thought about what I have learned and seen. That I have used language to achieve all this is not to say I have been using language to make ideas, but that thinking and opinion-forming are functions of language. Talk about ideas and their relations is talk about things and what they are with the eyes averted, as it were.

We cannot find and isolate concepts within our own experience, but we can trace the ideas that have been held by others provided they have been expressed, and the expressions recorded. This is also the only way we can discuss our own ideas apart from frankly discussing facts. Even in what is called the history of ideas, a personal selection has to be made, and the whole field from which the selection is made was called by Hegel 'objective mind'. When we talk about someone's idea that is recorded, we can only do so in words that require other ideas for their comprehension. Thus we cannot speak of the history of an idea, but only of the history of ideas. Since we must express the meaning of an expression by other expressions,

[1] 'Are there *a priori* concepts?' *Proc. Ar. Soc. Suppl. Vol.* (1939).

concepts tend to appear in constellations, a number of which must be elucidated together if any one of them is to have any relation with any other (see page 110 above). We cannot elucidate or give the history of, for example, "democracy" without also elucidating and giving the history of "liberty", "individual", "constitution", etc. And here we find ourselves back at our original difficulty: we had, by Austin's method, and by an experiment of our own, a group of words, which purported to represent ideas. How then, as Ryle has put it, 'map' out their meaning? If we cannot answer this question, neither can we say that the meanings 'exist'.

(2) To attempt to maintain that concepts, when empirically, or inductively, acquired, have necessary relations may be an attempt to show that concepts are acquired as units which are constant, and in this case, we shall leave the matter for the following section. Or it may be to assert the logical consequence of the argument that, if we can only investigate concepts that are acquired, then it is only *as* acquired that their relations can be investigated. This would merely require that, during the investigations, the concepts were not modified in any way, that they would be taken as a given set of ideas.

Plainly this is trivial, for it asserts the tautology that when perception ceases or is suspended, the content of perception remains what it was.

However, it may be that the discovery of what Ryle has called the 'logical powers' of concepts is a method of inquiry into our accounts of the world in abstraction from it. Now if several observers compare the accounts they have composed of some one thing, or subject, they will not only find their perceptions of it vary, but they will also find they allot different words to different features of that subject. By comparing, criticising, reconciling, their accounts they may throw light upon the subject they were all anxious to understand when they observed it. In discovering the logical powers of the relevant ideas, these observers would be able, presumably, to find out where ambiguity of expression had misled them in inferring from their observations. That only one account of facts, only one set of propositions can be correct, or true, is a necessary truth, and that where conflict occurs between accounts, there one or both are necessarily false, is undeniable. This procedure appears to be another version of Carnap's thesis that philosophy has only to say what kind of words are being used in statements of perception. And to say that statements about logical syntax are necessarily true is, we saw, a device to turn matters of empirical fact into matters of necessity.

If concepts are inductively acquired, then the relations between them are contingent, and can only be described in statements related by material implication, not by sentences entailing each other. Only if concepts were given *a priori,* could their relations be said to be necessary.

3. THE SOCIAL TRANSMISSION OF IDEAS

Finally we have to ask whether it is tenable that ideas are constant, are units of some sort, so that when they are acquired, they are acquired as similar from person to person. To say that concepts are acquired inductively, and variously, is no objection to a view that society is a repository of ideas from which we all help ourselves. If our account of the acquisition of ideas only covers what Frege (see page 113 above) called "the associated idea", then there might still be the objective sense he believed in as a perquisite of society. We could qualify society as a relevant, a particular society, and still allow for common access to certain ideas within that particular group.

The most convincing case for the social existence of ideas has been constructed by Pareto.[1] He expressly declared that 'not even logic supplies necessary inferences, except when such inferences are mere tautologies' (volume I, chapter I). He regarded ordinary language as a kind of bad photograph of the world (volume IV, Appendix III*f*). He made full allowance for the selective nature of learning; for, according to him, ideas belong to social life, and an individual takes from those available to him the ones that suit his dispositional self. There are certain fundamental ideas which persist in society, and which correspond to the instinctual needs of people generally. These ideas are constants, they survive changes of custom, outlook, and linguistic usage. They appear as elements in theories, if theories are taken to be groups of ideas, that differ widely in content and reference. Propositions stating theories are analysable into three discernible elements of basic drive or need, of social forms serving as vehicles for these, and of the resulting

---

[1] V. Pareto, *The Mind and Society* (4 vols, 1917. Eng. trans. 1935).

theory which might also reflect an attitude of the contemporary society. At times, Pareto maintained, society tends to expand and to integrate its ideas, and at other times to disrupt and separate them.

Clearly this view involves regarding 'ideas' as 'there' in society for anyone to acquire, and even if we accept that concepts are acquired from instances, we need only postulate that enough instances occur for the idea to be transmitted.

There is much to be said for Pareto's thesis, which is worked out in the most minute detail. It allows for the immense diversity of opinion and interest, and yet gives some account of how ideas are used as norms and thus as reasons for manipulating things in one way rather than in another. But it does not answer the question as to whether the concept or the word comes first, it may rather be said to avoid this issue. If we learn to use a word, we cannot in fact use it until we have some sort of concept, but surely we can only acquire the concept through language. This difficulty leads one to think of language as the application of the right expressions to the right situations, an ability acquired by imitation, and thus purely a matter of convention. On this view, the acquisition of concepts is a minor affair, and entirely subservient to the correct use of words.

However, although Pareto's theory is attractive, there is at least one argument fatal to it: if ideas are acquired from society and appear and reappear in different theories, under different guises, then how can we be sure they are the *same* ideas? That they are the same depends upon Pareto's account of human nature, its components, as investigated by psychology and sociology; but it is analytic that if a certain idea, X, appears *only* in a number of different guises, then, unless we know and can recognise some feature by which to identify X, we cannot say for certain that the different guises are guises of X.

In general, as an inadequate summing-up, we must say that there is little evidence that can help us to decide whether we should regard concepts as a common fund of ideas and words as incidental to it, or that words are a common fund and the ideas incidental. And we have found nothing, beyond assumptions, to justify us in supposing that there is a sense, an objective sense, for words and expressions, apart from the objects to which they are actually used to refer. Unless we 'legislate'. But if we legislate, we are in effect adopting a technical language, on a par with those used by the sciences, with regard to which it is mere tautology to assert a necessary correspondence between word and sense, since we have prescribed it.

The most we can do is to endeavour to approximate what Frege called 'the associated idea' as between one person and another, with the aim, not of producing sets of concepts with necessary relations, but of identifying the more accurately the objects of which we speak when we use words. And this is another way of saying that we can free our perception of the world from the bias imposed on it by emotional associations and the effort to prove some favoured theory. We can create, or establish, our own conceptual schemes by studying, not the relations between ideas, but the evidence given to us in support of those ideas.

We might dismiss the distinction between talking of words and talking of concepts as trivial, were it not that Frege's hypothesis, or doctrine, of an objective sense has had serious consequences. For if we adopt a method and practise it, our actions in doing so tend to implant in us the implications of that method. And in practising Frege's logical techniques, in employing his notation, philosophers have been led to think they can turn to ordinary language, examine it, and find *the* sense of an expression. This is especially dangerous with regard to such words as "action", "responsibility", "freedom". Philosophers also come to assume they can investigate their own conceptual schemes and yet remain within necessity; and thus it is that much of what passes for philosophical analysis in the so-called Philosophy of Mind is formally indistinguishable from the phenomenology of the traditional thinkers. Phenomenology might be described as unscientific empiricism, pseudo-empiricism. It is unfortunate that methods which expressly disown metaphysical implications should re-introduce them in a way that escapes notice; for from the hidden assumption there is little effective defence, and the empirically minded student is led blindfold into the very centre of the Platonic camp.

We have left ourselves with no guide as to how to investigate 'responsibility'. On all sides, if we try to meet the word or the concept face to face, we fall into error. We have found no argument that could lead us to forsake Bradley's rejection of the abstract universal and the floating idea; we cannot accordingly embark upon an analysis of a set of chimeric entities.

When one's knowledge fails, and one is aware that it has failed, then is the time to seek advice; and fortunately it is to be had in this instance. Kant remarked that a science should be left to determine its own technique, and that to lay down some method in Applied Logic would be useless, 'nay, even mischievous. One would thus begin to build before he has the materials; and provide the form where there is no content'.[1] We have reviewed the main methods and presuppositions of contemporary philosophical inquiry, and now we have to decide upon the method we will ourselves make use of. To do this, and to heed Kant's warning, we shall have to find out something about the concept of responsibility. We have failed to find statements about responsibility with which a critical method could deal, or which could, for example, enable psychology to devise experimental inquiries. Finally, we have not even given a sense to the expression "the concept of responsibility", since we cannot say what we mean by a "concept", except that it only exists when used, or in its application, which brings us back to the problem of how to obtain statements where it is applied. We could list applications which have been recorded, but we would then have to interpret responsibility merely as the ascription of responsibility. This would be a matter of precedent, and would, since recorded instances give us only a vague indication of context, bring us no nearer to an understanding of the grounds of its ascription, or make it easier to locate instances in future.

In chapter I, we referred to Wittgenstein's analogy of the drawing of sharp outlines over a blurred picture and the apportionment of meanings to ethical and aesthetic concepts. We should now note that his account continues thus: 'In such a difficulty always ask yourself: How did we *learn* the meaning of this word ("good" for instance). From what sort of examples? In what language-games? Then it will be easier for you to see that the word must have a family of meanings' (*Philosophical Investigations*, 77). In due course, then, we may ask how we learnt the word "responsibility", but first let us be clear about learning to use words generally.

It is immaterial, if "concept" is a name for our use of an expression or expressions, whether we speak of words or ideas; and the 'idea' is certainly the 'concept'. We learn the names for

---

[1] *Introduction to Logic*, II. 4.

objects by being told what they are, or by hearing the names used by others. But we cannot learn the name of an object we do not yet distinguish as an object, and so we must say that the learning of words goes hand in hand with the perception of the world. To be told a name involves a proposition: "That is a table", etc. We do not distinguish between what a table might be and the tables we know of until we have experience of several tables. Thus, as Ryle says, the idea, the application of a name, comes as an abstraction from a family of propositions.

The propositions by means of which we acquire concepts are mainly of two kinds: those concerning material objects and their relations, and those dealing with social phenomena, and their relations. We do not spend our days looking at the inanimate; we turn most of our attention to animate bodies, we look at people talking, acting, and we try to plan our own actions upon what we predict others are likely to do. We find certain uniformities in social behaviour and events upon which we can base those predictions, just as we base our manipulations of material objects upon uniformities of size, mass, shape, etc. But there is a sharp distinction between the world of material objects and the world of social relations: for social behaviour demands that at least two persons be involved. It is not that two human beings are necessarily involved, for 'human being' is a biological notion, while 'person' is a sociological one. A person is someone with rights, with a viewpoint. He is, speaking in terms of society, or social relations, not only an agent of social development, but also a meeting place of social influences.

Propositions dealing with social phenomena yield concepts as do those dealing with material objects. But while the latter yield concepts which are concrete and tend to be static, the concepts derived from the former rely upon personal opinion which is subject to change. What we see of social phenomena is thus determined by the descriptions we have heard of them. We see social life through a scheme of categories, through the eyes of others, and social phenomena do not attract our attention unless we have learned to look out for them. Since, however, we do see and hear what is physically there to be seen or heard, social phenomena also are for us logical constructions, but the outlines of what we name and recognise vary with the distinctions other people have drawn for us, rather than with our own efforts of perception. It is because of this that social concepts become constellated, or associated amongst themselves, in the absence of any objective situation to which they refer; and they lend themselves to the formation of theories, and attach themselves easily to the wrong situations.

It is convenient to distinguish, on logical grounds, between three groups of propositions concerned with social relations:

(i) Propositions which can be said to be true or false; verifiable statements derived from records, public utterances, regulations, institutions, and the like;

(ii) Propositions which are personal descriptions of specific or of actual actions, purposes, intentions, opinions, etc.;

(iii) Scientific statements in an agreed and technical language. Of these, group (i) are statements of material fact, and group (iii) are statements of agreed sense, that is to say, they refer to certain specified phenomena and are prescribed descriptions of the relations of those phenomena. With group (ii), however, neither of these conditions pertain: for if propositions—or statements—in this group are to refer, they must be taken as including the speaker or the experiencer. The statement 'It is very cold today' cannot be verified, or be said to refer, by itself: it must either be extended to include the speaker, when the full statement becomes 'A says it is very cold today', or taken to refer to a specific measure, such as, in weather reports, the linking of so many degrees on a thermometer to certain expressions. In the latter case, the statement then becomes verifiable and falls into group (i). The former statement, however, becomes a different statement: the remark made by the speaker becomes a subordinate sentence, and the statement to be verified is now that 'A says . . .'. Should A be found to be shivering when the temperature is high, we should say that A had made a mistake, and had taken his own abnormal condition to be an indication of external circumstances.

Personal statements in their crude form cannot be verified, but neither can they be refuted: and this is of great importance. Ryle has made out a strong case in support of the view that "to know" implies that something can be done, that lessons can be applied and repeated, and other demonstrations made of knowledge. But suppose a man says he knows and refuses to demonstrate? We cannot accept an ability for which there is no evidence, and we cannot assert that he does not know on the grounds that he has not failed to show us that he knows. Accordingly, it is correct, in my opinion, to call such statements, taken by themselves, "pseudo-propositions", for they do not refer. We cannot infer from them, nor use them as major premisses. They are, however, statements, for they are meaningful taken in their context as statements of someone. I propose to call such statements "experiential".

It is here that I wish to continue the account given of Frege with regard to reported statements of this kind. Frege said, as we saw on page 115 above, that statements when they become subordinate sentences in reported speech, do not refer to a truth-value, but to a thought. I remarked on this point that it must be to a thought as an event, an occurrence, that the reference was made. Frege did not make the distinction clear, as Bradley, we saw, did, but at least it is consistent with his thesis to say that the reference is to a state of the person. If we stop thinking of people as entities which have states, and identify a person with his states, we can accordingly say that the sentences, or the statements of opinion refer to a person. If a man uses a sentence expressing his own opinions and feelings, then he himself *is* its reference. Consequently, when we come to talk about the verifiability of such a statement, we must take the reference into consideration, or we cannot say to what facts we would look for a criterion of its truth. A person plus what he says thus ensures that his statement refers to a truth-value. With the word "feeling" this is especially important, for it is contradictory to speak of feelings unless they are occurring in someone. We should accept, I believe, that experiential statements must, for purposes of analysis and verification, contain their author as reference: otherwise they cannot refer.

Plainly, since the same sentence can be used to express an observation statement which is verifiable, and an experiential statement which is not, taken alone, it is upon the context that the onus lies of showing to which category the statement belongs. Very briefly, we can give criteria for the recognition of experiential statements. A statement is experiential if:

(i) The sense of what is said contains an element of particular awareness, so that it would be incorrect to use such a form of words unless a personal experience was being described, or a personal opinion declared.

(ii) The accuracy of what is said depends at least partially upon the criterion that the speaker is being truthful.

(iii) The meaning of at least one expression tends to vary according to the person using it. To say, for instance, 'Stratford-on-Avon is a place of great historical interest' is an observation statement, and it can be objectively verified. But to say: 'The Avon is a fascinating river' is to speak experientially; for the application of 'fascinating' to a river or to this river is certainly a matter of personal opinion, and rests upon some person's particular knowledge of it.

(iv) To take the sentence or expression to be classified and put it into the mouth of someone other than the actual speaker would be an offence against truth.

(v) The concepts concerned have been acquired through social relations, through, that is, other people's descriptions of things, rather than by demonstration. There is thus an arbitrariness about the relevant definitions and their application.

We have not found any convincing reasons to suppose that concepts have any separate or independent existence, apart from our knowledge of language. But, in view of the foregoing discussion of experiential statements, we must admit that if a man says he "knows" there are *a priori* concepts, then we cannot refute his statement or remove his conviction. We can reflect that by *a priori* he only indicates he is unaware of their origin, or guess that the ideas are transcendental projections of his perceptive apparatus; but if we voice such views, he will only be the more certain that we are ignorant materialists!

At least we can now give body to our earlier suspicion that "responsibility" has no one identifiable meaning. It may signify more than one condition, it may figure in more than one kind of statement. But we still require statements. We have a choice now between reverting to method E in chapter II and selecting some philosopher's account for examination, and looking at the social situations in which statements about responsibility might be made. Or we can try both alternatives, in turn. Those philosophers who regard philosophy as necessarily normative would not admit that a practical situation had anything to do with a philosophical investigation, rather that it savoured of existentialism, or was frankly an empirical study, proper to sociology. So we might first challenge those philosophers to find us an account of the concepts relevant to responsibility which can provide us with practical criteria for its application. Can the building of a consistent and comprehensive account of social relations by the use of words in accordance with prescribed definitions relate to facts in such a way that we can recognise responsibility in fact? We must use definitions, since without them, we cannot investigate statements which do not refer to a real situation without supposing the ideas to be themselves real, and this we can safely rule out as a medieval superstition. No system of sense could be held to be valid if it could not be located in some way.

VI

BRADLEY'S ACCOUNT
OF MORAL RESPONSIBILITY

There is little doubt that, if we require a philosophical account of 'responsibility', that of Bradley is the most suitable. His insistence that a theory, to be good theory, must not only be consistent but also comprehensive, that it must take into consideration *all* the facts,[1] can be expected to ensure that the subject has been thoroughly explored. However, in *Ethical Studies*, Essay I, Bradley is dealing only with moral responsibility, and we are as yet hardly in a position to assume that it is the moral aspect of responsibility that is paramount. For we can speak of responsibility in a political, social, and a legal sense besides that of the moral. It has, for instance, sometimes been said that we have a moral responsibility to fulfil political, social and other duties: yet when we speak of duties we do not mean quite what we mean in speaking of responsibility, or of particular responsibilities. Bradley seems to have provided for all of these: for if we look at pages 3–4 of his Essay, we find he uses "moral responsibility" to indicate responsibility for "all" a man's deeds, for all he does. In whatever sphere a man may have acted, his action falls under the word "all", and we may assume that if we can discover what responsibility is in this wide sense of 'moral', then we should, by subsumption, know what is meant by any other kind. By definition, Bradley makes moral responsibility the category-word, with all possible subdivisions included within it as "deeds". 'Without lying,' writes Bradley, a man 'can disown none of his acts—nothing which in his heart or his will has ever been suffered to come into being.'

We must be clear that Bradley is not stating moral responsibility to be a social fact; for it *is* a social fact that men *are* held responsible for what they do. Given a legal or a moral fault, we find out who has been responsible, and, when found, the offender is punished. So much is evident. But it is not this

[1] *Ethical Studies—E.S.*—pp. 74 and 251.

aspect that Bradley is stressing: for we might blame the wrong person, and Bradley stipulates that it is only when a man *has* done the deed that he *is* responsible. His whole argument hangs upon this stout subjective rope, and we shall have to see what limitations it imposes upon his theory.

Such questions should not occupy us yet. We have committed ourselves to examine a theory, and so long as we are doing this, we cannot go beyond it in our criticism. Any difficulties there are must be found within the theoretical 'given' itself. When we are in doubt about Bradley's use of a word, we must look to his own definitions for guidance. If we are presented with theoretical examples, we have not the right to treat them as if they were actual: we are to confine ourselves to what is given us, and take care not to extend the contextual implications further than is analytically contained in the expressions Bradley himself uses. Only in this way can we obtain a reliable account, which we can afterwards submit to tests of our own devising.

The view of responsibility that Bradley gives us purports to come from the 'plain man'. He is not intellectually gifted, according to his sponsor. Although he can say when he thinks a man is responsible, he may not be able to explain why he does so in adequate phrases. He is perhaps uneducated, by which Bradley seems to intend 'unsophisticated', and he may even (page 3) be said to be unenlightened, in the sense that his native or "ordinary" consciousness has not been set over against the views of others, in an effort to acquire opinions of his own. This, then, is the plain man who has a notion of moral responsibility.

To say that men are morally responsible for their actions requires support from supplementary statements about what responsibility is, and about what is meant by "action". Thus Bradley's account involves (1) a consideration of how a man can be responsible, to whom and for what, and (2) the criteria according to which we can say whether a man is responsible or not in particular instances. Unless we know, for instance, when a man can be said to act, we cannot say when he is responsible for his act, for men often have to meet a difficult situation in ways they themselves deeply regret.

I. MORAL RESPONSIBILITY

'For practical purposes', says Bradley, 'we need make no distinction between responsibility, or accountability, and liability to punishment'. If an action X is imputed to A, then A is accountable for it, and liable to be punished. To be accountable, one must have someone to account to, and Bradley supposes a moral tribunal which is also a court of conscience, 'imagined as a judge, divine or human, external or internal'. He argues that 'to give an account to a tribunal means to have one's reckoning settled', but adds 'It is not necessarily implied that the man does answer for all or any of his acts; but it is implied that he might have to answer, that he is liable to be called upon'. He then asserts, that even though we may not know the meaning of the word "right": 'It is *right* that he should be subject to the moral tribunal; or the moral tribunal has a *right* over him, to call him before it, with reference to all or any of his deeds.'[1]

If a man is to be called to account, it is reasonable to say that he should know what it is he is to answer for. Bradley makes no distinction between what a man is and what he does, as he considers it is by what a man does that he becomes what he is. 'What he ever at any time has done, that he *is* now', he says on page 4. A man's standards of conduct are to be acquired by contact with instances of the morality of the community, which Bradley supposes to be a concrete universal. By fulfilling the duties of 'his station', a man comes to understand not only his own part in the moral order of his society, but also, in comprehending it *as* a part, he senses the moral order itself as a 'felt whole', and can then recognise what is right by making 'intuitive subsumptions' (page 196) to this whole. From his own observation and from personal example he builds up some notion of perfection against which he can test the goodness or badness of the actions he proposes to himself, and this notion is his 'moral ideal'. As we are not dealing with moral ideas, but only with their formal conditions, we should not explore these points any further.

We can now see that, when Bradley speaks of responsibility, he is not regarding it as a mere social convention, nor is accountability a social device for the apportionment of praise

[1] *E.S.* pp. 3-4.

and blame. His notion of responsibility is a great deal more subtle. The man who is responsible is answerable for everything he does, not only for duties with regard to his station, but also for systematising all his interests and activities in the light of an ideal of personal perfection. According to Bradley, when a man does succeed in acting in accordance with his ideal, when his acts assist him in the ordering of his life as a good life, then he experiences pleasure; and this pleasure is the feeling of expansion he has when he realises himself as he ought to be. If a man is not called to account by society for his faults, then not only do his wrong acts bring him no pleasure of the true kind, but also he has no opportunity for rejecting his wrong act. It is here that Bradley's view of responsibility as liability to punishment becomes intelligible: for a guilty person becomes, on that view, a standing assertion of wrong, which can only be superseded by an assertion of right achieved in punishment.[1] When a wrong is recognised as such, it is a duty on those who recognise it to cancel it out, thus manifesting the right.

Bradley speaks of justice being suppressed in guilt, and being restored in the giving of what is due, in punishment. And if we are to follow his thought, we must pause and consider the implications of what he is saying. We must assume from his account that a man's progress towards the moral ideal is expedited by punishment. But the word "punishment", Bradley makes clear, is only applicable when man *is* punishable, that is, when he *has* acted criminally. To say this is either to utter a tautology, or to require that the code of the offender is or can be the same as that of the judge who punishes, or orders the punishment. What is difficult here is the question of that code: for if a man builds up his ideal by the instances of communal morality that he encounters, it is analytic that coincidence of moral ideals as between one person and another will be accidental. No-one apprehends the whole objective

---

[1] If this seems a strange doctrine, it should be borne in mind that it is consistent with Bradley's treatment of opposites, which do not stand over against each other, as Hegel would have it, but which are alternatives in thought, so that in asserting the one the other is thereby denied or negated. The trouble with such a view is that, being in effect a choice of words, or description, it tends to conceal the *facts* as successive events of wrong act and penalty. Bradley speaks of "good" and "bad" mainly with regard to good and bad selves of the agent; but, except for the phenomenological account of their emergence, *E.S.* pp. 276–97, he treats these as matters of principle rather than of fact.

moral order, it is merely 'felt', and as, according to Bradley, each person is a distinct part of a system, an organic whole, each person's felt whole might in principle be the same, but in practice it would not exert the same influence.

The most we can say is that, on Bradley's view, a man has to be prepared, if challenged, to justify himself in acting as he has acted, by reference to his own moral ideal, and that if he fails to do this, he is punishable. This is both unconvincing and unsatisfactory. But on the other hand, if the justification is to be left to an all-seeing eye, some projected principle, such as God, we are altogether out of the moral and social sphere and into that of religion. It is hard to see what Bradley intends by his use of 'court of conscience', and the judge, divine or human: for a human judge is certainly fallible, and punishment that is unmerited Bradley calls 'monstrous' and not punishment at all. Our practical experience, however, insists that wrongful punishment is apt to be deleterious in its effects on what we suppose to be moral progress. And again, if a man is merely to be prepared to be his own assessor, then he would have to have, for the purpose of assessment, a basis of judgment, a standard, which was not exemplified in the act to be assessed. Presumably, Bradley expects the moral ideal to provide this basis, but we are not given any precise account of how it does so.

2. THE CRITERIA

These are the essentials of moral responsibility, and we now require criteria for saying when a man is responsible for what he has done, when he has acted, and can be held accountable. Of such criteria, Bradley gives five: (i) that a man has done the act himself, (ii) that he was, at the time of acting, the same person that he is at the time of accounting, (iii) that he had been himself at the time of acting, (iv) that he had sense enough (a) to know what he was doing, (v) and (b) to be able to tell good from evil.

In acting, according to Bradley, the agent's accountability follows of necessity, and the contingent matter of an actual charge is irrelevant. We are still concerned with a moral agent, not with an assessor, who remains a mere possibility.

(i) *Acting*

Bradley describes an act as the translation of mere thoughts into corresponding external existence,[1] and again, as the self-realisation of an idea.[2] He develops his account phenomeno-logically by requiring that an idea must, to realise itself, banish or subdue any idea contrary to itself, and develop its own content, that is, it has to specify and individualise its own proper nature. Thus the process of translating idea into external existence is prolonged. The idea, 'what we have in our minds', as he puts it on page 82 of *Ethical Studies*, must be the same before and after the translation occurs, the intention and the action must correspond. The word "intention" Bradley uses as the idea of a not-self which particularises itself until it is identified with the self in action. It is thus distinct from mere resolve.[3]

I think we should interpret Bradley's notion of action in this way: if an act is to be an act, it must have been seen as a possible act by the agent when he embarked on it, for if he had not seen it as such, in its true character, he could hardly have chosen it. He must have it in idea as it will be in practice. One cannot choose unless one can see what is to be chosen, and if the choice is to be made by comparison with the moral ideal, there must be something to compare. It is not an empirical question of not having time for such processes, but the logical impossibility of bringing two things together if one of them is not to be found. 'The doing *what* one wills is acting, and nothing else is acting', declares Bradley on page 152 of *Ethical Studies*; for the action cannot be what the thought was not, and to speak of action is the sufficient condition for speaking of the thought. Action is thus self-conscious volition, where volition is the empirical aspect of intention.[4]

It follows from Bradley's account of acts that a responsible agent must apprehend the situation in which he is involved.

[1] *E.S.* p. 7.
[2] *Collected Essays*, p. 488.
[3] *Collected Essays,* pp. 483-4.
[4] There is no way of distinguishing in practice between intention and action, but 'volition' covers both terms for theoretical purposes, since it *means* action following on a corresponding intention. Ryle's attack on 'volition' in ch. 3 of *The Concept of Mind* is fully justified, for it is a cover-word for concepts which could never be applied separately in practice.

But to say this is not to say he *is* responsible *because* of this awareness. Nor does a man escape responsibility *because* he did not
fully know what he was doing, or *because* he thought he was
doing something else. For Bradley expressly makes provision,
on page 9 of *Ethical Studies*, for culpable ignorance: 'Where
ignorance is wrong, not to have known does not remove
accountability.' Robinson[1] has called such inadequate thinking, occurring when one could have improved upon it, by the
expression 'wilful thinking'. Using this convenient term, we can
say that accountability, on Bradley's view, is analytically
related to intended acts, where intention arises in non-wilful
thinking. Wilful thinking is itself connected with the act that
issues from it, and thus the agent is answerable for it.

If the intention and the act are to coincide, a man must act
from his own will without compulsion.[2] Bradley argues that
compulsion is only relevant where there is a will. To force someone to be in or to produce a certain state without reference to
his will he calls absolute compulsion, for there is no question of
the compelled person willing at all. But if a will involves seeing
an action as possible before acting, it does not make sense to
speak of forcing a will, for no one but the agent could see the
act in this way. Where a conscious will has either no control
or no time to exert control, or where the deed is known and yet
the will against it cannot be implemented owing to physical or
psychical conditions, then a man is only responsible in so far
as he has himself brought about such a state of affairs. Again
the compulsion may be absolute. There is also relative compulsion which depends upon a man's attitude to the terms of the
compulsion. What Bradley means by this is, for example, that
if a man were careless of death, then the threat of death would
not constitute absolute, but merely relative, compulsion: for he
himself would will the compulsion, if he acted under the threat.

Compulsion, as influence upon the will, should by its very
possibility encourage a strengthening of the will against its
occurrence. Bradley discusses in some detail the difficulties of
applying his doctrine of compulsion, since in practice it is
possible to plead extenuation on the grounds of undue influ-

---

[1] N. H. G. Robinson, 'The Moral Situation', in *Philosophy* (1949).

[2] *E.S.* p. 6. The following argument on compulsion is taken from note A to
Essay 1 of the same book.

ence or psychical conditions.[1] The issue must, he admits, turn on the man himself as witness of his own moral life: how far has he endeavoured to make himself one with the good? At what point did his will fail, and why? It is upon a man's own answers to these questions that in the end the verdict rests.

Before leaving the question of agency, we may take an example in order to illustrate the remarkable flexibility of Bradley's position. Suppose A and B bring about X, and A alleges that B influenced him psychically so that he co-operated in the action X. It would then appear that A is responsible for X only to the extent to which his own will was overruled. The rest of the agency, if we can use such an expression, belongs to B, or is imputable to B. Thus the action X is imputable to both. On the other hand, if B drugged A, and A produced a result Y which was not in accordance with B's will, then, although the result must have been produced by A, he is not responsible, and neither is B. It was not an action, on Bradley's view, and it is idle to look for agents. What it is will depend on the particular circumstances, whether accident, or irresistible urge. But A remains the kind of man who, when drugged, might produce Y, and on Bradley's doctrine it could be presumed that unless he took some steps to ensure either that he was not drugged again, or that, if he were, he would no longer be the kind of man who, when drugged, produced Y, he would in a second case be responsible. For, as Bradley emphasises, it is only when compulsion, ignorance, and weakness of will are in no way due to the failure of a man to correct them, that he escapes responsibility.

(ii) and (iii). *'The same man'*

These provisions are usually combined under the heading of "self-sameness", and (iii) is in any case a subsumption of (i). On page 5 of *Ethical Studies*, Bradley describes self-sameness as being 'throughout one identical person'. Even if the character and disposition of someone alters, we do not say that he is not the same person, in a common use of "person". The 'I' who did the act is to be the same 'I' as is now here, the one 'I' that

[1] That Bradley was fully aware of the practical difficulties in applying his account of responsibility in general must be assumed from the unequivocal statement of his doubts on this point with regard to compulsion.

is distinct from any other 'I'. The act must have been an act, and must have belonged to 'me'.

On pages 33–41 of *Ethical Studies* Bradley discusses the nature of the self with reference to the question of its identity. If a man has to answer for an act, then to be responsible he must be 'the identical self' who did the action; there must be identity of will, 'the will, which is now, is the will which was then, so that the contents of the will, which were then, are the contents of the self-same will which is now existing'. It would be easy, on this and other passages, to say that if the will contains the whole self then we have the identity which is a necessary condition of responsibility, but it would not be in accordance with Bradley's philosophy. What we want for the criterion of self-sameness is a logically coherent account of an agent, so that we can say exactly what identity means in regard to him. Given he does action X at time t, and that we are to find him answerable for X at time $t+$, what is it about him that will enable us to say he is 'the same person'? Since we are dealing with matters of principle, it does not make any difference whether the time lapse is great or small, for that is contingent: the criteria we want are such that they could be applied to any periods in a life-time.

We find no simple definition, as in the case of 'action', or 'intention', to help us. The question of the self and of personal identity arises over and over again in the writings of Bradley, but nowhere does he attempt to co-ordinate and systematise his remarks on the subject. From the unity of immediate experience, from feeling, we abstract, and thus introduce relations into what is, in the first instance, unrelational. We abstract and objectify ourselves, and also that which is over against ourselves, the not-self, the world and other selves. Since there is one reality which lies behind all that we perceive as divided and relational, and since we progress in knowledge of what we succeed in abstracting, objectifying, and co-ordinating, there is always a felt background to our everyday living which contains all that we have been and have done. Bradley spoke of 'a certain basis of content, ideally the same', and so long as it remains in the self 'so long may the self recall anything once associated with that basis.'[1] But he admitted that he failed to perceive 'the metaphysical conclusion which comes from a

[1] *Appearance and Reality*, ch. x.

consciousness of self-sameness', and in his later collection of essays he tried to remedy this. 'Our personal sameness', he writes,[1] 'consists in the ideal identity and the continuity of the experienced'; and his criterion for the accuracy of memory in any particular case is that: 'I do not see how to reconcile the fact of its error with my accepted world'.[2] Thus we know that there is self-sameness, but we cannot account for it as a matter of principle. A man, as a man, is, in Bradley's view, a concrete universal,[3] since he is in all that he does; and he is particular in his relations with others yet identical in all his attributes. But, taking all Bradley's remarks together, we still cannot say that, in one body as located and identical, there might not be more than one 'accepted world' and 'basis of recall': more than one set of propositions constituting self-knowledge.

Yet we can so far accept Bradley's attempts to account for self-sameness as to say that one of the necessary conditions of self-sameness is that a man *can* give some explanation of himself when asked, and that he can remember himself as acting when he is required to justify or describe that act at a later time. A man cannot avoid the consequences of what he has done by alleging forgetfulness; or unawareness; for Bradley expressly says on page 4 of *Ethical Studies* that 'he cannot put them (his acts) on one side, and himself on the other, and say, "It is not mine; I never did it".' In practice, however, we know that this is precisely what great numbers of people do attempt to do in self-exoneration.

(iv) *Sense*

When Bradley says that a man, to be accountable for what he does, must have the sense to know what he is doing, he includes intelligence in his notion of an agent. To say that a man intends an act is to say that he is aware of himself as agent; intention is thought, ideal, and to think what one is doing is to be aware of doing it. But to know what one is doing goes further: it implies that, when asked, it can be described to others, or at least approximated to some description given by another. Knowledge is not a mere vague looking on, it involves

[1] See *Truth and Reality*, ch. VI and Appendix.
[2] *Op. cit.* ch. VII.
[3] *Principles of Logic*, p. 188.

at least some comprehension. If A acts in a situation S, he must be able to describe his action X in terms of the situation. So he must be able to objectify enough of S to discuss it. Otherwise it would not make sense to speak of 'what he did'.

It might seem that, on this argument, it is not so much what a man does as what he sees of what he does, that is relevant to responsibility. Is Bradley asserting that responsibility for actions varies with apprehension of them? A man must be accountable for the act for which he is responsible as agent, and this, we have seen, requires his having intended it, and so having apprehended it as a possible action before realising it. We thus appear to be limiting responsibility by what can be known of 'the particular circumstances of the case' as Bradley puts it on page 6 of *Ethical Studies*; or should we say that to speak of an action at all presupposes the conditions of its occurrence, those conditions which could have been used as premisses by the agent in order that the idea of the action could have occurred to him as a possibility, as a solution? For example, if Icarus had known more about wax, and we do not know how much he did know, his flying towards the sun might be described as suicide rather than as youthful zest.

(v) *Moral knowledge*

That an action may be good or bad in the moral sense is so much a part of our everyday knowledge that it is almost inconceivable that any normal person should not be aware of it; yet, Bradley asserts in a note to page 7 of *Ethical Studies*, if there were anyone ignorant of this simple distinction, he would not be accountable. On this, although Bradley does not mention it, we should note that to hear others use such words as "good", "right", "bad" etc. is not in itself to learn to apply them, or to infer that they are used with reference to moral, as distinct from linguistic, rules. The difference between 'good' and 'bad' implies a criterion, a standard, and it is the possibility of applying some standard that is the possibility of the moral life. *Qua* "external existence', as, that is, an action for which we have a name, an act may be right in one situation and wrong in another, wise in one, foolish in another, and a too narrow vision may fail to weigh up the harm and the gain. For intelligence varies. With regard to moral values, however, Bradley insists that an agent, to be accountable, need only be capable of knowing 'the moral quality of his acts'. If he is intelligent enough to perceive such values, even to know that there are moral distinctions to be drawn, then he is accountable. Not to draw such distinctions, being capable of it, does not exempt him from liability to punishment.

Before leaving the exposition of the criteria, we should note that the account of responsibility they allow is essentially sub-jective. The description Bradley gives of the conditions of the moral life on pages 298-9 of *Ethical Studies* and quoted below, suggests that the number of persons who *are* in fact *morally* responsible may be very limited. Now this limitation may be in respect of morality, and not necessarily of responsibility: for we are not able, within Bradley's theory, to distinguish between them. Morality may be wider than responsibility, or respon-sibility may be wider than morality. If we take mere knowledge that standards may be applied to conduct as permitting the *ascription* of responsibility to an agent, as Bradley seems to require in Essay I, then we must reserve the *meaning* of respon-sibility as something much more complicated, even remote. For Bradley appears to hold that to be really responsible a man must be living, or trying to live, a moral life; and this goes far beyond the mere knowing that there are right and wrong ways of acting. Good and bad are not, he says, just two identifications of the subject which can be separately or severally known, for a man 'can not know them, unless he knows them against each other; and for that he must have them both before him at once. He must have before his mind himself as desiring two things in opposition to each other at one moment, each being seen to belong to a certain class;[1] he stands above them, and in his conscious identification of his whole self in act with one or the other arises the knowledge of himself, as asserting himself as the good or bad will. This is the condition of imputation and responsibility, and here begins the proper moral life of the self'. I do not think it can be doubted that here "responsibility" is used as 'holding oneself responsible', and it suggests that Bradley, when he talks of the 'moral tribunal', and the 'judge,

---

[1] 'Each being seen to belong to a certain class': this qualification, which I take as indicating seeing the two things as right or wrong, good or bad, brings Bradley very near Kant; for the action which is seen as good is chosen because it is seen as good.

divine or human', regards 'being responsible'—as against being held responsible—as 'acting *as if* one did in fact hold oneself responsible, or accountable'. The confusion between ascription and self-imputation is very marked.

It might be said here that Bradley, in giving the criteria for responsibility, and the account of responsibility, is giving what he assumes to be a commonsense view; while in working out his moral theory, he is applying logical standards that may not be applicable to the plain man's outlook. But from Bradley's obvious reference to Hegelianism, on page 41 of *Ethical Studies*, as 'a philosophy which *thinks* what the vulgar *believe*', I cannot doubt that his account of responsibility, when fully cognised, is expected to form the basis of the moral life in its fullest sense.

CRITIQUE

It remains to comment on Bradley's treatment of 'moral responsibility', and I propose to do so under the two heads of: (i) Bradley's theoretical account as theory, and (ii) its inclusion of the relevant facts.

(i) *The account as theory*

We should consider first, the question of agency; second, the practical consequences of the account of agency; and third, the applicability of the theory in practice.

(a) *Agency*

Bradley's account of moral responsibility consists of a number of inter-related words, for which either definitions are given, or at least definitions are admitted to be required. The definitions are so arranged that they cover the facts Bradley regards as relevant to his discussions. Thus the ideas of 'intention', 'volition', 'act', 'will', are apportioned out among the facts that concern agency in such a way that, although they are consistent among themselves, we could not point to some fact at a certain moment, and say which one of them applied. We would have to conduct such an operation in a hypothetical way, and say: 'If he so-and-so, then we can speak of —'. This difficulty arises mainly because Bradley straddles his subject like an all-seeing awareness: he, that is to say, assumes that an observer who wants to apply his theory can avail himself of information which is only available to an agent's personal consciousness, and for which we could have only his word. Consequently, if we have to ascribe responsibility without the co-operation of the agent, we are only able to do so by means of a decision expressing an approximation of the truth, never the truth itself. For instance, let us suppose that, through a series of misunderstandings, two or more people produce an effect which they none of them intended should come about. This is not to say they did not produce the effect, that they, and only they, were not the agents. Theoretically, their part in it can be determined by saying they acted according to their knowledge and with certain intentions, but that there was a disparity between the intended and the actual outcome. In practice it is almost impossible to sort out the issues involved.[1] Bradley would have dealt with it thus: If X was not intended, then it could be said that X never appeared to any one of those concerned as a possible action, X was not *what* any agent was trying to do, or was doing.[2] From an observer's point of view, these distinctions would be impossible: X was done, it was achieved by A, B, and C, and so they must have done it. If they did it then they were responsible for it. That is inevitably how a spectator sees the matter, and he then proceeds to assess, to judge, X. But it is difficult for an observer to find out whether A, B, or C could have had X before him in the way that actions should be before a man according to Bradley's definition of action. In criminal cases, the agent is allowed to try to show absence of intention, but in moral theory the difficulty does not arise. Should it occur in practice, an assessor may follow legal methods or he may risk making a mistake. But in theory there is no possibility of such a mistake. In theory it is assumed that the action as committed by an agent and as seen by an observer are one and the same: in practice this is seldom the case.

In theory, then, the question of agency is largely a matter of the description of the action. If an action X cannot be said to have been intended, what was thought to be action X must in fact have been part of an action Y. What is done must have

---

[1] For an excellent description of the confusions in such a case, see G. E. M. Anscombe's *Intention*, paras. 23ff.

[2] It has, for instance, been pointed out by W. H. F. Barnes that we do not speak of "accidental actions", since the action would in fact be different from a mere description of what apparently occurred. Lecture, Royal Institute of Philosophy, 1 Nov. 1957.

various descriptions to fit the knowledge of those concerned, and this introduces almost insuperable difficulties with regard to fact. The reduplications inevitable in describing contingent events have been logically investigated by Wisdom[1] and by Pears,[2] and it is an argument in favour of the coherence theory of truth that such duplications are avoided, whereas in a correspondence theory of truth they are not. When Bradley used the word "translate" in his definition of action, it is inferred that the 'external existence' must of necessity reflect or embody the intention, for this is what translation means— the assertion of meaning or sense in another medium, another form. There can be no blurred edges, the one *is* the other. Theory escapes these complications just because it is theory, but that is no reason for refusing or neglecting to admit their existence; or for assuming that, because they cannot strictly be brought against the theory as objections to it, this escape is any merit of the theory and not in itself an objection to it. Even Bradley himself made it plain that he believed all the facts must be taken into consideration: to select only those relevant to the support of a thesis is to make a mockery of truth.

(b) Practical consequences

A more serious consequence of this purely theoretical account can be seen in the following situation. If an act is the translation of an idea into external existence, then, given an external existence, we can in theory work back to the idea. But we cannot do so in reality. If someone should say: 'This is an external existence, it is the realisation of an idea,' he is, in effect, saying: 'A does X, so he must have a reason, or a motive'. But it is not sound logic to suppose that the reason was ever before A's mind as intention, or as determining intention. The idea may be a necessary condition of the action, but although that makes the action a sufficient condition of *an* idea, the action as such is not a necessary condition of the idea. The two, according to Bradley, are equal. But given a description of some act we cannot say the idea corresponded to it. That there was intention, yes, but not that the intention was equal to what we can see of the action. We need the inner side to determine what the action *was*: the relation is asymmetrical.

---

[1] 'Logical Constructions I and II', in *Mind* (1931).
[2] 'Time, Truth and Inference', in *Proc. Ar. Soc.* (1950-1).

Here again we see the limitations of theory, and the ambiguity in 'action'. For we *do* label actions as such, and we *do* use "action" in ordinary language to cover all sorts of happenings, without conducting lengthy inquiries into intentions. Bradley is looking at the processes, mental and physical, which are involved in acting, but he can not escape the difficulties of description by doing so. What he wants to say here is 'It was *A*'s act' with the full implication that *A* intended it, and that no-one else intended it but he. But to want correspondence between what we see a person do and what the agent actually foresaw is not necessarily to find it: and in any case to want it is simply to seek another way of equating responsibility with a technical use of "action".

It is easy to say that we are incorrect in consulting contingency, and that such complications need not arise in theory. But it could be said that if theory is to consider all the facts, among the facts that it should consider is the desirability of describing the moral life in terms of entities which are never recognisable in practice. If we accept too wide a definition of "action", then within that definition we have to distinguish sub-classes of actions according to whether we include the agent or whether we accept descriptions of actions, as for example events. If, on the other hand, we make use of too narrow a definition of "action", we find that whenever we use the word, we apply every element in the concept, so that what we say necessarily becomes a succession of tautologies: for, if it does not fall within the concept, then we are not talking about actions, but about something else. If theory is to avoid circularity it must *be* theory: and theories are constructions out of facts, such that deductions can be made from its hypotheses, and put against more facts. Where moral theory differs from scientific theory is in having as facts what are already general terms and universal propositions; but that does not mean that when moral theory fails to account for moral behaviour, or fails to allow for all the contingencies of the moral life, it is still valid in the theoretical sphere; for it may or it may not be bad theory.

(c) Applicability

As a theory derived from the plain man who, presumably, is concerned with practical living, Bradley's account of responsibility is often quoted with reference to practical difficulties in ascribing responsibility. Thus we may ask how it can be applied in practical situations. And we find that the question of agency is not the one which presents the most difficulty; for in legal practice there is provision for joint culpability, while in morals we often apportion blame and praise among several agents. It is the difficulty of deciding how far a man is capable of controlling what he does, how far he is aware of his motives and of the nature of his act, that constitutes the chief problem in law and in social life generally. The problem is not solved by some easy formula which draws a line between sanity and insanity, for men may be remarkably sane in some respects and remarkably lacking in restraint and judgment in others. Attempts to measure and classify the factors in the personality which, when disequilibrium occurs owing to some unusual pressures either from within the personality itself or from the environment, or both, appear decisive, suffer from the difficulty of establishing a norm. The range of compensatory habits available to persons of high intelligence probably deprives research of its most fruitful field of inquiry. A mere scoring on a psychiatric scale is not likely to prove a reliable guide as to a man's actual, subjective, responsibility, at best it can provide a little extra evidence to an assessor. Bradley is in the main dealing with the question when a man is truly and necessarily to be held responsible. And it is not enough to say that responsibility is a conceptual affair and it therefore follows it is also a matter of necessity, for as we have seen, all we learn from this is that it is an affair of words being applied to the correct situation. But it is precisely how we find the correct situation that is the problem, for situations are matters of fact. We have to use the words, not only to know of their uses, and we have to use them in our everyday life, rather than in seminars.

Is it possible, we might ask, to establish 'responsibility' as an empirical concept, by relating Bradley's criteria to fact? Now according to these criteria, a man, to be responsible generally for his actions, would have to act, to be aware, or conscious, to have sense or intelligence, and self-sameness. Suppose we could find verifiable statements which, made by an agent, would determine the applicability of the concepts, could we then definitely say, and without error, that the man concerned must be responsible for whatever he has done?

To do this, we should have to accept an objective account of actions, by which they became recognisable forms of social behaviour. Intelligence tests we already have, tests of physical control are easily devised and are plentiful. For awareness, some principle might be logically valid, as to say, for instance, that feeling-states being wholes, then if a man could compare his feelings as from one time to another, he must be aware of himself as distinct from any one of them.[1] With regard to self-sameness we could use records and memory tests. But what would we then have gained? That is the crucial question, not the contingent problem of the verification of certain characteristics of responsible people. For it can never follow that a man, however set in his ways, however assured his reputation, does not, finding himself in an unusual situation, act in a way that he himself could never have foreseen. When we speak of self-sameness, we do not mean to point to a particular aspect of a man, rather we mean to suggest that there is something about him that enables him to be *known*. And for this we have no grounds whatsoever. Leaving out of account that all contingency is only describable in terms of probability, there is the undeniable fact that what most characterises a man is his unpredictability. However well we may acquaint ourselves with what goes to make a human being, consciousness, sense, habit, prejudice, etc. we can only speculate as to what result will ensue from them all at some one particular moment of time. As a convention it could be laid down that a man who conducted himself in certain ways as a rule should, when he failed to do so, be regarded as responsible; but we should never be able to make a statement to the effect that he was necessarily responsible in a subjective sense: we should find it difficult to show that we were not merely projecting upon him the conditions of our ascription of responsibility to him; and even if we succeeded in doing this, we would find it hard to show that what we were holding him responsible for was something that he logically could have been reponsible for, in Bradley's sense of having intended what we believed him to have done. Bradley avoided these considerations because he was dealing with moral responsibility, and he appears to have equated 'moral' with a kind of inner reflection of 'legal' procedures.

---

[1] On this point see pp. 302ff. below.

(ii) *Comprehensiveness*

We have now to consider—briefly—whether Bradley's theory can be said to be comprehensive, in the sense that it covers the contingencies that arise in practice. Here again we are in a difficulty owing to Bradley's assumption that responsibility relates to morality, for we are not able even to ask whether it makes sense to speak of 'responsibility' without further qualification. If a man is morally responsible for all his acts, and it is only what can be said to be his 'acts' that constitute the moral life, then it might seem trivial to differentiate between moral responsibility and responsibility in any other sense. For social and political responsibilities might be said to be allotted rather than assumed by a man: yet I am far from satisfied at this arrangement. If a man is responsible for what he does, does it follow that he is morally responsible? For Bradley at least it is evident that it does. And in asking whether Bradley's theory is comprehensive, we are in effect asking whether it allows for the furtherance of the moral life, for it would be absurd to say that a man was morally responsible if, for example, he was unable to make use of any kind of moral guidance. There are three questions which are of particular importance on Bradley's theory of the moral life:

(*a*) If a man is to conform to standards, is it assumed he has the opportunities to acquire them?

(*b*) If he has acquired standards, does it follow that he can apply them? Is having a standard the same as applying a standard?

(*c*) If he is to be responsible for resisting compulsion by strengthening the will, *can we say* that he *can* strengthen his will?

(a) *Standards*

A man's moral standards are to come from the morality of the community, which is a concrete universal, and thus is something given to us by sense. Bradley maintains that if a man is capable, by sense and opportunity, of acquiring standards, of knowing moral rules according to which some acts are good and some bad, then he is culpable if he fails to act accordingly. Now failing to find out, or to acquire standards—that is, moral knowledge—*if* it is to be culpable must, on Bradley's view, have been intentional, even if only in the sense of being a recognised meaning of what he was doing. Thus it would seem that, when presented with the opportunities of learning about morality, he must have intentionally disregarded them. This is a very difficult point, for it begs the question of morality: if a man who is given an opportunity, disregards it as an opportunity, he must surely have seen it as an opportunity for gaining moral knowledge and have intended to disregard it as such; and this presumes he knew what moral knowledge was before he disregarded the opportunity. Thus we appear to have a regress. To be told, warned, impressed, have one's attention drawn, and so forth, to certain facts or opinions, is to be enabled to form intentions in accordance with them. But if a man does not avail himself of these opportunities, who is to say whether or not he could have done so if he wished? This is not merely an empirical question, since it does not follow that because certain moral rules are pointed out to a man, that he ought to subscribe to them. He may, for example, observe that there are differences of opinion about the rules, and fail to decide whether they should be accepted or not.[1] In itself, this is an exercise of a moral sense. By speaking of a man's 'fault' we again beg our question, for if we assume an offence, we must also assume the code against which the offence is judged. If *A* joins an association and offends by breaking its rules, it can be said that he is to blame either for failing to find out the rules, provided he would have kept them, or for deliberately breaking them. The rules are there for him to acquaint himself with, and it does not make sense for a man to join some group if he disapproves of its rules. In speaking generally, however, of the moral life, it is not easy to maintain that the rules are there for a man to learn, if he will. What people think ought to be done, what principles ought to be observed, is as much a postulate of moral theory as intentional action. To say that a man had reasons for what he did, that he can justify himself, is to say that he did have some regard for rules, that he has adopted some principles of action, that he acted as a moral agent even if condemned and repentant; but it is not to say anything about what rules and principles he has or knew or could have acted upon. If we say, then, that a man's ignorance is culpable, whether ignorance of relevant fact, or of convention, how can we say that what he does, his actual achievement which is material, is a logical

[1] See *E.S.* p. 204.

consequence of some omission which is formal? In law, knowledge is presumed, but in morals, it cannot be presumed: for who could fail to see the inconsistency of the moral principles of even a moderately sized community?

Again, if a man who has failed to acquire standards and learn the rules, acts and is called to account for his act, he must of necessity give that account in terms of the code under which he is to be judged. His reasons will be unconvincing and inadequate because of his failure to understand or abide by the code. His reasons, his account, is thus defective. But 'that his account is defective' is a formal concept, and once more we see that it is difficult to bring the material act as such into the category of an intentional act. These difficulties, which I can not resolve, serve only to show that the concept of culpable neglect in terms of the moral life, of 'wilful thinking', is very hard to locate and apply, and that the difficulties to which it gives rise in practice may be the result of logical weaknesses within the theory itself.[1]

(b) The application of standards

To *have* a standard, in the sense of knowing it to be one, and to *apply* it, are two different things. If a man regards actions of type X as morally odious, it does not follow that he never does acts of type X. Some philosophers might argue that if he did such acts, then he had no such standards; but this is open to the objection that if a man acts on principle, then he must be aware of it, and to say that a man's actions reveal his standard is to use "standard" as conventions implicit in actions rather than as principles according to which choices are made. To say a man's standards are revealed in his actions is more properly to say he has a certain character. Any theory of objective rightness —as Bradley's is—has to admit that a man may do right without knowing it, and Bradley expressly says a man may be unaware of the principle upon which he is acting. But in the main he insists upon awareness: 'You can not have the moral world unless it is willed', he says on page 177 of *Ethical Studies*, and goes on to remark that if the moral world is willed it must be willed by persons who not only have it as the content of their wills, but who also are aware of themselves as willing it.

---

[1] An answer to these two problems is suggested on pp. 214-5 below.

If we can speak of intention, we can say an act is contemplated before it is achieved, and if it is or can be contemplated, it can also be assessed. It is here if anywhere that we would find the opportunity to apply principles. For it is at the stage of reflection, of contemplation, and thus possibly of assessment, that Bradley requires that there be "two things in opposition" to offer a choice. For this, it is only necessary to have an act, foreseen as ours, and ourselves as not acting, to fulfil the condition of choice. To reject an act recognised as bad, on Bradley's account of a possible action as a not-self, good or bad, is to prefer ourselves not having done the act. Our difficulties with regard to assessment by the agent would thus be solved by Bradley with reference to the self: for it is the acting self that is objectified in thought rather than the action as such. Bradley does not speak of an action as distinct from the agent, or, if he can be said to do so, he unifies them for purposes of moral assessment. Thus the code, or standard, of the self, its relation to an ideal, is carried into the proposed action as a necessary condition of the inclusion of the self. The disparity of the code and the proposed act appears as an instance of 'the bad self', and, in consequence, the self is not identified with the act, the action is not willed.

If we accept this account, we must say that moral assessment by an agent is assessment of himself rather than of an action. But this cannot apply to the actions of others: for the good selves that a man hopes to realise are not apparent to another as to himself. What others see is what a man does, and though they may judge him for what he is by his actions, they cannot do so on one or two of them, and even then, they cannot be sure of his reasons for acting as he does. On Bradley's view we see that a man has the chance to assess his own actions before committing himself, but that he must assess them in a different way from that by which others will assess them. To speak of intended acts as selves widens the gap between ourselves and others and results in the difference being one of kind rather than of degree.

(c) *Strengthening the will*

If a man can look at his acts before acting, and assess them in the light of any code he pleases to apply, does it then follow that he can strengthen his will? When Bradley speaks of the identical will that is a condition of responsibility, and again of compulsion, we are led to ask whether, if a will is to change, and to be strengthened, it must not be done from beyond or outside itself. How should the content of a will change otherwise? Compulsion comes from without, and yielding to it weakens the will, so must not the source of strength also come from without? The answer, one supposes, lies in the objective moral order, from which a will derives its moral direction, and also perhaps, although Bradley does not say so, its force. He does, however, seem to have held that if a child, and then the man, accepts and fulfils social duties, obeys precepts and the like, he will grow in due course into the member of society that he 'ought' to be. But is this an assumption that any moral system should make without careful exploration? Admittedly, if a man finds there is conflict between the interests that he forms and the life he is expected to lead, he has the opportunity to make a choice, and to attempt to reconcile the incompatibilities. But suppose he is caught up into a scheme of rules and practices which are not likely to bring about any satisfaction or realisation of himself, since they are not genuinely suitable to his nature? Is he to realise himself in opposition to what others regard as his duty? Bradley offers no solution, except that there is no need for one, since such complexities are avoided when a whole community is ordered into one moral scheme. He does, however, recognise that such a difficulty would arise in connection with communities "in a confused or rotten condition".[1] No one can assess from a standpoint that they have not experienced, certainly not on Bradley's account of experience, and our social victim would be engulfed in a fog from which he could not hope to escape. We cannot assume that even in an advanced community education would offer by contrast all that is needful to the choice of a new way of life.

We must leave this question with the reservation that it is unsatisfactory to speak of precautions against yielding to compulsion and of moral progress without a more detailed account of how a will is to be strengthened. The consistent and conscious application of certain principles must, we suppose, lead to such strengthening, but to say this is to assume the application. To give an account of the way a man realises himself in the light of an ideal is not to say what he might have done without that

[1] *E.S.* p. 203.

ideal, and a moral ideal must grow with a man as his experience increases. Should a man wish to change his ideal, he must
know that the strength to do this can only come in some way
from beyond himself, from the morality of the wider community. Yet, in practice, how does a man set about looking for
what he wants, when he does not find it ready to hand?

CONCLUSIONS

Certain results have emerged from this short inquiry into
Bradley's treatment of 'responsibility'. One of them is the
danger of taking a number of ideas and arguing that, since
ideas emerge from experience, and are thus essentially linked
with the actual, they can be so manipulated as to provide
guidance about facts themselves, about what is actual. If ideas
are derived from occurrences, experiences, events, then they can
add nothing to those occurrences and experiences once they are
derived: for that is what "derived" signifies. Thus theory based
solely upon ideas needs to be constantly referred back to fact.

To apply logic to a theory based upon contingency is sound,
for such inconsistencies as appear can be directly attributed to
perception, to the selection and classification of the facts. But
when we apply logic only to the products of selection and
classification, the case is different, and we invite circularity.
The principle of self-contradiction, operating in a given conceptual scheme, can only function if there are ambiguities, and
such ambiguities will necessarily be schematic, and not lie in
the concepts themselves. In other words, the ambiguities arise
from the abstractions made from contingency, from failure to
distinguish true from false propositions in classifying the facts,
the phenomena. Differences and inconsistencies in theoretical
exploration must, accordingly, at some point lead to the re-
investigation of fact, and thus cease to be purely theoretical.
This is especially so in regard to ethics and the philosophy of
mind. With respect to the latter, if might be said to constitute
its *raison d'être*.

Bradley's thesis that responsibility is accountability and
liability to punishment may be said to be vulnerable as follows.

(1) If men are regarded, on Bradley's criteria, as responsible
for their actions, they require: (*a*) to be able to assess their own
actions both in prospect and retrospect from some viewpoint

alternative to their own; (*b*) to postulate some ultimate metaphysical principle which, if they fail in respect of certain unspecified rules, will exact, perhaps, a penalty, at least as the burden of being what they have made themselves by their actions.

(2) If a man is accountable, he must be judged against a standard or code; and on Bradley's moral system, a man is expected to subsume his moral decisions to a concrete universal of which he can, by definition, only be partially aware through sense.

(3) While purporting to hold men liable, the criteria for responsibility and the moral system of Bradley are in general inapplicable in practice without certain provisions: (*a*) to be liable, a man must, when answering, be 'the same person' as when acting; (*b*) a man should be able to progress morally by comparing his actions with his moral ideal.

Now on these two points:

(*a*) There is no principle of personal identity which extends beyond and includes the moral self, the good as distinct from the bad, self. Three anomalies follow from this.

(i) If responsibility depends upon identity, to say that the creation or particularisation of a moral self is the result of responsible action is to argue in a circle, for the identity consists in the growth of the moral self.

(ii) To say that if a man is responsible he is accountable for those actions which can be called his, is a tautology, since 'responsibility' and 'action' are here analytically related.

(iii) Also, to say that if identity consists in the sameness of the acting self, the moral self, then a man is responsible for those acts which are his, is another version of the tautology.

(*b*) There is in Bradley's system no indication whether a man can, or how he can, act in accordance with his moral ideal and so realise himself. We are told that there must be no compulsion, but not at what point in the process of intention becoming volition he is to assess what he is about to do in the light of his ideal. Nor do we know how, faced with the range of his station and its duties, he is to select from them when they conflict. He is to systematise, but how can he be sure he is systematising with the guidance of a realisable ideal, and not under the influence of a dream that, although derived from instances of actual life, from example, is entirely unsuitable to his own abilities?

With a theory such as that of Bradley, we have no chance of reconciling it with observed facts for which Bradley has not already made provision. The ideas are so related in the theory that the distinctions between them are hypothetical, formal, and in any practical situation, their application would be impossible because there is no reference from which to start. When Bradley says that theory must consider all the facts, he omits to mention that, once all the facts are collected, and the theory built up, there is no point at which further facts can enter: for the theory consists of its original basis in fact, and, the ideas within it being abstractions from the facts as given, once the reference is lost it cannot be regained.

What then of responsibility? Are we to agree that it can never be accurately, contingently located? For what follows merely from words remains words and, given a sentence, we cannot tell where it should go, when it should be used. If we want to know what responsibility is and where we are to find it, we should perhaps look first for the facts, instead of contenting ourselves with what facts we already have. Bradley thought responsibility was responsibility for living a moral life, with a perpetual threat in the event of shortcoming. Thus, for him, responsibility was analytically related to moral standards, and the distinction between good and bad. But in view of the difficulties both in his theory and in his criteria, we might ask if we need make any assumption about morality when we speak of responsibility. There may be something about a man in virtue of which we may say he is responsible, even if he has never heard of morality, nor would care for it if he had. But we should not make the mistake, as I believe Bradley has done, of looking at him alone; for if we want to know what a man does and is, we must study him in relation with his fellows. And not merely marching along with his fellows towards some common goal, sharing some remote ethos, but living his life with them and, owing to their diverse interests, finding it almost impossible in practice to pursue any consistent policy in his actions.

VII

SOCIAL RELATIONS

Before continuing with our inquiry into 'responsibility' we should list what methodological gleanings we have to our credit. The results of these preliminary investigations must, we decided at the outset, be borne constantly in mind, so that we are able, in the event of our reaching any material conclusions, to recognise in them those features which result from the form of the inquiry itself.

(i) If an argument is to be valid, it must follow from premisses that are meaningful; and to be meaningful, it is required that the premisses refer to facts which can be tested in some way, not to facts that are merely verifiable on principle. (pages 22-8, 44-7, 74-9).

(ii) We make no special requirement about 'fact', except that facts are what we can know of the world through sense, that is, they are the world we perceive. If we are given that A is greater in size than B, and that B is greater in size than C, and we then conclude that A is greater in size than C, or that C is lesser in size than A, etc., this inference is the work of our reason upon what we perceive to be the case, and is, itself, a further perception of fact. In this example, 'that B is lesser (in size) than A', etc. is entailed by 'A is greater than B'; while 'that A is greater than C', or 'that C is lesser than A', are materially implied by A being greater than B, and B being greater than C. The non-ambiguity of B is a matter of fact. The same principles would apply in the case of universal propositions, for which the expression "formal implication" has been used: for entailment is the way our descriptions overlap, while material, or formal, implication is the way things are related.

We could say that fact is the reality of our experience, what we can try to state, or express. Where we can find alternative expressions for the same facts, there we have entailment; where we must look again at fact, or apply our knowledge of facts, there we have formal or material implication (chapter III).

(iii) We distinguish "awareness" or "experiential" statements from statements verifiable by observation. Our usual mode of verification, we should admit, is to corroborate by another sense organ what one has provided. When I hear a sound, I come to know it is a 'real' sound, that is, part of the external world, because I recognise it as resulting from the movement of objects that I could see and touch. So the sound would not be a ghostly murmur. If we fail to account for a noise in this way, then we may begin to invent supernatural causes, but only after we have tried to relate the noise to material events of some kind.

The first class of statements I have called experiential statements, or propositions; these are in principle declarative statements requiring the speaker or author to be included as reference. In making such statements (expressing such propositions), a person asserts himself as a social fact. We have to admit the positivist claim that these statements, by themselves and without their reference, are pseudo-propositions, and lead to the acquisition of pseudo-concepts; but this is no reason why they should not be accepted as statements: for it is analytic that they are not statements unless they are said, and if they are said someone says them. If we say 'A says p' when p is an awareness statement, then this is a historical statement; the statement to be verified is that A says p. Nothing is implied as to the truth or falsity of p,[1] which is merely A's opinion (chapter v).

(iv) To analyse sentences with a view to establishing their meaning, or the meaning of the expressions contained in them, requires a distinction between: (a) saying what other sentences are entailed by the sentence, and (b) saying what is materially implied by the statements made by the sentence.

(a) is linguistic analysis, and makes the assumption that the conventions of a living language have the status of rules, and that the meaning of a sentence can accordingly be found to follow analytically from the meanings of its component expressions plus syntactical implications.

(b), on the other hand, is usually known as logical, or conceptual analysis; it requires (i) that knowledge of the world as given by observation and science can be used to enumerate the further facts which are involved in the statements made by the sentence; or (ii) that the concepts involved in the statements can be elucidated by exploring or discovering their mutual relations. The logic of (i) is that of material implication, or formal

---

[1] This might be said to be the principle of authority.

implication, that of (ii) is falsely thought to be entailment, but in fact it is merely a discussion of personal conceptual schemes.

(*a*) and (*b*) (ii) are complementary in so far as they are both concerned with language, the former from the aspect of learning language and using language correctly, the latter in that of applying concepts acquired by means of propositions of perception. We saw that, if used together, there is great risk of overlapping and circularity.

(*b*) (i) is different in kind: it is still a matter of knowledge and of personal experience, but it does not disguise these as concepts common to everyone except when dealing with the agreed social concepts of science, that is, technical terms. The knowledge is material, not knowledge of language as a means of describing the world, but knowledge of the world as an object of perception.

In some philosophical studies no clear distinction is drawn between (*b*) (i) and (*b*) (ii), with the result that the expressions of everyday discourse are mistakenly thought, when severed from their context, to yield information about the nature of the world and of ourselves in it (chapters IV, V).

(v) With regard to moral, legal, and political theory, such words as "responsibility", "action", "intention", "will", "self", "person", etc. have been defined in terms of their interrelations rather than given any application in fact. Thus they have formed the hypothetical background against which decisions should be taken in particular instances as to whether they should be applied or not. Accordingly, such statements as '*A* is responsible for his action', '*A*'s intention was . . .', have had no possible defence against the allegation that they were meaningless because they did not refer, or because there was no means of their verification (chapter VI).

A RECOURSE TO FACT

If the terms mentioned immediately above, "responsibility", etc., are to meet the attack made upon them, they must meet it on its own ground, namely in that of fact. We shall accordingly once more take the advice of Wittgenstein, and look at the ways in which we learned to make use of the words that interest us. Our main object is to give a sense to "responsibility", which is generally taken as the ground of ethics and the necessary condition of the moral decision. In discussing the account of moral responsibility given by Bradley, we found we were not convinced that responsibility is a sufficient, as well as a necessary, condition of morality, and we must take this dissatisfaction into account. If we cannot argue from responsibility to morality, we must take society as the starting-point and look for responsibility where we know morality is also to be found. A man ascribes responsibility for what his fellows do, and he also asserts that he feels responsible for what he does himself. We must look at the complex of social relations in which we acquired the notions of responsibility, morality, and also that of action. That complex we will call the social situation.

But we must be warned: for we have seen that if we come to lay down uses for words, we are legislating, adopting technical terms or idioms, while if we merely try to find out what the ordinary use of such words is, we are encroaching upon the territory of psychology or sociology, and conducting an empirical inquiry. Psychology is making great strides in acquiring techniques for conducting such inquiries, and it will not be long before we are given an account, at least in topological terms, of the acquisition, application, and inter-relations of moral and kindred concepts.

Such an account will not, however, satisfy the moral philosopher. He may even consider it irrelevant on the grounds that it deals only with signification as a system of what Bradley called 'psychical facts'—the occurrence of a thought, not its content. The moral philosopher is interested in the logic, not the psychology, of moral discourse; he does not want to know where such concepts as he wishes to elucidate are to be found as plotted in an n-dimensional space, but why they should be found at all, anywhere. If he knows what are the grounds of their occurrence, he believes, he will be able to say precisely how the concepts should be applied and made use of in practice. For this is not a matter of material evidence, but of principle. And if it should be said that principles, and deductions made in accordance with them, are ultimately scientific, then the principles the moral philosopher seeks are likely to be akin to those of physics rather than to those of the so-called empirical sciences. For in physics we only perceive effects, we never isolate their grounds. Nor do we ever succeed in isolating ultimate moral principles, though we have to deal with the effects of moral action.

Yet it seems odd to accept moral philosophy as a philosophy of practice while denying it any direct application to practical situations. It is now seriously doubted whether we can accept a set of concepts, consistent and comprehensive though they may be among themselves, as a valid field of study while they remain incapable of reference or application to empirical circumstances. We are beginning to look for a bridge from theory to fact. If we require to say that a person *A* is morally responsible for his act *X*, and we can indicate act *X*, we still have to consult empirically recognisable criteria in order to apply the word "person" to *A*.

And, further, if we should make 'moral' a matter of motive, we have another formidable problem in its application. For Kant wrote: 'In fact, it is absolutely impossible to make out by experience with complete certainty a single case in which the maxim of an action, however right in itself, rested simply on moral grounds and on the conception of duty'.[1] We do not need to equate moral action with action for the sake of duty to retain the force of Kant's argument; and Hume also stipulated that an action, to be virtuous, must of necessity spring from a motive that existed naturally before it came to be considered moral, since, had it not existed naturally, it would not have been available to become a precept of morality.[2] We can see that the odds against the empirical identification of a particular moral action are indeed heavy. We shall even have to establish a claim to have before us some example of a moral situation.

THE REMOTENESS OF ETHICAL SYSTEMS

At least we can ask why ethical systems, or moral theories, remain aloof, and add little or nothing to our understanding of the practical moral problem. I propose here to adopt the recommendation of Jackson,[3] and speak of the moral problem as the "object" of ethics; for this distinction leaves "ethics" as

---

[1] *Fundamental Principles*, tr. Abbott (1923), pp. 27–8.

[2] *Treatise on Human Nature*, III. II. I.

[3] Reginald Jackson, 'The Moral Problem—The Problem for Conduct', in *Mind* (1948).

an objective discussion of moral principles, and of the nature of the moral problem itself, while enabling us to reserve the use of "moral" for precise reference to the practical problem that is solved by moral action. Ethical systems attempt to give substance to our use of such words as "good", "right" etc. They presuppose freedom and responsibility. They conceal the gap between theory and fact, between the logically and the contingently possible, by the use of hypothetical statements. Can it be that in this difference of type between the logically and the contingently possible we have a clue to responsibility and the relevance of moral discourse? We saw in discussing Bradley's theory that it is not enough to lay down certain principles which should be applied; it is also necessary to show that they can be applied, that, in the world of contingency, there is an opportunity and the possibility of such application. Such possibility must be contingent possibility, it is not guaranteed by mere cognition. Let us state the difficulty thus: theory tends to ignore the difference between logically possible and actual choices. According to theory, one can attempt to act on a principle if it is there present to us, in our thought; but in practice what one achieves is somewhat tawdry, and we should not assume it is justifiable to dismiss the difference as a difference between a 'good will', a good intention, and an external result. May not the introduction or attempted introduction of an unsuitable principle into a situation be in itself a wrongful act?

In general, ethical systems supply reasons for the ethical codes they advocate, or prefer. In effect they assert that actions, for example, *a, b, c,* are good, while actions *x, y, z* are bad, and if they do not openly assert this kind of opinion, they assume it. *When* confronted by an action *a* or *b* one should pronounce it "good" on the grounds of *M, N, O.* And if one does actions *a, b, c* and does not do actions *x, y, z* then one will become similar to, or acquire the characteristics of *M, N, O.* What such systems and codes tend to assume is (i) recognition and (ii) opportunity. Possible actions are taken to be recognisable as falling into certain moral categories; while we are supposed to be constantly able, in our everyday lives, to find the means and the occasions for living according to the given code.

Further, it is usually a feature of those codes which are based upon some metaphysical system or theological vision to regard their recommendations as universally applicable. The moral principles they support contain a covert "Everyone should act so". And everyone does not, and we are not sure what would happen if they did. In practice a decision has often to be made as to whether it is better to express one's own principles in one's actions, and risk losing on a short-term view, perhaps, *only* perhaps, gaining in the long run, than to adopt the principles of an opponent in order to defeat him. For it is impossible to fight fairly—effectively—unless both sides come to grips on the same level. Many philosophers have suggested that moral decisions are as much decisions as to *when* to act on certain principles and *when* to disregard them, and this amounts to making decisions as to *how* to act, since it involves deciding to what principle the action is to be subsumed. In principle it can be argued that to realise or advance a principle it is necessary to act upon it even when apparently imprudent. But in this view there lies a threat to the possible autonomy of any code: for if it makes sense, in morality, to ask whether a certain code, a certain set of principles, should be applied, it also makes sense to ask which of available codes is in this instance the most suitable. It thus appears that codes, principles, and precepts become additional facts in the situation rather than influences, covert or overt, in motivation. The question arises, not what rule shall be followed, but what standard shall be adopted: for when we choose between rules we speak of a standard, and when we speak of choice between whole sets of principles, we are choosing between standards.

OUR THREE CONCEPTS ARE 'SOCIAL'

According to the distinction made on page 128 above, 'responsibility', 'action' and 'moral' are all social concepts, for we would have to acquire them from propositions about social phenomena, about the world of social relations. And it is clear that we must take the three together, since, if we do not, we are likely to fall into the error of explaining the one in terms of the others, which is a failing we have found to be characteristic of purely theoretical accounts. Ryle has set an admirable example in *The Concept of Mind* by examining each of the concepts most intimately concerned with that of 'mind'. It may be that we shall have to add to the three we have at present under discussion.

In saying that our three concepts are all 'social', we imply that, when they are applicable, there will be more than one person involved in the situation. By saying that more than one person is involved, we may mean one or both of two conditions.

(*a*) It may indicate that 'responsibility', 'moral' and 'action' require a prepositional expression. 'Responsibility' could be said to be triadic if one has to be responsible for something to someone, and it would hardly make sense to speak of "a responsible person", or "a sense of responsibility" unless a person acted publicly in certain ways. 'Morality' requires conventions, maxims, and the like, which are perquisites of societies, so that morality must occur within a particular society, and cannot be used in a universal context. 'Action' is applicable to what occurs between people, so that actions affecting oneself only are either fictions, or require an ideal dissociation. To speak of actions with regard to oneself may be called a metaphorical use of language.

(*b*) It could be argued that the individual as individual is excluded from 'action', 'responsibility' and 'morality'. 'The mere individual', wrote Bradley on page 174 of *Ethical Studies* 'is a delusion of theory'; and what indeed could an individual be without society? We can also accept Bradley's condemnation of 'group' and 'society' as abstractions, for they can be nothing apart from the persons who are their members. Yet 'Man is not man at all unless social, but man is not much above the beasts unless more than social', we read, this time on page 223 of *Ethical Studies*. If we try to imagine a man behaving in a way that has no effect at all upon anyone but himself, we find it very difficult; for it can always be said that what he does affects what he is to become, and that what he becomes affects all those with whom he comes in contact. On the metaphysical argument that a society *is* a society only in its members, it follows logically that whatever any member does modifies the society. It is very difficult to conceive of a man being unaffected in himself by what he does, yet if we agree that everything we do affects what we are, it becomes necessarily true that all human activity is causal. Against this, there is the diversity of a man's relationships: for, from observation, it is hard to see any justification for saying that, for example, *A*'s behaviour towards *B* influences in any way *A*'s behaviour towards *C*. The relation *AB* may in itself be consistent, and so may the relationship *AC*, but we cannot, especially in view of the lack of any principle of personal identity, from the fact that *A* is common to both *AB* and *AC* assume any similitude between the two. Nor does it follow that, in practice, if *A* has an intimate, friendly relationship with both *B* and *C*, that *B* and *C* are going to be friendly, suppose they meet. In this case, can we say that anything *A* does will affect his relationships with *B* and with *C*? We need to remember those many criminals who, after serving long terms of imprisonment, revert at once on release to a former way of living. It might be true in some sense that the possibility of *AB* affects *AC*, and *vice versa*; as the possibility of pleasant pastimes may affect, we suppose, the application and energy of a man at work.

Again, even if we think we have a part of our lives which is our own, and which affects no one but ourselves, we have been so influenced by those with whom our life, from its first day, has been shared, that in whatever we do, we have to make use of social forms which have been imposed upon us. Bradley seemed to identify the moral self with character: 'The character', he said on page 217 of *Ethical Studies*, 'shows itself in every trifling detail of life; we can not go in to amuse ourselves while we leave it outside the door with our dog: it is ourself, and our moral self, being not mere temper or inborn disposition, but the outcome of a series of acts of will.' These considerations, now that we have paid some attention to them, may be left aside for the present. Since we have to learn about actions in a social medium, we can at least assert that names for actions have an interpersonal reference. For actions are done with reasons, with purposes, and the generation of purposes is dependent upon a social medium.

ACQUIRING THE CONCEPTS

We should return now to the question of how we learn these terms: 'responsibility' 'moral' and 'action'. We must distinguish here between learning the use of the words, that is, learning to apply the concepts, and learning to act morally. We are not going to consider moral instruction, as contained for instance in educational treatises or religious manuals, but we are going to look at the ordinary human situation in which men act and others criticise their actions.

From behaviour, certain stretches—to use Austin's word—are abstracted as actions. '*A* did *X*', '*B* did *Y*' etc., are the selected and objectified actions. These actions, once objectified, are praised and blamed, and often the same action is praised by one person, blamed by another. Praising and blaming are themselves acts, and as such are also subject to justification. If *M* blames *A* for *X*, but *N* praises him, the resulting dissatisfaction usually leads to an analysis of *X*, in the course of which it will transpire that *M* is objectifying one stretch and *N* another, or that *M* is regarding certain features of what *A* did as under his control, while *N* is excluding them from control. Such attempts at reconciliation deal with facts, and it could be said that *M* and *N* are judging in different situations. Or again, *M* and *N* may have different codes of behaviour, different standards for judging. What *M* regards as a skilful business manoeuvre, *N* may regard as an underhand trick. From such differences, we learn (*a*) that a person is morally judged for what he does, assuming it lies within his power, (*b*) that people may have different standards, and (*c*) that within the social complex of interpersonal relations, it is possible to assign to individuals the responsibility for what occurs. From these again come the more abstract ideas (i) of acting freely, (ii) of actually being responsible as distinct from being blamed or held responsible, and (iii) of the logical examination of moral codes.

Listening to adults discussing the players in a football match, and arguing as to whether or not mistakes have been made, could instil into a child the notion that right and wrong are matters of skill. It may be that there is a stronger case then is generally recognised for regarding morality as an affair of skill in personal relations. We easily recognise the person who 'must always be right' and one who tries to persuade himself of his own ability and wisdom. "Wisdom", properly used as the Greek φρόνησις, does mean knowing what to do and understanding what is likely to happen. Much of what passes for moral discourse is self-defence occasioned by uncertainty and fear of rebuff.

It might be that if we could discover *why* it is that morality is *not* just skill in manipulating one's social relationships we should come nearer to the actual differentia of the moral situation, of the moral 'ought'. If it were skill we required, we should seek to attain it by psychological insight and prediction; yet we do not in fact pay special attention to these in moral assessment, we are more likely to discount them before assessing a person's act, and his character. It is still consistent to deplore someone's lack of or disregard for practical insight and yet commend his moral courage. When we praise someone for giving a fine moral example, however, we usually assume he has a high degree of practical insight and also that he has a very good reason for acting. And this reason is not concerned with mere skill, but is an expression of purpose which transcends the immediate situation.

To have a good reason for acting is to be able to justify an action, and this justification must be offered if required. For if actions are interpersonal, reasons must be interpersonally available. On Bradley's view of responsibility, a man should not even be praised or blamed unless he is in fact responsible. Yet we do not in practice often weigh up the likelihood of a man's responsibility when we apply praise or blame to him. As a matter of psychological fact, in some people swift processes of subconscious assessment result in indignation or approval which, since they appear to occur in a disinterested way, they call "moral"; and if they have learned to trust to such feelings, they will permit themselves to make a moral judgment without being fully aware of the circumstances. Others again will not notice the indignation or approval, if these occur, but will produce a verbal judgment as to the moral nature of an act as an intuition, because the sensory processes involved are unperceived, and only their end-product is cognised.[1] In saying this, I am committing myself to the view that moral assessment may issue equally or alternatively in words or as feeling.

I have also to assume that our moral judgments do not

---

[1] I am not going to defend this view here, because it seems to me that the present achievements of psychology, and the evidence, e.g. of the greatest playwrights, support it beyond question. The so-called intuitionist accounts for his intuitive judgments by supposing them to be based on recognition of a quality of acts, which is objective, i.e. it is 'there' to be recognised. The relativist, on the other hand, accounts for his moral indignation and approval by reference to attitudes which are derived from and built up by his more intimate personal relationships. I do not think either of these 'theories' can maintain itself against logical or ethical criticism, but as it follows from the description I have given of them that those who hold them are not in a position to doubt them, they remain as data, as 'facts' of ethical thinking.

necessarily relate to responsibility, unless we suppose them *all* to be hypothetical in form. If we blame a man, and he then excuses himself, we may retract our disapproval and accept his explanation, or excuse, but we do not thereby alter the fact that we did blame him, and we did express a judgment to that effect in the first place. We are content to have voiced our views on the action we believed to have occurred. We should note here that there is constant confusion in ethical discussion between the moral judgment as made in a situation and the voicing of it. We often, in practice, do not declare our moral judgments aloud, and our reasons for this restraint are themselves reasons for actions which have to be morally justified. With children we apply sanctions according to certain rules, provided they have been told of the rules in advance, and when we do praise or blame them for acting in ways unspecified, we can usually bring these actions under such general principles as 'being helpful or unhelpful', 'causing or preventing harm', 'using their heads', 'being sensible' and so on. And this is surely morality, since we imply that the children had alternative courses of action and could choose. But again it does not necessarily relate to responsibility. Children, lunatics, and the senile are often excluded from the category of responsible beings, yet we give children moral training by praising and blaming them *as if* they were responsible. A lunatic who did some routine job and kept it up to standard—it being perhaps a matter of pride with him to do so—would have to be conceded as responsible for his achievement. He would have a just complaint if everyone took his performance as a matter of course.

If moral training consists of the imparting of a set of rules, or a standard, or code, by means of experiences of praise and blame, do we say a person is responsible when he can and does act according to those rules? Few would maintain that we had sufficient reason to suppose responsibility here: what has occurred is rather conditioning, as dogs are conditioned, or trained, to obey the shepherd or the gun. The sight of an unattended dog using a 'zebra' crossing in a busy London street, is relevant here. He has probably picked up his technique from observation, not from praise or blame. His sanctions are life and death. His unwitting principle is his survival. He survives because he keeps the rules, but he does not keep the rules in order to survive. The zebra is his 'how' to reach the other side of the road.

CONDITIONING AND RESPONSIBILITY

From this homely example, we begin to see the difference between the conditioned being who keeps the rules as laid down by a social group, and the responsible being who keeps those rules on some principle, be it survival, or ambition, or love for others. Children are beset by social forms, ways of behaving in every detail of living, from babyhood; but there comes a time when a passage has to be steered amid a multiplicity and redundancy of conventions, and the pilot becomes, not a good memory, not a conditioned reflex, but a set of principles. It is the principle that bridges the gap between social expectancy and the conventions that will satisfy it. By understanding the principle that lies behind certain conventions, suitable conduct can be improvised in strange surroundings. Thus a man can be relied upon to 'fit in', and not offend. Awareness that one's own group has its ways leads to the inference that another will also have 'its' ways. Conventions are, for the individual, converted into rules by being given as commands in particular instances. It is thus that a convention acquires the sanction, the formulation, the authority, that is a necessary condition of speaking of rules. That the rules imposed as such on a child are not rules of society in general, but a personal selection from encountered conventions, is itself a recognition marking a stage in maturation.

It could be said that knowledge of conventions should normally generate the principle that there are rules to be consulted when in doubt as to how to proceed. We thus reach the more commonplace, and frequently stated, position that morality proper is a second-order consideration of what rules should be accepted as such. This amounts to saying that in any pursuit one is given a choice as to means, and that in this choice lies the possibility of decision and of action to be distinguished from a random trial and error method of dealing with a problem. For the rules themselves are but norms of response in social situations; they arise out of decisions made by those who came before us. There are occasions when a well-recognised rule is followed for the reason that it represents a traditional, or tried-out, solution; for, even though other possible solutions may appear, the agent does not feel justified in taking a risk and departing from custom in this particular case.

On this, we should have to allow that a child who failed to acquire a principle as distinct from learning a set of rules of conduct, and whose behaviour remained purely repetitive or imitative, would, so long as this condition persisted, be exempt from responsibility. And it follows from this that if we want to know the criteria for responsibility, we have to ask how such a principle is in fact acquired.

There is a serious logical difficulty here, to which we must pay especial attention. Children are taught rules with concrete examples, and they hear criticism of behaviour that they witness. But the examples they see and the criticism they hear is part of the world external to them, it is in the 'third person' all the time, and there is no guarantee that it would look the same if it should be transferred to the first person. On the other hand what they learn by praise and blame of their conduct is seldom consistently related to moral precepts. To see the action of a person A, is to see A acting, not to see A's problem as it confronts him, and which he has to solve by his action. How then should a child recognise a recommended action when it is actually before him as a possibility?

In my opinion this question is unanswerable. The most that can be achieved is that, by verbal discussion, the description of an act by an agent and by an observer should be approximated. But if we agree that an action as seen by an observer and the same act as seen by the agent cannot be approximated except by verbal descriptions, then what guidance can a child obtain from being told or given examples of, social rules? In his own world, confronted by the need for action, the possibilities before him cannot fall into the patterns of the actions of others. He sees his situation as a projection of what has just happened into the future, and what he does not only fits into the pattern of that past, but it is limited by the social forms he has learnt. Thus the actions he can take are restricted to actions falling within his previous experience; and, more limiting still, they are morally labelled, not by what he has been told, but by the experiences of moral success and failure, of praise and blame, of encouragement and frustration, that he has actually felt. He may, for instance, fail to perceive, or to consider, certain actions, because to achieve them would involve some minor activity for which he has been severely censured or injured (for example, accidental burn). In later years, his reluctance to take such action might attract his attention by its lack of rational support, and he would perhaps discover that he had rejected the whole because of an inhibition of some part of it. He would then be in a position voluntarily to overrule his former decision, and by doing the action he would break down the inhibition. But children cannot do this: they are restricted in their perception of their world to the experience they have had of it; and exhortations in terms of another world make no impact upon them.

The barrier between an observer, or a critic, or an adviser, and the personal awareness or consciousness is thus seen to constitute an ambiguity in the word "action": for the words by which we describe actions may be misapplied as between one action and another, seen by different people. Factual description and evaluation of any action will both rest upon the previous experience of the persons concerned, who will see it *as* different actions. To say that the two accounts might logically be reconciled by argument and analysis is not to remove the difficulty from ethical discourse: for it is a matter of fact that to reconcile such differences is an affair of some maturity and altogether beyond the power of many adults.

PERCEPTION AND REASONS

If the actions of an agent are limited by and to his own experience, it would seem that, even if he is aware that different people and different societies have different sets of rules for the same purposes, he will not be able to see any such differences in his own world. For his perceptions of practical situations are in terms of his previous experience, and his experience is exclusively, with most children, we may suppose, and even many adults, within, or dominated by, one set of rules. Thus he sees, if he watches other social groups, what they do in the light of his own classifications and assessments. What he cannot explain becomes "odd". Plainly, he must have, *in his own experience*, positive contact with different rules, or social forms, or customs, in respect of *the same activity*, if he is to relate them as 'different' codes. It is conceivable that a child or young person dislikes and wishes to repudiate practices to which he is accustomed and habituated, yet has no positive ground upon which to reject them: there is nothing to take their place, and the motive for this behaviour is such that it has to have expression. In spite of his dislike he is forced to act in accordance with those practices. Can we say that such a child, or man, has a genuine choice in moral matters?

The logical asymmetry between the act as seen by the observer and the agent implies similar asymmetry between the reasons for those acts. For an agent either *has* a reason when he acts, or he makes one up afterwards. His reason satisfies himself. But this does not by any means ensure that it satisfies anyone else. Conversely, the only reason an agent can think up may not satisfy him, yet appear quite satisfying to an observer. It is clear that reasons for actions are linked to those actions in a person's own logic; and while it may be possible for an agent who is satisfied to explain to an unsatisfied observer why he is satisfied, and for the observer to accept his explanation, yet even then the observer is not necessarily going to be satisfied. Logically, an agent A may regard reason M as sufficient for action X, while an observer B will regard X as sufficient for there being a reason, that is, it is a purposeful act, though he does not consider M as sufficient for X. It is only if A is himself prepared to admit that X presupposes a sufficient reason that he can discuss with B the sufficiency of his supposed reasons. And it is only thus that he can find in himself that disparity between what he does, viewed objectively, and what he intends, or thinks he does, viewed subjectively, which is the only possible means of increasing his knowledge of his own self. He can school himself to suppose B, and thus objectify his own behaviour as he would, for example, objectify B's, or anyone else's, but it is a necessary condition of the success of this procedure that he first reduce the ambiguity in 'action' by applying words with recognisable concrete meanings to his own behaviour and to that of others. And again, if he is to agree on the description of an action, he has to be able to distinguish between description and appraisement, evaluation.

ACTING ON PRINCIPLE

So far as the relevance of 'responsibility', 'moral' etc. is concerned, we have found that the moral element in a situation relates in some way to acting on principle. An ethical action might be said to imply a socially habitual—or conventional—action, but not necessarily an action on principle. Such an action might occur without responsibility, if it is the result of conditioning, or training. It has been said that a man may not be aware of the principle upon which he is acting, and if so, when challenged, he may deny that he is acting upon a principle that observers find exemplified in his action. A man who is conscientious, when challenged in this way, may be willing to look at what is said about his actions, and, finding certain principles, debate within himself as to whether he proposes to continue acting upon all or any of them, or whether he will seek new ones. But on the other hand there are many men who are not conscientious and who 'justify' their actions to their own satisfaction and for their own convenience. Such men will not be willing to admit to the principles that others find in their actions, and such men may often be generally agreed—for example, in a court of law—to have acted unethically, against the accepted rules of their society. But can they be said to have acted on principle, and if not, can they be said to be responsible for their actions? This, it seems to me, is the very crux of the problem of the moral situation, for example, in the case of a confidence trick, is it seen by the agent *as* a form of dishonesty?

The present tendency to regard "action" as a cover-word for "responsibility" or "responsible", conceals the difficulties of the ethical act as distinct from the moral decision.[1] If "action" is limited in this way, then what could we mean by "ethical actions"? To use such an expression would reduce responsibility to a mere matter of convention.

I am proposing that the statement 'The moral act, or the responsible act, is an act done on principle', should be regarded as a synthetic statement, which means that we must find a meaning for "on principle" which is not contained in "action". We should also note that, in this statement, though both the responsible act and the moral act may be said to be on principle, they are not thereby themselves identified. They might form overlapping elements, or they might form stages of a process. The statement may be false, in that acting on

[1] That there is a necessary connection between 'decision' and 'choice' I take as beyond question, for it is absurd to speak of decisions, and then to doubt the presence of alternatives in respect of the same situation. No one would attempt to question the use of "decision" as relevant to the discussions of committees, although committees may in fact be so dominated by one member that the others meekly accept his ruling. But formally their decisions are decisions, and formally there is the right of opposition.

principle may not be a necessary condition of responsibility.

Let us accordingly look at "principle". What does it mean to say 'it is a matter of principle', 'he would die for his principles', 'we stand for the principle of, for example, human rights', or 'in a matter of principle, there should be freedom of conscience' etc.? The word itself seems to indicate not so much the essential nature of something, but the way that nature works, its logic, one might say. Principles are not true or false, but rather they are existent. When a man stands out for something he believes to be right on principle, he is not necessarily saying anything about acts, or kinds of acts, except by inference; but he is preventing something from being realised in fact that he believes to be wrong. If he were to give in, it seems to him, he would be assenting to some principle he does not wish to endorse. If he betrays himself over this—it may be a trivial incident—he is betraying all. Matters of principle are not matters of principle because they are the same for all men, but because in creating the world of social relations with its bearing upon life in general some principles are furthered by our acts and some are not.

To say that principles are existent, rather than true or false, is illuminating: for if we are correct in this then we are also correct in saying that the principles of actions are facts, they are there to be cognised, *if* there are principles of actions. But to say that actions may be actions on principle is not to say that *all* actions *have* principles, unless, as indicated above, we lay it down that it is so by definition. However, one thing we can be sure of here is that *the principle is instanced in the action* and not merely in the account of it, or the idea of it. Thus if a man acts for a reason, his reason may not be the principle upon which he acts. If it is, it is contingently so, there is no necessity. And a further result of this analysis is that there are no principles in intentions; an action must occur before the principle is there. Principles of actions must accordingly be part of the world.

Further, we may say about principles that they stand or fall as one: we cannot compromise with principle, either we apply a principle, exemplify it, or we reject it. There are no half-measures, no 'mean' with principles. If principles conflict, we choose between them; if possible actions conflict, we may perhaps be able to compromise, but with principles there is no compromise. For example, if the principle of verification *is* a principle, that is, if it is possible to establish and formulate it, it must apply to *every* statement in some way.

THE AGENT AND HIS ACT

If we say that 'the principle is in the action', and that a man's reason may not be the principle upon which he acts, and again that responsible action or moral action is action on principle, are we not in effect suggesting that action on principle is merely knowing what one is doing? The principle upon which the action is based should be the same as the one on which a man believes himself to be acting. In other words, the account that a man would give of this action would tally with that given by an observer; for it would not be possible to give the principle of an action without an accurate description of it. Thus the objective character is given as well as the subjective: both coincide. But they more often do not coincide, and there we have the morally responsible act. If a man recognises the need for justification, for giving an account of his act, then he falls within the sphere of morality and responsibility. If he does not see any need for justifying his actions, are we then to say he is amoral? It seems to me the answer has to be in the affirmative. For if a man takes the view that what he does is his own business, and that so long as *he* thinks his acts are right there is no more to be said, then he may be said to disregard, or fail to perceive, the claims of the society he lives in; he has, so to speak, contracted out of that society. While, on the other hand, if he fails to understand what justification is, if he cannot perceive that the principles of his actions are questionable, that they may or may not be justifiable, then he appears not to have any knowledge of morality. If a man cannot apply the notions of good and bad to his acts, is it possible for him to act on principle? For if it is the action that he deems right or wrong, it is the principle of the action he calls good or bad. Their reconciliation occurs in the principle that what is right is also good.

It is as well here to remind ourselves that a principle of an action is not a maxim: a maxim is a rule, and rules are concrete. Rules, we have seen, are conventions adopted by someone as rules. Maxims or precepts are rules recognised as such. Principles are ways of choosing, are the formal conditions of choosing what must be adhered to as rule or convention if the concrete situation is to be successfully ordered. The word "successfully" here relates to the judgment of the agent. As examples of such principles, there are (i) Kant's Categorical Imperative, which is purely formal in character, (ii) the principle of doing those actions which fall under social rules, or the law, *because* they *are* ruled by society, and (iii) the pleasure-pain principle, as stated by Freud or Aristotle.[1] If we do not accept (iii) as a "good" principle, then we should be able to withstand pleasures and pains that are morally misleading.

Have we succeeded in showing that 'acting on principle' is something more than 'acting'? Does awareness, or cognisance, add anything to the act? It does not, we must admit, if 'actions' are permitted to yield principles just because they are actions. To act on principle is to do something more than merely to act; for when a man acts on principle at least he asserts the principle by his action. He puts it into the world; he makes it evident; he strengthens it by identifying it with himself, or by identifying himself with it. It is in this sense, I believe, that Bradley could speak of the wrong act, of guilt, as a standing assertion of wrong: the guilty agent is one who has identified himself with a wrong principle, and this position can only be rectified by asserting, in the act of punishment, the principle by which the former one is wrong. The assertion of the second principle is the assertion that the first one is wrong.

If acting on principle is an assertion of a principle, it is true that the self which asserts the principle asserts its own character as being of a certain kind. If we apply this to the moral judgment, which is itself an assessment and so an action, we can say that the moral judgment is the acceptance or rejection of the principle of an action. When a man gives his opinion on someone else's action, he is asserting a principle, quite apart from any other motive in declaring himself, such as, for instance, the desire to praise or to blame the agent. When he makes a retrospective judgment on his own acts, again he identifies or refuses to identify himself with the principle upon which he then acted.

There are objections to speaking, as Bradley did, of good or bad selves rather than of good or bad actions, as seen prospectively by an agent, but at least this way of speaking emphasises the indissoluble union of an agent and what he does as agent.

---

[1] *Nichomachean Ethics* Tr. Ross, 1105a: 'And we measure even our actions, some of us more and others less, by the rule of pleasure and pain.'

We have found it more convenient and informative to stress the elements within this union: to distinguish the agent as agent and the action as action. For this distinction permits the recognition that an agent's view of his action may not coincide with an observer's, or an assessor's, view of the 'same' action. The 'sameness' of this action may only be its identity in space and time. To admit the two accounts of an action in this way escapes the effete ambiguity of 'intention', a notion that Kant accepted in defining 'the good will'. For what sense can be given to 'intention' without action? It cannot even be established as idea, for if we have an idea of acting we must at least work out some of the practical details, or abandon it. Yet intention as a notion contains no practical indication of its content. In legal procedure 'intention' must be proved by overt signs of an impending action, and thus 'intention' in effect becomes part of the action itself. But in theory this cannot be done, nor is there, in moral discourse, any way of proving an alleged intention retrospectively. The word purports to indicate the subjective idea or meaning of an action, and by a succession of uses it has—since the slicing up of actions by Adam Smith into 'three different things', that is, intention, physical movement, and result—become separated from action, and an 'entity' in its own right.[1] Its use in this way has prompted the curious idea that morals is mainly a matter of language, and that, if one uses that language, one is thereby exempted from proving anything at all about morals; the main content of the subject can be assumed, and its relevance to the world of fact can be left aside.

Are we then to look for the principle of action within the formula 'A-doing-X-to-B-in-AB' rather than in either the agent's intention or idea, or the action as a material change? Here we have A acting towards B in a situation that occurs within their relationship, and the principle of A's action derives in part from B as well as from A; for B contributes to the situation in which A acts. But here we have several concepts: that of a situation, of A and B as agent and recipient, of their relationship. Can we deal with these in such a way that we overcome the difficulty of applying our moral discourse to the world of fact? Let us first look at 'action'; not as A's action, but as anyone's action, to see whether we can find in it some linkage between the world of theory and that of fact.

[1] *The Theory of Moral Sentiments*, part 2, sect. 3.

VIII

THE AMBIGUITY IN 'ACTION'

TWO USES OF "ACTION"

It is the prerogative of the theorist to define his own terms, and it is only through these definitions that we can be sure we come to share his thought. Unfortunately there are, in moral discourse, many words which seem too ordinary to single out for definition, and some also whose meaning is so clear to the theorist that he neglects to ask himself whether they are as obvious in those meanings to the reader. With the word "action" we have the two-fold difficulty that not only are there different meanings but also a fundamental source of confusion in its application. We will take two examples of the former before turning to the latter.

That "action" is sometimes used to refer to stretches of interpersonal action or behaviour, and sometimes to indicate an agent acting, can be shown by reference to Kant and Bradley. We have already remarked on these uses, and all we need to do now is to put them side by side for purposes of contrast.

Kant distinguished between the maxim as the subjective principle upon which an agent acts, and objective law which consists of principles upon which everyone ought to act. If reason, he argued, is the common sense of all rational beings, then its dictates must be universally valid, valid for all rational beings. He believed there must be an objective law binding upon all those rational beings; but, since rational beings in fact tend to follow subjective principles, the objective law has to be posited as ordering or commanding what *ought* to be done, but which often is not done.[1] For a test, Kant advocated the application of a formal principle that could reconcile the action contemplated by an agent with the action ordained by reason. If the act contemplated could be found to fall under the wider notion of a universal law of nature without contradiction it would be 'right'. This is another way of saying that everyone should be able to adopt the same rule without causing

[1] *Fundamental Principles*, tr. Abbott, notes to p. 45.

anomalies in the social structure. For, in speaking of contradiction, Kant had in mind such contingent possibilities as the
negation or the making futile of property laws that would occur
if everyone started to steal. The institutions of society are taken
as the positive criterion of the moral law, and it could be said
that society itself set the barrier between right and wrong. But
Kant, in saying 'if everyone did . . .', implied that everyone
might, and makes the essential distinction between the act as
such, and an agent doing it: the agent only comes in as the
person acting and those affected by the action only enter in as
affected; the persons themselves are irrelevant to the act, they
are only part of its occasion. If the criterion of one man doing
something is based on everyone doing it, then it is only contingent that one man *is* to do it. The reference of the action does
not contain the reference to an agent.

Kant used simple descriptions for actions, such as "lying",
"stealing", "borrowing". He assumed that a man could
classify what he intended to do as properly falling under one of
these recognisable social forms of behaviour. The agent has the
possibility of action before him, he has also his knowledge of
social conventions, and he understands something of the
structure of society. He sees under what description his act
would fall, and whether his own reason for doing it tallies with
the description it might be given. He then considers what
would happen in society if everyone acted in the same way. By
supposing everyone acting similarly, an agent dissociates himself from the act, and it becomes more difficult for him to pretend he is doing a harmful act under the guise of a just one.
For instance, if he is going to act in retaliation, it would be
hard to imagine his act done without the motive of retaliation,
and others would not have, in his knowledge, such a motive of
personal revenge as he himself has. If the maxim on which he is
going to act survives the test, he may proceed to act. If it does
not, the agent can consider other possibilities that arise in the
situation.[1] What is very interesting about Kant's view is that

---

[1] It may be that Gellner is mistaken in applying his own account of a maxim
to the moral philosophy of Kant. Gellner virtually includes the whole situation in
his definition of "maxim", with the result that the particular maxim is so detailed
that the action becomes apparently unique, although the description is generalised.
Kant's account of the moral situation and the moral problem is very much more
simple and straightforward. See E. Gellner: 'Maxims', in *Mind* (1951), and
'Ethics and Logic', in *Proc. Ar. Soc.* (1954–5).

it relies on the logic of material implication. The rational law, if it is to consist of natural laws, is concerned with the contingent, and if it were not, no Categorical Imperative could bring it within comparative reach of an actual maxim. Logically, it does not follow that *because* a maxim is found to involve contradictions in society as a man knows it, it is not compatible with a rational law. In practice one must be practical: Kant may presuppose social institutions like property and contract to be analytically related to society in general, but in practice it is only what a man knows of society that he can use for purposes of reasoning. If we have a possible act X which is under maxim M, then the act is right if, in a society, or in society, for example, society S, $S = SM$; it is wrong if M materially implies not-S. That is, if the proposition 'All citizens act on M' is compatible with the proposition '$S = S$', then they together imply that X in this instance is right (that is on maxim M) in virtue of their compatibility. If the two propositions are incompatible, then X on maxim M is wrong.

For Bradley, the agent has before him, not two possible acts, but himself as acting in one way and himself as acting in another way. The agent is building up the idea of himself as if he were actually doing the action, producing the change, or effect. He then compares what he foresees with his moral ideal, and if he finds some inconsistency, he should reject the action containing it. If the moral ideal is the ideal of behaviour proper to the conservation of the objective moral order—society, that is, in its moral aspect—then in practice there is not much material difference between the respective tests of Bradley and of Kant, especially as, for Bradley, the agent's ideal is necessarily derived from instances of the objective morality he experiences. But we are not interested here in ideals, but rather in the distribution of words over the moral experience. For Bradley, an action is not distinguished from the self acting, both are one for purposes of assessment. It cannot be said that an action, as a change in the environment, in the world, had any meaning for Bradley except as the difference between himself and himself acting in a certain way—the "not-self", as he called this difference, is nothing but a mere contrast between the agent's world as seen as present before him and as seen or imagined after the action.

In that world which is not yet, the agent is playing the role of observer of his own action. Bradley's agent is asking himself whether he will realise himself as a member of his own society if he acts in a certain way; while, for Kant, the agent must ask himself whether it makes sense to do such an action in any society. Virtue, for Bradley, lies in choosing correctly in accordance with the moral ideal; for Kant it lies in trying to act in accordance with the desire to choose the right, whether that choice is realised in fact, or not. In both accounts of virtue it is clear that knowledge and experience of society is a necessary condition of right choice. We should try to illustrate these two theories.

If A decides to place a bet, having refused to refund money borrowed from B on the ground that he is too short of money to pay, then on Kant's account, A, when he places the bet, acts on a maxim that he can speculate with money he owes, or has borrowed for some other purpose. Since if everyone did this, confidence would rapidly evaporate in society, we can say that Kant would regard it as incompatible with universal law. Again, the refusal to pay involves a lie, for it is plain that if A can place a bet, he can refund the money at least to the extent of his bet; for even if A wins, he makes the initial outlay before either gaining or irrevocably losing.

Bradley would, we may hazard, give this account: A would have before himself two things: (a) A placing the bet and becoming the sort of man who, when he owes money and has refused a demand for repayment, proceeds to speculate with what he has, and (b) A not betting but keeping his money in the hope of being able to repay B, perhaps returning to him the amount of the bet. Strictly speaking, the result of the bet is irrelevant, though A may not think it is so.

There can be little doubt that action as regarded by Kant would be very much more easily seen to be right or wrong than action as described by Bradley. The excuse that A has a better use for his money than repaying his debt would be less effective against the Kantian than against the Bradleian account; for the latter, containing as it does the reasons for the action within the concept of 'action', is the more readily condoned.

THE NATURE OF THE AMBIGUITY IN 'ACTION'

Kant's descriptions of actions lend themselves to discussion in a way that those of Bradley do not, and we should try to see why this is so. There is a distinction to be drawn within 'action', but it is not between physical movement and the purposive or motived co-ordination of movements. There is no such distinction to be drawn in fact: for to lift an arm is to lift an arm, and since all movement is conditioned by its point of departure—one can only start from where one is—it would be absurd to try to isolate 'lifting an arm' as any kind of unit of physical movement. This is as true of physiological description as it is of purposive action or moral behaviour. The detail of physical movement can at best be inhibited, for instance, an irritating twitch of fatigue can be stopped, but it cannot be controlled below the level of purposive behaviour, of action. Logically, we can demonstrate this through noting the time factor: for while co-ordinated movements are composed of many simultaneous occurrences and changes, simultaneous and interdependent in the very structures they involve, willing or starting to act must consist of consecutive units; for it is impossible to think of and start two things at once unless they are contained within one, or contained within each other, and even then, they could not *both* be thought in the identical time. The fact is that movements have to be abstracted out of a continuous series of positions which does not cease even when a body is at rest—rest being, physiologically, a comparative term—in precisely the same way as actions are said to be abstracted out of behaviour (see also pages 196-7 below).

What those philosophers who do attempt to distinguish physical movement and action as two different ways of describing action are misled by is, I believe, the disparity between the observer's method of describing actions and that of the agent. For an agent cannot look at a long, continuous series of actions in the way that the observer looks at behaviour. He cannot do this for the obvious reason that he himself constitutes a barrier between the past and the future, and when at any moment he looks forward towards that future he must—logically it is impossible that he should not—see his future actions as wholes. An observer can halt the process of behaviour at any point, and in so doing he may arbitrarily determine what "stretch of action" he is concerning himself with; but it remains a stretch of action and not a series of movements. An agent cannot do this. Even if he does attempt to do so in retrospect, he is by then in the position of knowing about circumstances of which he was not aware at the previous time, at the time he is trying to investigate, and thus it is logically impossible for him to see that earlier occasion as it was when he was part of it. The observer, on the other hand, has his own purpose which must—again necessarily must—enter into his method of observation. The sentences in which the observer describes what he sees of the behaviour of another may have no significance for the agent who is behaving under circumstances that only he can fully appreciate.

We return here to the difference between the experiential statements of an agent and the observation statements of the onlooker. It is this difference, in the moral, or supposedly moral, situation which is now beginning to attract the attention of moral philosophers,[1] and which has either been taken for granted or overlooked in the moral systems of the past. One of the devices for overcoming the disparity is the notion of an impartial observer, but, leaving this aside for the present, we will see how the distinction and the difference in outlook is dealt with in language.

At first sight, the agent and the observer are equally limited by their own experience in making statements about the moral problems that confront them. The onlooker, or assessor, may regard the agent and what he does as his—the observer's—own moral problem, the problem being what judgment to make about what he sees. But at least he has to describe what he sees in the conventional, that is, in suitable, action-words, and thus he has at some point to make a decision about the facts. He has to name the stretches of action as they appear to him. And, since it is part of our perceptual function to have a comprehensible account of the world about us, he will want to reconcile what he sees, in the terms in which he describes it, with his pre-existing knowledge of the world in general and this occasion in particular. If the agent's actions do not seem consistent with what is known of his character, the observer will look for some unnoticed factor to explain this. If the actions do not seem suited to the occasion, then he will ask himself whether he has misinterpreted what he sees. Thus his account will inevitably be in the form of an explanation. Only as an explanation will it satisfy him.

[1] E. g. N. H. G. Robinson: 'The Moral Situation', *Philosophy* 1949; J. M. Hems: 'Reflecting on Morals', *Philosophy* 1956. See also D. M. Mackay: 'Brain and Will' —II, *The Listener* 16.5.57.

It may be said, against this, that for purposes of moral assessment, it is enough for an onlooker to name the actions he sees
by applying action-concepts, and that, having made his judgment according to his own standards, the affair, so far as it is
moral, is finished with. The judgment is final, unless challenged
either by the agent or by another observer. Here we must, I
think, distinguish between types of observers. And we can best
do this by considering the circumstances under which a man
may make a moral judgment. For although he may produce
what appears certainly to be a case of a moral judgment, yet it
may be that the final form is deceptive. It is conceivable (a) that
he may be indulging a desire to express his contempt for, and
thus disapproval of, or alternatively, his admiration for, and
approval of, a certain kind of act, and that this desire may lead
him to 'recognise' that kind of act more readily than is
warranted; or again (b) that he had delayed his judgment long
enough to go deeply into the facts, and that it is attenuated
and—one could say—secondhand as a judgment; that is, it is
not genuinely the result of any direct personal contact, but
rests upon a set of hypothetical, factual propositions. Finally (c)
it is possible that the judgment is misleading because the onlooker tends to find excuses when he recognises fault and to
seek baser motives when he feels himself drawn to praise. Some
distrust of his own reactions and feelings may lead him to suspect appearances, and attempt to turn the situation into something it probably is not. When we are confronted with what
appears to be a moral judgment, are we to assume that is what
it is? Again we see that the onlooker, according to theory, is
assumed to have a simple nature and that his moral judgments
are what they seem to be, a sure basis for further analysis.

In the event of (a) it would be correct to say that the moral
judgment was, at least in part, an expression of feeling, in (b)
that it related directly to a set of rules, or a standard, and in
(c) the observer fails to objectify the agent and confuses the
issue by introducing all sorts of considerations that may or may
not be relevant. He may be said to mix himself up with the
agent in some way, so that he attributes to him as possible
motives ideas of desires and aims that have occurred within his
own experience.

In view of these difficulties, we shall have to say that a moral
judgment by an observer cannot be accepted as such on the

mere evidence of its form and because it happens to occur in
what appears to be a moral situation. The observer who makes
a moral judgment will have to be given the same status as an
agent, that is, he is himself making a moral decision in making
his judgment, he is acting and his action falls within the concept
of 'moral'. According to the account of 'action' given by
Bradley, the observer who gives a moral opinion identifies himself with, asserts himself in, his judgment. He declares that he
himself has a certain attitude towards the action he judges.

We have said that an observer must have a factual account,
or some impression of the facts, on which to base his moral
judgment. Otherwise there would be no occasion for a judgment. An account of the facts which contains no moral judgment may be said to be psychological, or scientific. The distinction between the psychological and the moral may be more
clearly marked by noting that the moral situation is a practical
situation, that is, it calls for action. Thus, when moral judgments occur, they may be taken as indications of how the
observer is urged to intervene. If his reaction to the situation is
to join the agent happily and to encourage him, then his moral
judgment will be that the agent's action was good; while if he
desires to turn away, to make gestures of disgust, and so on, his
judgment will be one of disapproval. Yet to say this is not by
any means to say that the judgment *is* the substitute for, or the
sign of, these behavioural characteristics, or these actions. Nor
does it follow that the moral judgment is an expression of feelings, with gestures etc. as alternative forms of expression. That
the moral judgment is not merely the expression of feeling is
shown conclusively by the fact that we make moral judgments
about events which occurred in the past and events which may
occur in the future. It is absurd to say that we could have feelings of something which had not yet happened.

We are now saying that an observer, if he is to make a moral
judgment, must be involved in the situation to which that
judgment is relevant. For the situation in which he makes his
judgment *is* a situation only in being limited as a context of
action. This leaves aside the observer, *qua* observer, as a
scientifically interested observer only. In the rest of this study he
can, accordingly, be forgotten. To him, moral judgments are
as much phenomena as anything else, and their occurrence is
just as factual as falling down and breaking a leg.

Let us now attempt to codify the ambiguity in the word "action". First let us take the personal account, the account of an agent. Suppose A has acted in such a way—M—that X is produced, and that X is generally regarded as unfortunate, by A as well as by others concerned. A's account, assuming that he is a man of goodwill, is that he chose M as a means to Y, but that, since there was another, and an unexpected, interference with the situation, X occurred instead of Y. And by the time A realised that the circumstances were changed in such a way as to give a different meaning to his action—M—it was too late to prevent the incidence of X. In this we find the following propositions:

(1) A's action was the production of X;
(2) A's intention was the production of Y, he believed Y would be the result;
(3) In the situation as seen by A, M would produce Y;
(4) In the actual circumstances, M resulted in X;
(5) The difference M—Y/M—X was the result of an unforeseen event;
(6) A regretted X and would have prevented it;
(7) A became aware of the changed circumstances of his action, of M, too late to withdraw it, or to compensate, or to change it.

If this account is to be acceptable, A must admit that he did intend M, and it must appear from the circumstances at the time that M is consistent with Y. It must also be clear that the kind of intervention M—Y/M—X was a genuine intervention from beyond the immediate situation, whether it was someone's action, or some natural occurrence known legally as an 'act of God'. A's regret for X must be genuine enough to support his statement that he did not intend it. In addition, his contention that he perceived the changed circumstances too late has to be supported either by material evidence, or by his reputation for goodwill. Out of the propositions 1—7, then, 1, 3, 4, and 5 are verifiable, they concern matters of observation; but propositions 2, 6, and 7 do not: they concern A's own perception and thought exclusively, and, as we found on page 130 above, their reference is supplied by A as a person, not by objects to which we can point.

Let us look at the affair as it would appear to an assessor, to a man who judged A's action morally. This assessor, we have said, would have to be in the situation in some way, were it only through sympathy, if it could be said to relate to him morally. If he is not to assess it, then he would merely be the scientfic observer, who by his own purpose, contracts out of the situation as a moral one.

The assessor sees the action X, with A as the apparent agent. He notes that events converge to produce X, but if he wishes he can objectify A's actions at the M stage, and regard X as fortuitous. Or he may not notice any changes apart from A's action M, and draw the conclusion that A is either very stupid or that he is malevolent. His moral judgment may express indignation against A and repudiation of X. He decides to study A's behaviour and to attempt to discover his motives in doing so unworthy an action as X. Since this study occurs after X is completed, the more remote results, one of which may be A's attempts to make amends in some way, are also available for observation. It is possible that he will not consider an action X at all, but name A's activities by some other purposive term. For instance, if A has made some gain by action X, the assessor will have to ask himself whether the unfortunate effects of his action were disregarded in the service of this gain.

All this is familiar enough as the material of case-law, and I am not here interested in the difficulties of decision, but in the logical characteristics which contribute to those difficulties. For there are many factors in the affair which serve to confuse the moral issue, the moral judgment, so that it is difficult to be sure what is relevant to the moral issue, and what is not.

The action X achieved by A may, so far as the assessor can tell, have been an act of revenge against the person injured by X; the action A intended, Y, may also have appeared to have another aim. A might, by speaking in terms of X, Y and M, succeed in excusing himself from intending X, whereas in the alignment of events as seen by the assessor, the excuses made by A would not apply. Here we can see that A's personal statements have no logical force unless they can be supported by some kind of verifiable statements. For instance, if A says that he intended Y at a certain time, the fact that it could be proved he stated his intention to someone would count as evidence provided he did so at a time when it was not materially probable that X would result from M. But the time when it would have become obvious to anyone in A's position that X

would so ensue might be very difficult to establish, and an assessor could, by assuming malevolence instead of goodwill as characteristic of A, regard "Y" as a fabrication, as a rationalisation. A will then be required to account for his interest in Y, either by showing he *had* an interest in producing Y, or by demonstrating that Y was the sort of action he would be likely to take in that particular kind of situation. He will have to justify his doing M to produce Y, and will also have to justify his failure to observe that X was in fact being produced. The assessor, on the other hand, will relate what A says about what occurred to his own knowledge of the world—and of those in it—and it is against this background that he will assess A's actual behaviour.

In theory it is usual to take some example, and argue from the wording of the example to the contextual implications— the setting. In practice, an assessor has two methods open to him: the first, the way of theory, to take his impression of the agent's action, to name it, and to look into the situation for relevancies to that kind of action; the second, to look at the situation and attempt to reach an accurate account of the action. In so doing, the question of relevance is secondary, for every circumstance must be looked into before some pattern emerges which will allow a criterion of relevance to be set up. In the first method, we start with a criterion, although it is, of course, possible to question it as a criterion later. But to adopt one criterion, try it out, then adopt another, savours of trial and error, and, in any case, the only way we could come to doubt the original criterion would be through opposition to it, through the setting up of another as a challenge, as indeed the defence challenges the prosecution in a criminal process. It is then up to the opposition to draw attention to sufficient facts to throw doubt upon the original hypothesis. The adoption of one account rather than another thus becomes a matter of decision.

With the second method, the results are equally hazardous. For the assessor takes, not the act itself, but the agent acting, as his starting-point. And here, logically, there is no limit with regard to relevance. A person acting has a character, interests, a life to live, and so on, and his action can be related to all of these. That he took one action rather than another within the range of those possible, or open, to him can be explained by an onlooker in terms of the man and the situation as they lie before him. But the onlooker, or assessor as he is here, only sees as possible those acts which an agent could have taken according to the natural sequences involved in the situation. Yet the actions apparently possible to an agent according to the facts may not be present to him as possibilities: they may not have occurred to him. It is here that we begin to see how divergent are the situations as seen by an agent and as seen by an assessor. It is a trick of moral theory to throw a cloak over these divergencies by talking of 'impartiality'—a trick that we cannot afford to employ here. But it can be seen that, unless moral theory starts from the descriptions of actions used by an agent in the form of intentions, it is in danger of floundering in an endless controversy as to how particular action-words are to be applied at all. If the attempt to limit the use of "action" to action-names were successful, it would enable these to be applied both to the agent's and to the onlooker's accounts, thus giving both of them some minimum of common reference.

Hope of this survives, even if we concede that it is difficult to confine the reference of action-words to one person. For if A acts towards B, B has some part in the affair, in the situation. Similarly, if B's action is under scrutiny, A is inevitably in the situation in which B's action occurs. Actions do not occur in an impersonal vacuum. We have seen, on page 165 above, that the concept is a social one. In the example given on page 183 above, the attitude of the man who lent A money would influence A's decision. If a person's actions seem odd to us, then it is reasonable to suggest that we are not fully aware of the situation in which he is acting. And when an assessor has to look at an agent acting in a situation, it must be remembered that in the person of that agent are all the previous situations in which he has acted, is the long process of conditioning that he has undergone since birth. The assessor who delays his moral judgment in order to be truly just, delays it for ever if he restricts it to one person: but if he rejoices in, or deplores, what happens as between members of a group of people, be it only two, then he is on the firm ground of actual moral participation. In a deplorable situation, he need not seek to condemn one agent but to apportion the blame on those concerned in it. For by saying that the situation is "deplorable" we introduce the evaluation that implies some one at least to have been at fault.

ACTION AND RESPONSIBILITY

As an assessor, the man who makes a moral judgment makes it
upon a certain section of social behaviour. He sees certain
people doing certain acts, he sees the resulting situation, and in
assessing it he implies it might have been otherwise. If it is not
as he thinks it should be, he condemns the actions of those concerned, in different degrees, maybe, and if it is as he thinks it
should be he commends it and commends those who have
brought it about. He judges what he sees, and he does not ask
whether what he sees is inevitable, because, as we have seen, if
he did so, he would never reach a position where he was
justified in making his judgment. In making his judgment, he
introduces into the situation he judges an element of praise or
censure, and if he feels very strongly about it, and is sincere in
his own acting, then he may take some steps to enhance or
destroy what he sees. His judgment then motivates his action in
the situation, and his influence upon those concerned in it. If
there is, as some intuitionists maintain, an element in action
itself which provokes praise or blame, then the assessor's moral
judgment may be said to be the reaction to this element. The
assessor must accordingly be said to perceive the element in the
action which provokes the judgment, and to perceive it as we
perceive things and their relations in the external world. His
feeling of moral approval or indignation may provoke his
judgment, and, in this case, we must say that the feeling is the
reaction, resting on and part of the perception itself. But since,
as we have found, the assessor, to make a moral judgment at all
must be himself involved, or be *ipso facto* becoming involved,
we must go further and say either (i) that this intuitional or perceptual moral judgment includes perception of the agent's
responsibility, or (ii) that the question of responsibility is
irrelevant to the making of the judgment. But on (i) it seems
absurd to suppose that there is some element in actions which
arouses moral feeling, or reaction, and that we have some immediate moral sense which perceives the rightness or wrongness
of certain actions, and yet deny that we recognise an action as
the action of a responsible agent when we make moral judgments. This argument seems to me to be fatal to intuitionism.
For if we judge an action, surely we must judge it as a kind of
action, yet if we do not know an action as being that of a

responsible agent when we are confronted with one, or until we consider it carefully, how can we immediately judge it as a kind of action? Again, the only escape—an undignified one— seems to be into the hypothetical way of speaking: 'If there is anything that is an action, then if it is wrong, we would on seeing it judge it to be wrong . . .' and so on. The fact remains that we do make moral judgments, and that it is mainly because we do so, that, as a further matter of fact, we try to analyse the moral situation at all. The intuitionist argument can hardly apply to the agent, since, if he recognised actions as right or wrong in advance, the man of goodwill would be infallible, and we do not especially notice him about the world. We have accordingly for the present to accept (ii), though we shall consider it again on pages 241-5 below.

Let us now return to the agent. When an agent is faced with the need for action, he does not see himself and his action as one, for his action is not yet done. He may contrive to imagine himself as acting, but he cannot look at this objectively in the way that an observer could. He is imprisoned in the present, and he only ceases to be confronted by the need for action when the action is completed, and he can survey its results. At no time can he say 'I should have chosen otherwise' except when it is too late for him to change his action. But when his actions lie in the future, he can only say to himself 'This is surely what I should do', and proceed to do it, even then finding he regrets his choice. It may be argued that if a man makes his choice with every possible care, then he should not regret it, once made, yet in fact, in practice, this does occur. It is not always because there are unforeseen results, or because he did not look carefully enough at the situation to find out what kind of changes his action would bring about. There are times when it is impossible to believe we have not been misled by our very efforts to do what is right. As Kant said: 'Those among mankind, who proceed according to *principles*, are but very *few*, which is no doubt good, as it can so easily happen to err in these principles, and then the disadvantage which arises therefrom extends itself the farther, the more general the principle and the more steadfast the person is, who has laid them down for himself.'[1]

---

[1] *Observations on the feeling of the beautiful and the sublime*, tr. William Richardson (1798), sect. II. Let us also, as light relief, note his remark in sect. III: 'I hardly

There are thus three divergencies between the agent's account and that of the assessor. The first is that it is logically impossible for them to isolate and objectify the same action. Hems has expressed this point cogently: 'Moral agency requires that an action has not been done, while moral assessment requires that an action has been done; and it is impossible to regard oneself as agent and assessor at one and the same time in respect of one and the same action' (*op. cit.* page 185 above).

The second divergence concerns choice: for it is analytic that if an assessor cannot see an action as the agent sees that action, then an assessor cannot see the alternative actions that confront the agent as the agent sees them. The assessor may have a more accurate perception of what an agent is capable of than the agent has himself, and consequently, the assessor will rule out actions as impossible which the agent foolishly attempts and fails to accomplish. Or this provision can be reversed, and the agent be aware of powers that an assessor could not discern. Such considerations not only limit and direct what actions shall be taken as 'possible', but they also are germane to the descriptions the agent and assessor respectively give of the actions in question: as instanced by such damning remarks as, for instance 'No doubt he thought he was being kind', which are of sufficiently frequent occurrence to warrant mention. What may be indicated by such a remark is not that the agent and assessor disagreed as to what constituted a kind action, but that the action intended by the agent as a benefit did, in fact, do some harm. Since benefit and harm, in a material sense at least, are matters of elementary observation, we can assume here that the agent was only partially aware of what he was doing, and beguiled himself into believing he was acting on a principle of benevolence. The logical difficulties in knowing what *is* good or bad for another person, in any but a crude sense, again follow from the different viewpoints of the person himself and an observer, however friendly.

The third divergence is that no one but the agent can know the relative strengths of the claims exerted upon him in any situation. An observer can see that there are certain claims, since these follow from the social relations of the agent, and to some extent are matters of convention. But the observer cannot

believe that the fair sex are capable of principles, and in this I hope I do not offend, for these are very rare with men.'

know the actual intensity of the claims as exerted in a particular situation at a particular time. This question concerns situations rather than action and must be left to the next chapter.

We should attempt to sum up what has been said, and to see whether we are any nearer to isolating criteria for 'responsibility', 'moral' and 'action'. The positions of the agent and assessor, who here includes the observer, can be schematised as follows:

What is most striking about these two aspects of action is the difference of direction: for an agent must proceed from his intention to his action, and inevitably to the results of it, whether they are anticipated, or not. He may account for disparity between his expectations and what actually occurs, what he in fact achieves, by trying to find an adequate explanation of his own mistaken forecasting, or he can argue that some intervention frustrated his efforts. The observer, or assessor, on the other hand, starts with the overt behaviour, with or without the full consequences, and works backwards in time to the probable motive for the action. We see here the dangers of supposing that word-forms used both by the agent and the observer have the same reference, which is another way of saying that the two viewpoints are confused. On the other hand it seems to be equally dangerous to regard the two sets of word-forms as constituting different languages, as, as such, indicating or sanctioning different kinds of inquiries, or different kinds of worlds, of facts. We should consider these and other points under separate headings.

(a) Intention and motive

Only an agent can make a proper use of "intention", and to express this condition he would introduce it in some such way as this: 'I thought of doing so, but did not really want to', or 'I might have done so, it occurred to me'. Intention is the sense of action, as the proposition is the sense of a sentence. Bradley distinguished between 'intention' and 'resolve' by saying that the latter does not specify any time for fulfilment, whereas 'intention' implies the action to be starting.[1] Similarly an observer cannot distinguish between a motive and the action which incorporates it: for without the action he could not know anything of the motive. To say a person has a certain motive, is to say his actions embody it, show it forth. To restrain a desire recognised in oneself is to act, but the act passes unnoticed—usually—by others. Desires, wants, wishes, one might have these without acting upon them, but to say a want, or wish, is a motive is to say it motivates behaviour, and it is analytic that there is the behaviour. The difficulty arises because of the confusion between means and end. One can speak intelligibly of doing X to bring about Y; one can call X the means, Y the end. But Y only occurs with the incidence of X, even though X is only a sufficient condition and is not necessary, in that, for example, M might also bring about Y if chosen to do so. In this we see that within any particular action we can, if we like, make smaller and smaller abstractions from behaviour, calling them by their appropriate names; but we still have intentional action, or motivated behaviour, according to the viewpoint. By analysing intentional action, or motivated action or behaviour, plain physical movement can never be reached; for there is no possibility of 'reaching' it, the barrier is logical. As said above, it is a matter of empirical fact that we do not directly innervate our physical movements except with regard to ends, that is, to the effect desired. Arguments which assume a real distinction between means and end are based on the misguided notion that all events are arranged in a sequence which can be broken into at will and one event taken without another. But means and end only become real when we are separated from our goal by obstacles which cause us to plan how best to reach it. It could not be said that Fafner killed Fasolt 'by mistake' when trying to get the Ring: he wanted to get the Ring and he wanted it so much that Fasolt's death as a means was unimportant in comparison.[2]

[1] *Collected Essays*, p. 484.
[2] And see Kant, *Fundamental Principles,* tr. Abbott, pp. 40–1.

(b) Morality and psychology

To lay it down that "behaviour" is a word for actions occurring as part of a causal process, and that "action" is reserved for intentional, or moral, action, is to beg the whole question of morality. With 'action' we remain within the concept of morality, trying futilely to find what is outside by examining the inside. As if concepts had windows like Leibnitz' monads!

Nor could it be maintained that morality has one language and psychology another. It is not here that the distinction in reference lies. The words "intention", "action", "good" and "bad" in the sense of moral commendation, and "reason" are taken as constituting the main signposts in this language, and they all point backwards to their origin in 'responsibility'. The 'other language', that of psychology, as in the other sciences, rests, it is supposed, on the assumption of the uniformity of nature, and regards actions as abstractions from a continuous flow of activity. As such, they fall within a causal process, and are hence not to be regarded as 'free'. Yet the moral judgment of the observer would be 'free' in its aspect of being an act of judging by an agent. We should look at these views more closely.

The language of an agent, the language of intention, decision, of foresight, and so on, must mainly consist of experiential statements. These, as we have seen, contain an element of awareness, and, since awareness is personal, the objects of that awareness, or in that awareness, must be qualified by 'as I see it'. 'My situation' is what I see of what is the case. The elements in that situation I can combine as I wish, those elements under my control I can, within the limits of that control, manipulate as I choose. The limits of my control are the same limits we speak of as "the principle of uniformity" with regard to all natural phenomena. That my control is also provided within this principle seems to escape notice. For nature produces according to her own laws, and the result is what Hegel described as an endless multiplicity and variety of forms. No classification is recognised by nature herself; the profusion and variety of instances requires that we must have the idea of some invariable types, by reference to which we can speak of border-line cases, of good and bad specimens, and so on.[1] Surely we

[1] See *Philosophy of Nature*, para. 250.

can also say that the very profusion of nature gives rise to our control, in that we are presented with a choice, and our reasons for choosing are based on the comparison of what we see before us. Each of us, for instance, can only occupy one point in space-time, and, since we move about, we have to decide, or let ourselves be persuaded, where we will be. Similarly, the profusion of our social relations is such that we cannot meet all the claims upon us, so we have to decide, or let ourselves be persuaded, which to fulfil. If this does not fall within the principle of the uniformity of nature, then one wonders what this principle can be. But these arguments have their dangers: for example, those philosophers who tend to fall back upon sociological concepts in default of moral ones, have been led to suppose that freedom is relative to the range of choice, and to make the further 'deduction' or 'speculation' that self-realisation is more probable when the provision of choices is more extensive. This materialistic account of the moral life and of freedom confuses realisation with satiety. The principle of 'choosing from' rests upon a restriction of the person choosing to some fraction of the possible choices. To increase power of choice one must increase the person who chooses, not the things to be chosen, and even then one may only be increasing caprice. Who can tell? No-one is likely to gain in freedom by acquiring the ability of writing long lists of coveted objects for use on a Friday evening.

(c) Choice and freedom

To increase freedom is one thing, to say what freedom is, or consists of, quite another. Freedom is not something quite apart from action that 'action' acquires, unless we rule that it is so. If a man has a choice between going to the cinema and going to the dogs, and he chooses the dogs because that is where he wants to go, we do not say his action in going to the dogs was not free because his want drove him there; we say he wanted to go to the dogs more than he wanted to go to the cinema on that particular occasion. The fact that he had three dog tracks and about fifty cinemas to choose from is quite irrelevant to the choice, *qua* choice, between the dogs and the cinema. Nor would his choice be affected by the provision of all sorts of amusements and pastimes in none of which had he any interest. If people

are interested in something, it must have been there to encourage or initiate their interest, and after aquiring an interest,
they can extend it for themselves. Interests demand, not provision, but tolerance.

We begin to see that there are two sides to freedom, and it
may be that there are, to correspond, two sides also to responsibility. There is the social side of choice, provision, the offering
of choices, and there is the personal side, the choosing. We have
seen that responsibility is ascribed to an agent by an observer,
by society in the person of a representative, provided he can at
least assume that the agent was not acting under duress, that he
did in fact have a choice of actions open to him, even if it were
only the doing or the not doing of one thing. But responsibility is only admitted by an agent when he knows that he in
fact planned and intended the action to be as it was. The
difference between foreseen or intended results, and unforeseen
results, he describes as "chance", "bad luck", "accident",
"interference", the latest term is "sabotage". His knowledge
and skill in his social relations increases his foresight and lessens
the sector left to chance or accident. In this sense he *can* be
said to be responsible for more of the effects of what he does,
and thus, more responsible for his actions. But this is a strained
usage: for it is another way of saying that a man has more
control over the situation in which he finds himself. To speak of
"more responsible" is to say that he takes responsibility for
more of the social world, that he makes himself responsible for
a greater area of change. He is accordingly able to take what
appears to others to be a greater risk; but to him the element
of risk is proportionately small owing to his more detailed and
accurate perception.

The element of risk in responsible behaviour—which was
found in the results of classifying sentences using the word
"responsibility" in the Appendix to chapter II above—is often
overlooked. But it is strikingly exemplified in ordinary discourse: 'I can always say that . . .' reveals that an agent, before
acting, likes to be sure he will not be blamed, and that, if he is,
he has a ready excuse, one that cannot be disproved. For, if
experiential statements about intentions cannot be verified,
and cannot be taken by themselves as premises, so also they
cannot be disproved. If a statement cannot be shown to be
true, logically cannot, neither can it be shown to be false.

In view of the strength of convention, it would be impossible in practice to restrict the use of "action" to responsible action, and we have seen that it has been used in one or other of its two main senses—as responsible action and as event—by philosophers who remained unaware of the possible ambiguity of what they were saying. If actions are taken as events they are still units of change due to certain persons; they follow from the social complex as the waters of a river flow from a physical one. If a man has no standpoint of his own, then he is carried along by society as the waters are carried along in the river. But if he *can* challenge his own actions by assessing them according to an alternative system of values, if he *can* ask himself whether his intentions are suitable or justifiable, then he can make a choice as to which way he will go, with which current he will try to swim. To go forward is compulsory, but the direction is not. If he chooses one direction rather than another, and can give his reasons, then he is responsible for the results in so far as they rest upon that direction rather than upon the other. If he acts on principle, that is, if he decides to make his choices with a definite end or plan, then to that extent he removes himself from the social stream of convention, and his actions on his principle, if they do not coincide with those already existing, provide a precedent for a new set of conventions. He withdraws himself from society in order to reshape the contours of his place in it for himself: and on that withdrawal rests the perception of the claims society makes upon him, and within which he can exercise his personal freedom. The logical gap between the claims of society upon him as he sees them and his position in social life as an observer sees it is reflected in the forms of language by which both are expressed. But we should be careful to say that, if there is a logical gap, a divergence, then there is also a linguistic disparity; for we cannot deduce that there is a logical gap *because* we find a linguistic one. The gap is in the reality we use language to describe.

APPENDIX TO CHAPTER VIII

ACTIONS AS EMPIRICAL CONCEPTS

Austin[1] believed that, by studying the ways in which actions may fail, or fall short of intention, it might be possible to make precise classifications of varying uses of "action". To me it seems unlikely that any precision could be reached without limiting the use of "action" to what is empirically recognisable; and 'legislation' would have to occur at a level where physical features predominate. Traditional ethics assumes such entities as 'kind actions', 'selfish actions', etc., but in aiming at precision, the method adopted would have to lay down rules for action forms, leaving the assessment open. Otherwise to have definitions of actions would add nothing to ethical accuracy, and would merely provide further instances of taking freedom, responsibility, and so on, to be linguistically implied.

Accordingly we should now pause to look at descriptions of actions, in an attempt to discover what arguments can be brought forward in support of these as recognisable units of social behaviour in the same way that we recognise material objects such as tables and chairs.

It is, perhaps, the same problem that confronts the agent and the assessor when they attempt to agree on their accounts of what has been done by the agent and observed by the assessor. Unless we suppose that one or the other gives up his point of view and comes to accept that of the other, the only way they can agree is by taking and describing the same stretch of action, as change, or event. For it is always open to an agent to say that the overt behaviour, the event, was merely the means to another, unrecognised and perhaps unattained, end. What they have to do, then, is to agree to accept the same stretch of action as an event. This may sound simple, but it is not.

Actions are social concepts, and as such they are limited to recognisable social forms. When the names of actions are learnt, they are learnt by looking at patterns of behaviour in social life. When we deliberate about what we shall do, we have to do our thinking in terms of those patterns. If we attempt to plan ahead, we must do so using such forms as the material of our thought, for there is no other way of distinguishing between phases of activity. Thus deciding what to call a phase of activity is deciding a question of fact. If A were to escape from prison, it would be no defence to say that B had come to fetch him. B might be punished for aiding the escape, but A would not be permitted to say he had been lured by B. If C sees a bundle of pound notes lying on a seat and spends them, it is no defence against stealing by finding that he could not bring himself to give them up. There are many people who, in such a position, would find it impossible to abide by the law. Yet the action remains the same. The action does not alter because it follows from an irresistible impulse. There is no difference, so far as actions are concerned, between a strong external, circumstantial opportunity, and a strong, internal urge to take it. All acts are the result of people being in certain circumstances, having certain opportunities; that sometimes the main opportunity comes from without, sometimes from within, is beside the point of the action itself. Nor, on the other hand, can it be said that any description of any action is free from an implication of purpose. For the essence of 'action' is bringing something about, for

[1] See page 37 above.

example, the simple verb "to run" implies a point of departure and, when it ceases to refer, of cessation. To say 'he ran part of the way', if taken by itself, and out of any context, can either be said to be nonsense, or to refer to some stretch of action which may or may not have significance in its context beyond what it actually says; in some contexts, it would imply 'hurry'. Yet such implications are not part of the action, but among the reasons for it.

Nor can actions be changed by the extent of the knowledge of the agent. If A does X, because he believes 'that p', then he can excuse himself, or attempt to do so, when he finds 'that not-p, but q'. But his action is the same, or he would not have to excuse it. In applying sanctions it might be asked whether A could have known 'that q', or whether he should have known 'that q' but was prejudiced against believing 'that q', and so on. He may have deliberately encouraged himself to believe 'that p', in order to give himself the opportunity to do X. But X remains the same.

If a man can stop himself from crossing a busy road when he is in a hurry to catch someone on the other side; if he can refrain from having 'one for the road'; if he can get up in the morning in time to go to work, then it is necessarily true that he has the mechanical means to stop himself from doing any action that is conventionally condemned, at least until he decides whether it is justified in the particular instance. It may not be true that he has the positive ability to do what society demands of him; but how can it be maintained that a man is responsible when crossing a road or travelling to the Continent or round the world, and not responsible in the sphere of business, for example, when he embezzles? Such habits as eating, drinking, driving, dressing, are other-trained, whereas moral habits are to some extent self-trained, but the same physical mechanisms are involved, and from an observer's point of view there is no difference in them merely because there is a difference in the uses to which they are put.

It can be asked how, if we were not to speak of 'action' in some contexts, we could speak of an agent. For 'action' can be said to be polymorphous. It may be taken as:

   (i) What a person does;
   (ii) What a person thinks he does;
   (iii) What a person is said to have done;
   (iv) What a person intends or intended to do;
   (v) What a person achieves, etc.

If A is walking over a bridge and he suddenly leaps over the parapet and is drowned in the swirling waters, surely someone must be doing something? If it was not A's action to leap to the swirling waters, or over the parapet, how did he get into the water? The difficulties arise because of the confusion between intended action and action as event: one cannot argue from 'He jumped into the river' to 'I must jump into the river'. 'He jumped' is a fact, 'I must jump' is an experience, a description of myself, an assertion of what I am at the moment. We would not say 'He must be jumped into the river' or anything of that sort. But he did jump. He was not, for example, carried off his feet. The two expressions "intended act" and "event" are of different logical type: an event is a change in the physical order of things, an action is a change due to a living organism. A wasp's sting is an action, the falling of a tree is an event, whether the tree is blown down or just rots. That "action" does not etymologically involve responsibility and deliberation is shown by the uses of "reaction", and the difference between "action" and "intended action, or act" is only a reference to an agent's awareness of what he does. "Intention" is merely the meaning of action. Intentions cannot be not-carried-out; actions may not be completed and then intention is the meaning of the action that has proceeded so far. The difference between an event and an action is that there is an element of interpretation in the latter, which involves sentience. The wasp stings because it encounters an enemy of some kind, danger. A ball cannot alter its course when in danger of rolling into a fire. The use of "event" in human affairs is metaphorical, an ideal construction out of the effects of actions.

From this we can see that actions as social forms must be distinguished from actions as manifestations of will. And that they are not has harmful effects upon our relations with each other. Actions may be regarded, for instance, as simple expressions of will: if action X is hurtful, and is done by a supposed friend, it 'must be' a mistake, it is argued, unintentional; if by an enemy, it 'must be' hostile. Consequently the friend gets away with behaviour that the enemy does not. The importance of this common confusion for the clarity of our moral thinking is obvious. A harmful act is an unfriendly act, no matter who is the agent; rather than slur over the nature of acts in this way, people of sense ask for explanations, but those of weak character do not seem to do so, and personal relations become unreal and forced as a result.

As a manifestation of will, "action" is used in experiential statements only, and these, as we found above, can only be considered as true or false if taken with the person who utters them. There is no act of will, since what is one act cannot be two acts, and a person's will *is* what he knowingly does. As such, it is part of the world, and can be seen, discussed, criticised, and so on.

My final argument in favour of actions as recognisable and tangible, is that if they were not, we would become involved in insuperable difficulties in trying to say what they are. This will become obvious when we discuss situations, but a brief note will suffice to show what I mean. Suppose A does an action X, and he argues that it was not really X but Y that he intended. His intention rested upon himself, his relations, his history, his knowledge, his anticipation of the future, etc. What he did, or believed himself to be doing was something superimposed upon the whole vista of the past, as seen by himself. It ushered in this whole long avenue of the future, as he foresaw it and as he still foresees it. How describe this action? It could have a million facets of significance. Surely psycho-analysis has shown beyond doubt that from one action alone a whole life can be reconstructed!

IX

THE LOGIC OF 'SITUATION'

Reasons for actions must, to be genuine, relate to, and to some extent reciprocate, the situation in which the agent finds himself. To make out that an action was done, for example, because it was kind to someone, in a situation which offered no opportunity for kindness, is plainly to mock at reason, and to try to impose principles upon a world that is alien to them. The situation is the context of the action. Therein must be sought all the relevant factual details from which the action takes its meaning. In theoretical discussions, when the description of an action is given, the situation is created from the contextual implications of this description as required. But if situations are relevant at all to the meaning of "moral", we cannot be content with a few hints dropped by the chosen descriptive words. Again we recognise that if we are to find criteria for "moral" and for allied words and ideas, we must be on our guard against methods which assume just what we aim to discover. In the practical moral problem, the situation is prior to the action.

"Situation" literally means where something is placed. In speaking of human actions, the human situation is how men are placed in their social aspects, and thus how the agent is placed with regard to society when he acts. Without society there would be no situation in the sense in which we use it here, the sense of a social complex.

There is no difficulty about the situation as seen by an observer or assessor, since he can continue to analyse what lies before him until he is satisfied he has the kind of account of it that he requires. A man looking at a picture can examine it in detail for as long as he likes. But in doing so he is limited to the picture. Similarly, an observer, whether he wishes to assess or merely to comprehend, is limited by the episode he wishes to study; it is the episode, the facts, which first engaged his attention, that determine how much and how far he shall investigate. As he looks, questions arise in his mind, and these guide him in looking for possible answers. These questions are prompted by his previous experience of occasions having something in common with the present one; and the greatest single factor is his knowledge of and insight into human behaviour, which he applies to those concerned in the episode under review. Thus he recreates the situation for himself in ever-increasing detail. He applies the theory of causation or the principle of evolution to the natural forces at work in the situation, and he applies the principle of sufficient reason within his own experience and knowledge to the human behaviour. Usually he will continue to probe and analyse until he is satisfied that he has a consistent account, and this account will include an explanation of the agent's actions in terms of motives. He may end by saying: 'Now that I know the whole story, *A*'s action was the obvious thing to do,' or some such general comment.

Robinson has said of the subjective situation that it is the objective situation as the agent sees it.[1] But I am not happy about using the expression "the objective situation". As Robinson uses it, there does not seem anything to differentiate it from the more modest "what is the case". For the observer does not consider the facts from some remote and all-seeing position: he, like the agent, is in his own situation, and if he assesses the action he is regarding, he is faced with the necessity for acting, just as the agent is, and yet their situations are not the same. Objects have to be manipulated differently by each of them, and because of this their situations are logically distinct: they cannot be said to be parts of some general situation. Yet to agent and observer, the situations are both "objective" if only because they are objectified. *A situation may be described as an ideal construction from what is perceived to be the case.* If we postulate "an objective situation" in the sense that Robinson speaks of it, who shall we say is perceiving the facts from which the situation is constructed? If an agent can have a subjective situation, then who is to have an objective one? We become involved in metaphysics, and find ourselves requiring the distinction that was drawn by Hegel between *die Sache* and *die Sache selbst*, which has defeated English translators, not because it is idiomatic, but because English readers of Hegel are no more sure than German ones what the difference is. For our purpose such questions are superfluous. But in constructing a

[1] See note to p. 185 above.

situation, some circumstances, for instance, that the yellow roses upon the garden wall are a blaze of colour, can hardly be said to be part of the situation in which a man has to act, even though it might be found to temper a man's impatience in dealing with his problem. A situation seems to be an interpretation of the facts rather than a mere description of circumstances: it is those facts which are to be perceived as relevant *only* from which the situation is constructed.[1] It is what the facts mean, what they signify to the agent, that constitutes his situation. A new interpretation of certain facts by a friend may change the whole situation, in so far as action is called for. Yet in a situation I do not think one includes that whole background against, and in the light of, which alternative interpretations of the same facts might stand out or emerge. By "situation" we mean the facts as relevantly abstracted, just as in speaking of objects we refer to what we particularly wish to consider or to which we point, themselves *in* themselves not markedly distinguishable from many other objects we might at another time wish to refer to in a similar scene. Indeed, the facts we assemble, interpret, and relate, are, thus objectified, a complex whole or unity of the phenomena of social relations, in an analogous sense to the complex wholes Russell speaks of as having a mind as a constituent and being the states of believing and those of judging.[2] Such situations are unique, and as wholes they are particular at any stage, though as descriptions they remain general. But, although as descriptions they are general, no description can adequately communicate their content, for such a description would necessarily omit the constituent of mind. And as unique, no two situations could be found to be identical, since there could be no way of comparing them.

On this, it appears that 'the objective situation' is a chimera. We may return to the example given on page 99 above, and use an analogy: if, for instance, we think of a house, a certain house known to us, we can imagine it whole, and we can visualise it vaguely as whole, back and front, inside and outside, garden, outhouses, etc. But as soon as we try to imagine ourselves looking at it to mark some particular feature—the porch

---

[1] Here I have particularly in mind Ryle's analysis of the expression "thinking of . . . as" in 'A Puzzling Element in the Notion of Thinking', *Proc. Brit. Academy* (1958).

[2] *Problems of Philosophy*, ch. XII.

and its climbing plants—we find that we cease to imagine, or think, the house as a whole. The more we try to imagine it as real before our memory, the less can we picture it in its entirety. This is perhaps because when we think of it as a whole, all the content of the descriptive statements, the propositions, we have made, becomes at once available to us; but when we think of particular details and have to imagine ourselves looking at it, then we begin to see it as we would see it in reality, if it were before us. In this way we might suppose that the meaning of all the descriptions of situations at a certain time might be available and that their assembled features would make up the objective situation. But since situations are ideal constructions, and because ideal constructions must be constructed by someone, they must, that is, occur as constructions in a personal consciousness, it is a matter of contingent fact that such a meaning picture could not occur. Further, it is inconceivable that it should occur. Loose talk about postulated ideal observers is out of place in philosophy, and indeed in any inquiry, and can be left to the special techniques of theology; for complete cognisance and ultimately true knowledge are matters of faith, not of logic.

There is, too, an element in the subjective, or personal situation which is never in that of any observer, unless he is moved to intervene, when his situation assumes a personal character, and he is to all intents and purposes another agent. This element is the necessity of action. It is necessary because the personal situation only occurs through involvement, and, once involved, there is no way of avoiding action, even if it be refraining from any positive manipulation of the situation itself. For here we must say 'He did nothing', 'He just waited', or 'He failed to take any action', or again 'He let everything go on as it was'. Given a situation, the very fact that a man goes on living means that he plays some part in it. And if he did not go on living, he would die, and the situation with him. All I am saying is that a man sees the world we all see according to his own understanding and need of it, and what his needs and understanding make of it is his situation at any particular moment of time. The significance of other people and things and events for him is how he thinks about them. And how he thinks of them is also how he will act.

It follows from this argument, if I am right, that *it is never possible to be certain of what situation a man is acting in.* It does not necessarily mean that he has a private world, but it does mean that if he wants to have a private world, he can construct one for himself. We can say that it is a contingent matter how far his world is private, how far we can know his situation, and share it. Thus we ordinarily do not accept a man's account of what he does and why he does it if it is at variance with our own in respect of features which are commonly verifiable.

These distinctions are vital to morals, because the disparity between the situation of the agent as seen by himself and surmised by an assessor makes it improbable that the decision of the one and the moral judgment of the other relate to one and the same action. Even if they agree about the action, in describing it, and perhaps if they also agree about its moral character, they may disagree about the reasons for doing it. For reasons depend upon how a man sees his action in terms of his situation. As remarked above, a reason that satisfies an agent need not satisfy an observer, and *vice versa*. In saying this, we come back to the definition of "action": for if 'action' be taken as what can be seen, and given its usual social name, then the agent and assessor, or observer, can agree about this and disagree about the reasons which justify it; but if, on the other hand, by "action" we mean to sum up the whole situation, as Gellner does[1] in formulating the maxim upon which a man acts, then it is analytic that if there is disagreement about reasons there is also disagreement about the action itself, and how it should be described. For, on Gellner's account, "situation" would merely be another word for relevancies to be included in the description of the action. Thus we are in danger of transferring, or shifting, the anomalies from "action" to "situation". It is only fair to the theorists to admit they did avoid this by disregarding the situation as such.

As we are considering a practical problem, we can take a practical way of finding a solution. To accept the traditional account is to say that a man acts in the world and that we judge his act in the same world. We are not going to be able to analyse the moral problem at all on this view, since it is all carefully contained in the ensuing action. We only come in at the end when the solution has been found, the deed done. What we want to do is to eavesdrop on the process which leads up to

[1] See ch. VIII above, n. 1, p. 181.

the solution, to see how a situation evolves as a man thinks it over.

In addition, it may be said with certainty that there is no precedent in ordinary language for taking 'action' as inclusive of the situation in which it occurs. When it is said, for example, that 'he did it in the hope of . . .', the meaning is that the action was done at least with the possibility that it would bring something about. On the more sophisticated use of "action" it would be impossible to make a distinction between the action as done and the action which could be said to include the further consequences. For if a man does something in the hope that something else will occur, then it is at least within his notion of the possible that his action brings about that something else. With regard to an expected action on the part of someone else, it might be said that, since we could not calculate that reaction, the response, all we could do would be to act ourselves and trust that he would act as we desired he should. But we do not make this distinction in ordinary speech as regards the actions of others. We might say: 'He did that to force so-and-so to do such-and-such', or 'to persuade', or 'to influence', etc. Then the original action is more accurately described as 'he attempted to force the issue' or 'he did his utmost to persuade him', etc. If the word "action" is used in the sophisticated way in which many philosophers do use it when they build up their moral theories, the action to which it is said to refer is the final description, having regard to all factors, that can be given: and this, ideal though it may be, contains what I am calling "the situation" within itself. It follows, accordingly, that to speak of alternative actions means that the same situation has been summed up in different ways, and that those alternatives are, and necessarily are, incompatible.

In most of the situations of every day, however, we have at least the chance of reconciling conflicts of claims, duties, and desires. Many moral philosophers have dealt with such reconciliations. But these details are lost if all efforts of problem solving have to be included in the over-all application of 'action'. In practice we do not cover some vast complex of thought and analysis by the word "action", and many features of one problem remain over to the next, since most of the people with whom we have to deal are with us over long periods of time.

Further, in this remote sense of "action", it would hardly be possible to bring the particular acts counting as actions in that sense under the headings of ordinary discourse; in any attempt to describe or name such actions, the original character would have to be well pruned to fit such names as "steal", "cheat", "give", "return", and so on. Several concepts would in fact be concerned in the one "action". Nor would there be any way of distinguishing between the immediate, foreseen consequences, and the more remote, unforeseen ones. It has indeed been suggested that we should give expression to the distinction by the two words "results" and "consequences";[1] but the distinction is at best a logical one; to speak of foreseen and unforeseen results or effects or consequences is to make an ideal distinction—as Bradley would call it 'to draw an ideal line'—for, practically speaking, what can we do when an agent refuses to admit he foresaw an event which, contingently, follows inevitably from results that he did foresee? To legislate in this way is to remove moral philosophy from the reach of ordinary language, and to admit the impossibility of dealing with a practical moral problem. The same objection applies to talk of reasons for actions: for in the extended sense of "action", the reasons are included as implicit in the "intention", which is the essence of the act itself.

What is unsatisfactory about many contemporary discussions in moral philosophy is that those taking part seem to accept a sophisticated notion of 'action' and yet introduce talk on a number of problems that arise within that concept. And in so doing, they neglect to ask themselves what they do, in fact, mean when they use the word "action" in their discussions. Austin's great contribution was that he did ask himself this question, and, as we have seen, he made practical suggestions for dealing with the problems connected with it. In noting the desirability of finding more detailed models for actions, he did not, however, commit himself to the limitation of "action" to what can be seen. It appears to me that such a limitation is inevitable if precision of language is to be achieved.

The question is of extreme importance: for it is to the action as such that the moral standards are to be applied, and it is of the action that the moral judgment is made. In the case of the sophisticated, all-inclusive notion, theory is restricted to the finding of reasons to justify one action rather than another,

[1] See *Ar. Soc. Suppl. Vol.* (1956).

where there is no question of reconsideration. In practice, two possible actions can both be discarded as unacceptable, and the situation reviewed.

FACTUAL AND MORAL REASONS FOR ACTING

If we now disembarass ourselves entirely of the sophisticated notion of 'action', and turn our attention to the less ambitious section of behaviour which falls under a verb or verbal noun, we thereby accept 'the situation' as the relevant context of such recognisable actions. The question, how to describe what a man does, under what action-word to bring it, may be itself a matter for discussion and difference of opinion, but differences which are in the main reconcilable. Whether the agent would admit his action to be of a certain kind is also to be decided in particular instances by the same sort of discussion that leads to agreement among observers on the nature of his action. The agent has to be able to produce some kind of evidence for his assertions; and in attempting to do this, he may fail to convince the observer.

Where an agent admits that any action should be justifiable by reasons, and yet fails to satisfy himself that his reason was good enough, he has two courses open to him: either he must search about until he finds more reasons, and does satisfy himself that his action was or was not justified according to his ethical outlook; or, he can invent reasons which would satisfy himself and justify his moral scruples if the reasons were in fact correct. The latter kind of reason is called in psychology "rationalisation", and it will help to show the relationship between a situation and the reasons an agent gives for his actions if we pass on, a little later, to consider the application of this term.

Reasons for actions may be of two kinds: they may be factual considerations which lead one to act sensibly, or they may be moral considerations. To raise an umbrella when it starts to rain is sensible, since an umbrella is carried for that purpose; to lend it to a friend departing in a storm has moral implications: to argue that, since it is raining, and the friend has no umbrella and is unsuitably clothed, *therefore* he takes the umbrella as a matter of course is not merely a factual argument. It could become so if the principle of loving one's neighbour as oneself were assumed, as it would then follow that the friend putting up the available umbrella was his response to the situation of rain just as the owner's would be. In this case actual ownership is factually irrelevant as the friends are for practical purposes identical. But that the moral principle is not just assumed is shown by the fact that it would generally be considered odd to go and take one's host's umbrella off its peg without saying anything, without, that is, some adjustment made in respect of its use. It could be argued that it was not a question of moral principles, but one of property: that personal property is associated with one person rather than another, and that it is here that the adjustment has to be made. The principle of property being not so much formal ownership, but priority of use, if A took B's umbrella then B might want to go out in the rain and need the umbrella himself. A might say: 'Look here, old man, I'm taking your umbrella, but I'll bring it back at once when I get mine', supposing he lives within half-a-mile of A. In general, it must, I think, be admitted that B is making a concession, and that his lending of the umbrella to A would fall under a moral principle of one sort or another. A might be a notorious collector of umbrellas, and B only consents to lend his because he can go to A's house and take it back; or it may be that B prefers to risk being let down than either to admit to himself that A is unreliable, even over umbrellas or to act on what he thinks is a principle of mistrust. These two 'reasons' are not at all the same, but their difference does not concern us here, as this is not an ethical treatise.

This trivial example illustrates the difference between factual and moral 'reasons for acting'. The situation presents certain features, response to which has to be made, and possible actions represent those responses; the possible actions also represent certain moral principles, and it could be said that the choice is as much between the moral principles as between the actions. But to say this leaves out of account that it is only contingent that such principles are recognised at the time the choice is made. For it is itself a moral principle to act upon the factual indications; no one would deny that the formulation of this principle by Heraclitus, 'Act according to nature with understanding', was a statement of a moral principle. Yet the agent, led by his insight into the situation, might not admit he was acting on a moral principle of any kind.

REASONS AND RATIONALISATIONS

If an agent acts on the facts of the situation, and is unaware of the question of moral principles as such, are we to say he is acting in a moral situation, and that he is morally responsible for what he does? When he is asked to give reasons for, to justify, what he does, he will have to say that the facts indicated to him that the best, or the most promising, or the sensible, or the obvious action to take was the one he did take. On this, it seems impossible to say that he was not acting on principle, or that he was not morally responsible for what he did.

Suppose, however, that an observer does not agree that the facts warranted the action the agent took; under such circumstances, it might be argued, against his account, that another course of action was 'plainly' indicated, was the 'obvious' thing to do. The agent may stick to his account, and maintain that the facts of the situation could only point one way. He might produce all sorts of reasons to 'prove' that another action was not called for. In this event, either the agent must be said to be inventing excuses for his action, or there must be a difference of opinion about 'the situation'. The observer may not perceive some of the facts that are perceived by the agent, or the agent may refuse to take note of factors which the observer regards as vital. The observer may suspect that the agent had 'a reason' for sticking to the action he chose which he is not willing to admit, whether he knows it to be true or not. It is clear that the observer cannot disprove the agent's point of view, since it is logically inaccessible to him. All he can do is to take the fact that the agent is giving a certain reason for his action, and consider whether a statement to that effect is consistent with other statements about the agent and about the situation. The agent's own statement of his reason, an experiential statement, can, of itself, yield no inferences; but a statement that the agent makes such a statement, is significant. There is always the possibility that it is the observer's perception that is at fault.

If an agent does rationalise, in the technical sense of the word, then it is analytic that he cannot say of himself: 'This is what I say is my reason for doing X, but it is not really my reason, I am rationalising.' He could say: 'This is what I say is my reason. Please yourself whether you believe it or not.' Or: 'If you want to know, I hadn't any reason, I just did it. It never occurred to me not to.' In this latter, the reason expresses itself, for the action must in this case have been 'the obvious thing to do' in the light of his other activities. But to rationalise he must give a reason which he thinks will satisfy himself or his questioner, and which if it was present in his mind at the time of acting, was—by definition—there only as an excuse for an action that he could not bring himself to do without satisfying himself that it was justified. If an agent admits later that he was rationalising at a certain time it is because he now sees his action in a different light, and his admission is tantamount to acknowledging that he acted without fully understanding his action. It makes sense, then, to wonder what a man's reason could have been for doing something, but it does not make sense for an observer to say: 'He says he did it because . . ., but of course that was not the reason. He really did it because . . .'. "Reason" is being mistakenly used for "motive" in such a context. It is impossible for an observer to assert, against the evidence of an agent, that the agent's reason was other than what he said it was. For, again by definition, if a man has a reason for acting, it is his reason or it is nothing. An explanation of why an agent did what he did by an observer is not in terms of reasons, except in the sense that explanations may be given either as causal or as necessary and sufficient conditions.[1]

If observers are speculating as to why an agent acted in a certain way, they may speculate as to his reasons, and if so, they are in fact speculating about the reasons he may have had; they are not speculating about the explanation of his conduct, except in so far as there is a gap in the logic of the facts which they cannot bridge: then they will try to supply a link through the inadequacy of the agent's understanding of his position, the disparity between his reason and the nature of what he did. In the observer's account it will be this disparity which forms part of the causal explanation, not the agent's supposed reason. It is thus correct for Bradley and other philosophers, notably Robinson, to say that, in so far as the disparity is due to wilful thinking, that is, that the agent could have remedied it, he

---

[1] It should be remembered that to speak of cause is in itself to pre-suppose abstractions from a continuous evolutionary process which are taken as data— i.e., they are not actually 'given', but isolated for purposes of experiment. The main advantage of speaking in terms of cause and effect is that it enables processes not apparently connected in time and space to be co-ordinated into one system. See ch. I, p. 15, above.

must be held responsible, and is, in fact, responsible for those actions which issue from it.

In this way, the difficulty we encountered in chapter VI, pages 152-3 can be solved: for we said that the ensuing acts would be material while their condition was formal; but now it appears that it is not the action *qua* action, but the action *qua* being what it is, taking one form rather than another, that is the consequence of the wilful thinking, and thus both ground and consequence are formal.

LIMITATIONS OF PERCEPTION

In the agent's situation there will be all that he perceives as relevant to his problem of acting. "Relevant" is the key word here, for it is within this concept that there lies the ability to include or exclude according to prejudices of which an agent himself is unaware. An agent who knows he is biased against something or someone—for example, the interests of an employee or student—will allow for that bias in making his decisions. An agent who is unaware of his unfriendly feelings in that respect, possibly because he has to keep up an illusion that he is infallibly just, will not, and necessarily not, be able to make that allowance. His act of injustice, if so it be, he will see as one which is just, according to the facts. The object of his prejudice becomes invested with the qualities that justify the poor opinion that led to his failure to advance the interests of that person. This is the phenomenon called "projection" by psychologists, though few of them take the trouble to explain the mechanism according to which it works.[1] To say that a man sees the world in terms of himself in so far as he does not know himself then becomes analytic. In his ignorance, he is, as it were, set against the world; as he comes to know himself, his knowledge puts his objectified self in the world alongside whatever else is there, and the distortions produced in that world by the necessity of accounting for his own prejudices disappear. A man's self, as feeling, is, when unperceived by himself, mirrored to him as the world, and it is in being against this world which is the image of himself that he is at the mercy of

---

[1] Hume put it thus: ' . . . when a passion, such as hope or fear, grief or joy, despair or security, is founded on the supposition of the existence of objects, which really do not exist.' *A Treatise of Human Nature*, II. III. 3.

what Spinoza called 'passive emotions'. They are not genuinely related to any world he shares with others, but he cannot escape their toils, their influence upon his judgment, because he cannot relate them to himself, or find their occasion in his own past experience. All he knows is that he has certain feelings, and that these must have some cause or other, some origin in events. In looking about him for the cause, he is not being unreasonable, only applying his reason in the wrong way. In the great majority of cases, one can hazard, the agent has been at some time in his life so strongly influenced by others against the recognition of any worth in his own being that he is no longer aware of that being, of himself.

What can be said to be a man's situation is, then, what confronts him, and what does confront him may contain knowledge of what pertains to himself or it may not. If it does not, it is analytic that it will be impossible for him to treat his own interests and those of others with any fairness: for it is a condition of fairness, or impartiality, that the objects to be judged are seen in the same perspective; and, as remarked earlier, it is also analytic that if objects cannot be set side by side they cannot be included in one and the same act of valuing.

THE INADEQUACY OF 'EGOISM VERSUS ALTRUISM'

It can be seen from this analysis of 'situation' how superficial is the theoretical restriction of moral choice to egoistic and altruistic actions. Butler, Hegel, and more recently Sartre, have delved beyond the mere opposition "self-and-other" in search of a principle which transcends both points of view. Butler found his answer in 'conscience', which arbitrates between the claims of the self and those of others, though it seems to be limited to choosing in accordance with the one or the other;[1] Hegel resolved his antithesis between self-identity and self-existence (Good and Bad, what could be and what is) by a principle of 'pure insight', which is able to view everything free from the bias of either, and thus to permit a truly rational decision;[2] Sartre, by replacing Hegel's "self-existence", as material self-expression, by the term "roles"—man

[1] 'Upon Human Nature III' in *Sermons*.
[2] 'Spirit', in *Phenomenology of Mind*, VI. By "pure" Hegel meant self-subsistent, unidentified and unidentifiable.

plus function—demands that a man keep himself, and conceive of himself as, distinct from his roles.[1] What they are all three protesting against is the selfish man who loses himself in the values of his worldly achievement, leaving no basis for future progress or adaptation in the recognition of himself as a source or fount of revaluing. At the point where his functions, his set of habits, becomes himself, his values are irrevocably fixed at a level where they must remain for the rest of his life.

If a man is to compare and assess the claims arising out of more than one role, or social relationship, it is clear he will have to distinguish himself from these. For how otherwise could he keep the issues separate, should loyalty to the one require disloyalty to another. If a man has more than one position of trust, it is almost certain that such a conflict will occur. If, for instance, in role A he has information X which is confidential, then in role B he should behave as if he were unaware of information X. In the situation which confronts him as B, X is not relevant, and should be disregarded.

It could be argued that, if a man so placed betrayed such a confidence for his own gain, he would be acting egoistically. Can it be said, however, that the man who observed the confidence was behaving altruistically? What the first man has done is to bring the knowledge of X into the situation which confronts him as an individual, rather than as a player of various roles. He has disregarded the barriers between them. But it is hard to call the action of the second altruistic, for there does not seem to be any opposition between the two procedures. Acting in accordance with various positions of trust is plainly to a man's advantage, since if he were to fail to do so the positions of trust would not continue. Altruism, when opposed in idea to egoism, might be said to be based upon respect for society, or for others in general, or on recognition of the obligations imposed by confidence; but in practice it is not the yielding of one's own interests to those of another so much as the ability to value, to ascribe meaning, in accordance with a larger complex than one's own self, or interests. The difference lies in the scaling of the factors in the situation rather than in the delineation of possible actions. For value is a function of perceiving with regard to feeling. Valuing is judgment of intensity, not of

[1] See for example the account by Mary Warnock in 'The Moral Philosophy of Sartre', in *The Listener*, 8 and 15 Jan. 1959.

extensity that can be measured. Intensities can only be scaled, *felt* to be stronger or weaker as they are surveyed in the light of the same criterion.

THE AGENT IN HIS SITUATION

I am here assuming a phenomenological account by which, when a man is faced with a problem, and has to decide how to act, he does *not* think out what actions he might take, line them up before him, weed them out by applying a scale of moral values, and finally make a decision between the surviving few according to some principle. If he did follow some such procedure, he would have to take the situation as static, and would be unable to return to an earlier stage once a new idea had occurred to him. What he does is to turn his attention to various features or aspects of his problem in turn, and as he does so, certain ideas of solutions occur to him, many of which are discarded as he considers another aspect. The problem is passed in review by a process, a series of perceptions, during which it changes in character according to the implications and possibilities that are explored. At the later stages it is no longer the same problem, it acquires a new sense, there appear many features which were not there at the outset, and finally a pattern emerges which gives definite indications of the way the problem may be dealt with, either by taking action, or by leaving it to develop further before intervening, or by postponing decision until some particular relevant information is obtained. What is important is that we should realise that at any time during the process of analysis and deliberation, the agent may stop and decide to act upon the problem as then before him. If he is, for instance, biased in favour of a revengeful action, he will halt his deliberations when the pattern of the problem is such that revenge is justified, and the act of revenge to some extent indicated by the situation as it is at the moment. I have refrained from using the word "situation" in the previous few sentences, but as deliberation continues, so, it is plain, does the situation develop. This development consists in the gradual coming into the agent's awareness of the material implications of the facts as given initially in the problem. His situation at any moment is his present account of his problem. Thus it is clear that the moral problem as such is a matter of contingency; it is what an agent sees his problem *as* that constitutes his situation. An observer to whom he describes the problem may see it as something quite different, and consequently offer advice which is unacceptable to the agent.

We may be mistaken in speaking of a 'moral problem'; for it may be that the moral element lies with the agent, so that we should speak of a 'moral agent' dealing with his problem. It is the pattern, we have said, emerging from consideration of the problem and seen within the developing situation that points to action. As the agent considers the possibilities before him during deliberation, he considers them as a *moral* agent, and, accordingly, some ideas of solutions are discarded immediately on moral grounds. Thus his moral standards operate in deliberation itself, and do not form a kind of ambush to censor actions in the final scene. The final pattern which emerges is compounded of all the decisions that have been made en route, and it does finally emerge because of all the detailed criticisms, on grounds of moral scruple and of efficacy, that go to make up deliberation. There is a sense, or feeling, of satisfaction or completion, expressed by 'That will do', or 'It's the best I can manage', when the point is reached at which action becomes both possible and acceptable.

Although it is generally recognised that the content of a moral problem, or of the problem of a moral agent, is material, factual, there is considerable interest in the logical relationship between a moral precept, or standard, and the action it permits, or forbids. It is held that a moral precept or principle is an imperative, and that it is because it is an imperative that it is a moral principle. But if an agent wants to know what he should do, and he looks to precepts and principles to guide him, then the imperative is a reflection of his demand for guidance, not any function of the sentence in which the principle is stated. Since a man must select from the great number of moral principles that people of piety and moral gnosticism litter our world with, to say that all principles contain imperatives is to leave 'imperative' totally without force. To say that moral principles contain imperatives is another way of saying that a man looks to them for guidance, and that they offer guidance in their very formulation. The desire and need for guidance is logically prior to the formulation of principles as imperatives, and whether those principles concern interpersonal behaviour, that is, whether they are moral, or not, does not seem to be of much moment. If the agent is moral in his asking, then the answer he gets must be moral too. On this view, there is only one moral problem, and it is formal: the problem of what to do. Thus to look for strict implication between the principle adopted and the act enjoined appears absurd. What is required is guidance as to procedure, principles for arranging the evidence so that the pattern which emerges from it, the indications as to action, will be morally acceptable, will give satisfaction to a moral agent. And this is precisely what Kant's Categorical Imperative aimed to provide.

THE PROBLEM

We have not yet reached the point where we could even hazard a definition of "moral", except to say that it may refer to some quality of an agent. In this we should find it similar to "responsibility", and we have remarked that if "responsibility" is applicable to a man, then there must be something about a man in respect of which we make that application. This consideration we may also bear in mind with regard to "moral".

At least we can ask what we mean by a problem, and whether there is any justification for distinguishing between 'problem' and 'situation'. A problem, we said, is the pattern of facts within which falls the necessity for action, while by "situation" we signify the whole complex of persons and things and considerations relevant to the solving of the problem. As the process of solving continues, the situation changes as more aspects of it are dealt with, and as more of the contingent circumstances are analysed. The problem alters as the contingencies are analysed and synthesised, and the agent's situation may be said to be the construct he builds round the problem, which determines what he sees the problem as involving. The situation may be said to supply an interpretation of the problem which provides the relevant facts, while the problem rests upon the plurality of ways in which the situation may develop, as a result of the action the agent is to take.

We should be sure what we mean by analysis and synthesis. Analysis of the facts consists in exploring the meaning of factual statements, and in finding other statements in which to describe them if these first ones are not found to be accurate. Statements of fact which describe social relations include statements of obligations or claims, for it is how a man sees himself placed in his various capacities—or roles—that determines what, at any particular time, he recognises as due to or from himself. Analysis is a matter of inference, and inference is a series of progressive perceptions as to the nature of the starting-point. Bradley expressed the problem of inference thus: 'If, on the one hand, the object does not advance beyond its beginning, there clearly is no inference. But, on the other hand, if the object passes beyond what is itself, the inference is destroyed.'[1] Earlier, on page 245 of volume I, he had remarked that the basis of inference, or the basis of the conclusion reached by inference, is 'something' we already know; and it is plain that Bradley here indicates what is now called material implication, the perception of what, in terms of our already existing knowledge, the statements before us can be said to imply. Once we have their full implications, as analysed, we can take any further steps we desire by putting together such of those implications which together, as premises, convey information. This is speculative synthesis, and it is also theorising, or forming hypotheses which are subject to some kind of test as confirmation. If we remember that the validity of the process depends upon the accuracy of the facts as first stated, and that it is limited by the knowledge and experience of the agent, we can formulate synthesis as follows:

$$\text{Propositions A — E together imply propositions } X_{1\text{-n}}$$
$$\text{,,} \quad \text{F — M} \quad \text{,,} \quad \text{,,} \quad \text{,,} \quad Y_{1\text{-n}}$$
$$\text{,,} \quad \text{N — S} \quad \text{,,} \quad \text{,,} \quad \text{,,} \quad Z_{1\text{-n}}$$

Provided propositions A—S are correctly known either as true or false, it will follow from this analysis that any combinations of the content of $X\ Y\ Z$ are factual possibilities. They yield by speculative synthesis what is likely to happen if certain acts are done, what certain people will probably do in the new situation, what will be thought of the actions contemplated by those in a position to assess and criticise. Some actions will be ruled out, as analysis and synthesis proceeds, because they are too difficult, because they may cause adverse comment, or because they are uncongenial to the agent, and so on. Fact and possibility meet in an ideal dimension. The opinions that may be

[1] *Principles of Logic*, vol. II, Essay I.

given as to an action's efficacy and those moral comments that may be made become facts in the situation, as implied by what is known of others, supposing that knowledge to be accurate. What is surmised has the status of fact in the situation, it stands on the same basis as facts which are perceived concretely. So far as practical problems are concerned, what one believes to be the case *is* so, and as such, forms the background of the action taken. Propaganda is based upon this phenomenon, and so, in a more dignified way, is persuasion. It is thus, too, that moral precepts, injunctions, social norms, the minutiae of convention, theological convictions, and the like, enter into the practical life of a man. Whatever their origin, their ground in belief, authority, or emotional appeal, they are all facts in the personal situation.

PRACTICAL ASPECTS OF PROBLEMS

Apart from the processes by which we deal with a problem, there is the problem itself. We have described the situation, not the problem, and we have seen that there is some case for conserving the distinction between the two. It is, at this stage of our inquiry, plain that some of the processes described may occur below the threshold of consciousness. The arousing of the associated ideas which enable inference to be made, for example, is a process of which we are never fully aware, for the same reason that we are not aware of the nerve impulses that innervate single muscle fibres when we make some movement. When we are thinking, our thinking acts as both stimulus and response so far as its material is concerned. The very use of one word rather than another in our thoughts may alter the sequence of our thinking. And control over the use of words is a matter of skill, it is acquired. A natural aptitude for writing does not include knowledge of words, but the ability to make good use of them once they are known. Knowledge of vocabulary in any language is a mere adjunct to knowing what to say, to have something to say.

It may be that we interrupt our thought processes by the use of words; for words, being part of the world, acquire emotional associations which become confused with their linguistic reference. They become significant in terms of love, anger, hate and fear, and when it is unsuspected, that significance tends to overrule the proper reference. At any stage, as we saw above, of the practical solution of a problem, the occurrence of certain words may halt the agent in his deliberations, and lead to a premature conclusion.

The problem arises in the first place, we saw, because there are many ways in which a situation can be forecast to develop, and human agency must play a part in directing this development. But a man does not stand alone in a situation; with him are those people whose lives his action will affect, directly or indirectly. He is alone, however, in that he can decide how far those others shall stand with him: for he may or may not admit the effect upon their lives of what he does as relevant or irrelevant to his problem. If he does not feel involved in their lives, he will not feel any concern for those lives, he will be unaware of their interests, one could say. For it is the feeling of involvement that constitutes the necessity for action in the first place. Otherwise one's attention would not have been drawn to the problem at all. How should it? One does not pluck problems from the wayside as one picks a bright flower from the hedgerow. Problems arise in the context of our lives as we live them.

A man who has a servant plans out his day for him, and allots him so much work according to his ability and contract. So, if he inadvertently sets him two tasks for the same period of time, the servant can ask what he is to do, and receive an answer. But an agent is an agent just because he has no one of whom he can ask such questions: if he is in doubt he has to work it out for himself. Where he is in the position of the servant, there he can ask, and it is one of his personal problems to know when he should ask and when he should not; for this follows from his various social relationships and from his lack of skilled knowledge in certain respects. As an employee, he is either directed all the time he works, or he is given a sphere of influence within which he has to make his own decisions. His understanding of that sphere provides the material of the situation when problems arise.

Similarly, what a man understands and accepts as the conditions of his life provides the material out of which his situation is constructed by him when confronted by the necessity of acting, when the issues are not clear enough for a quick decision to be made. As any problem demanding decision is a problem, even when, as in the case just posited, the issues are clear, and decision is in fact made almost as soon as the problem can be said to arise or occur, so easy problems should present the same formal features as those more complicated ones it may take almost a life-time to solve.

A man A may be said to have a practical problem to solve when a promise made to B in the relationship AB cannot be honoured without a neglect of duty in the relation AC. This might be regarded as a clear choice between two claims or obligations. But even so, there must be grounds for the choice. Let us say the duty arises in connection with A's paid work, that C is an easy-going fellow, while B is not. To annoy B will have unpleasant consequences in various ways, but on the whole A prefers to fulfil the duty to C. There are four actions that A can take: (i) he can use the duty to C as an excuse to let B down; (ii) he can ask C to excuse the duty, and keep the promise to B; (iii) he can fulfil the duty, and later explain his non-appearance to B as the result of compulsion; (iv) he can keep his promise to B and take a chance on C not noticing his absence, if he can find someone to do his duty for him.

I have specified these solutions, though of course there might be others, because it would be easy to say that A's dilemma was one of principle, that all he had to do was to look at the issues, and decide on priorities. Or alternatives might be ruled out since one or other of them involved a deliberate lie, for instance (iii). It may be, in the actual circumstances, that (ii) also would require a lie, if by chance C disapproved of A's association with B, or with the nature of the promise. A would then either have to be mysterious, or risk annoying C, or tell a lie. C's annoyance in this respect might be about equal to B's unpleasantness at being let down. Again, if A is a man who lets nothing interfere with his job, then, when he tells B he cannot keep the promise, B should respect his reason, or excuse: but B might then argue that A should only have given a provisional promise.

THE AGENT ACTS: ASSERTION OF A PRINCIPLE

I have said enough to show that, although a man may be said to decide a problem for himself, in accordance with the significance of the various factors and issues relevant to it, it cannot be said on this alone that his decision is taken on principle, or that it is a decision of principle. His moral views and scruples are, like his knowledge of current opinions on moral matters, facts among other facts in the situation. When I say his "moral" views, I refer to his ability to apply moral or social opinions about lying, deceiving, helping, etc., to physical descriptions of actions, as distinct from naming those actions. He will have, as a matter of necessity, likes and dislikes in his personal relations, and these are not matters of principle unless he can recognise that they are factors in his decisions. If he makes this recognition, he can act in accordance with them, or disregard them, if he prefers not to act towards an enemy as he would scorn to act towards a friend. He may then be said to be acting on principle in respect of his personal likes and dislikes. It is remarkable that a man, who has a double attitude towards another person, may try to act in such a way that he harms him, yet in some respects the same act results in benefits to him. The action is thus shown to be a compromise of some sort. Such a man will be deeply resentful when he finds out that his enemy has gained instead of losing on balance. The same curious effects may occur in reverse, when the positive attitude is the conscious one. It might be argued on this that the attitude of dislike prevented the attitude of liking from being recognised (or *vice versa*), since to feel like and dislike at the same time in respect of the same object is physically impossible owing to the structure of the autonomic nervous system. But there seems no reason why the agent should not become aware, or at least suspicious of the existence of the hidden attitude by studying the results of his act in retrospect. It would, however, be absurd, in such a case, for an observer to say that the agent acted on a principle of hate as well as on a principle of friendship. Yet on the traditional dichotomy of self-love and benevolence that is what would have to be said, although the traditional moralists would evade this awkward issue by ruling out the unconscious attitude as a motive on a theory, or by definition. A more recent view that the principles of actions, or standards of acting, are to be inferred from the completed action would, however, lead to this particular dilemma. For from the observer's point of view the difference in the agent's awareness is not significant or detectable. The act is what is seen, so the inferred principles are as inferred. If a man acts on principle he may be said to assert the principle by identifying himself with it in his act, but, by definition, he cannot identify himself with what he does not perceive. No inference as to a man's principles of acting is possible from the completed act. What can be inferred is information about his character. If an agent is asked why he acted thus, his answer must be taken together with himself as saying it: for, as we have repeated too often, maybe, the fact is *that* he says so-and-so, the fact *is not* that so-and-so.

When we say a man acted on principle, what we mean, it now appears, is that he acts in a situation ideally constructed by himself, whether the particular act merely happens to seem the thing to do in the particular situation, or not. The process of deliberation is the construction of the situation; it is not the prevarication of a man who cannot make up his mind. It is difficult, if not impossible, to say whether a man deliberates in order to find a *good* or *the best* solution, or whether he deliberates in order to find a *good* or *the best* justification for what he has already decided to do. In the first case the whole of the deliberation falls within the sphere of morality, whatever notion he may have of 'good' or 'best'; but in the second he may either be trying to persuade himself he is justified, and that he is not making some foolish mistake, or else he is sharpening his weapons against the social or domestic wrath to come. In the latter case, the agent is plainly well aware that moral issues are involved, and that he is in fact the agent and is not being compelled or driven, and it must be admitted that he, in both events, is influenced by considerations beyond his immediate self. He is not just responding as an organism to some external stimulus; in some way he is enmeshed in a social complex, and his decisions reflect its influence, even though to the very small degree that he decides what excuse to offer.

What then of this man who decides? Can he be said to choose between himself in his different roles, or between loyalties to others, or do these amount in practice to the same feature of social life? It is hard to see how a man could distinguish himself *from* his roles, since he must always be in one of them at any time. But the man who can organise the claims impinging upon him in his roles is already safe from losing himself in any one of them. So that "roles" as a term in moral discourse is misleading, for it suggests that we chop up our lives, and that there is something to chop up. What we do have is personal relations, and it is the personal standing that we have in our various spheres of activity that engenders the significance of what we do. In the example given above, it was not A's sense of duty that influenced him with regard to C, for if it had been, there would have been no problem; but it was the relationship with C, the social relation AC, that counted, upon which he placed value. Similarly, if B's friendship was unimportant to A, he would not have hesitated, we could hazard, to let him down, for he had a plausible excuse, and what would B's anger have mattered to him? Thus where we have a conflict of claims it is the value to us of the relationship in which the claims occur that gives the claim its force. If this seems an unpleasant thought, then let us also face the fact that in itself this constitutes a principle: for if we assess the value of our personal relationships in order to turn them into some sort of a hierarchy, this is only another way of saying, as Bradley did, that we schematise our interests and thus our lives: for the furtherance of interests is entirely dependent upon the personal relations in which they are pursued: a human being does not grow in skill without the emotional impetus of a personal relation. Things must be done within the compass of sentience, or they are not done at all. All motivation is fundamentally interpersonal.

THE CLASSIFICATION OF ACTIONS

If an agent and an observer are to be able to agree about the description of actions, when they cannot share the same situation in which those actions occur, we have to speak of actions in simple terms, as recognisable forms, or units of social behaviour. We have also to use action-words without the moral signification that is sometimes analytically ascribed to them. We may use words like "taking-from", "travelling", "seeking-out", on one level, and, with reference to the same occurrences on another level, "stealing", "escaping", "molesting". And still we do not reach the moral significance. The description must be free of implications as to praise or blame. We do, accordingly, have to admit a hierarchy of some sort in descriptions of actions, and we are entitled to try to group them according to their purposes. If, instead of using "action" and "agent" to cover the whole field of moral behaviour, we are going to try to locate the reference of "action", "situation", "reason", "problem", "moral", "responsible" or "responsibility", and "agent", we are going to require a far more detailed scheme of categories. So far, in these last three chapters, we have tried to give an account, a phenomenological one, of all that occurs when a man who is a responsible agent has to act. Now we shall have to attempt to delineate the formal differences that occur within our account, so that we find where one word applies or does not apply, where there is a distinction in fact which must be marked by distinction of sign. But before leaving our exposition of the characteristics of moral behaviour, we may find it instructive to give, in very broad outline, the different fields of actions and thus the bases of different kinds of reasons relevant to different kinds of situations.

Actions bring about changes in situations. It is thus to actions *as* changes that we should look for guidance in classifying them.

A. Acquisitive actions. A very large proportion of actions are taken to obtain something for someone. They involve economic values, contracts, and friendly agreements. A large variety of criminal activities fall under this heading.

B. Restitutive actions. We are pushed towards actions because we have unused energies, because we endure through time, and must maintain ourselves. Socially we can say we *are* because we *do*, and particular actions present themselves because we are involved in social relations. It may be that in our situation we see a dysbalance of social emphasis, or a disturbance of function, or an infringement of 'right'. When situations are seen in this way, the action decided upon tends to put right, or restore, a proper balance as the agent conceives it. Paying a bill is restitutive before it becomes a debt. On the physical level, attempts of any kind to save life are examples of restitutive action.

C. Initiating actions. Actions may disturb situations because they are directed towards some end which the existing situation cannot realise. Initiative is both useful and dangerous because, while it is essential for changes in the social field, in laws, design, invention, and so on, it often stems from a violent personal sense of grievance or exaggerated sense of mission, and consequently may overshoot its mark and cause a reaction which is more unfortunate than the orginal state of affairs.

A sub-class of initiating actions is that of those which do not directly aim at some end, but which aim at altering a difficult situation in such a way that a solution can at least be considered. Creating a diversion might be put in another subclass. In the case of a deadlock both these types of actions are of great importance.[1] They may be said to be ends in themselves, since they do not point to a solution, nor do they necessarily contribute to one. They should be carefully distinguished from expedient action in the accepted sense of the word. Ethical theory has hitherto failed to consider the status of such actions with regard to justification.

D. The reconciliation of claims. Finally, most actions, especially those of institutions and legislative bodies, are the result of the scaling of claims. When these have been relegated to what is thought to be their proper place, the prior obligation may or may not emerge. If possible, more than one claim is met when a difficult situation has to be dealt with. We will take an example.

Suppose the elements of a situation to be represented as a, c, $-d$, f, h, $-m$, while the personal or institutional claims relevant are A, D, $-H$ and M.

When

Possible action (i) would produce a situation $a\,d\,m$

    ,,   ,, (ii)   ,,   ,,   ,,   ,, $-a\,-d\,h\,-m$

    ,,   ,, (iii)   ,,   ,,   ,,   ,, $a\,-d\,f\,m$

(i) makes restitution in respect of D and M.

(ii) contains positive harm to A, H, M.

(iii) makes restitution in respect of m, but leaves D out of account.

Provided A, D, $-H$ and M are roughly equal, action will be decided in accordance with (i). But in a hasty decision (iii) might be selected, if M's claim had been considered more carefully or earlier than that of any of the others. This might occur in the presence of, or under the influence of, M. A foolish agent might be persuaded into doing (ii), and would thereafter reflect gloomily that everything 'seemed to go wrong'. It is evident, from all that has been said, that errors of perception and of judgment influence a man's choice of action, but that they do not of themselves influence the nature of the action itself.

---

[1] From an observer's point of view, an example of an action designed to force others to take some action was Eden's *coup* in Suez. It was very successful as an action of this kind.

X

THE APPLICATION OF 'RESPONSIBILITY'

If it is correct to speak of responsibility in some context, is it analytic that we can also speak of a moral situation with regard to that context? That is one question this chapter must discuss. It might be otherwise stated: Does any 'ought' imply responsibility, or merely one kind of 'ought'—the moral 'ought'? Whether we are correct in distinguishing between different kinds of 'ought' is a further question which will have to be considered later.

We have found that a man cannot be expected to act in accordance with a situation that, for him, does not exist; and also that an onlooker cannot assume he is acquainted with the situation in which an agent did act. Similarly, an agent, in retrospect, cannot without great care think himself back into the situation as it was when he acted, for his knowledge of what has occurred after his decision and his act is something of which he cannot rid himself—he can only attempt to discount it; and, even then, it will only be as an act of remembering that he can re-survey that earlier situation deprived of the significance it has since acquired. That an agent does attempt to look back in this way is evidenced by many expressions in ordinary speech, such as: 'I nearly did . . ., and how disastrous it would have been', 'Just think if I had . . .', 'I've always regretted . . .', 'I wish I had that choice again . . .' etc.

The lack of correspondence between the private and the observed situations is the sine qua non of most legal procedures. Morals differs from law in that excuses in the former are regarded with some scorn—as if a man who excused himself somehow admitted that he had been 'caught out' as unequal to his situation; while in criminal processes it is recognised as correct that a man should do his utmost to disclaim his part in felony. Civil actions are often the result of a man's attempt to evade his obligations under contract and are thus based upon a man's inability to excuse himself. It may be that an accused man, in pleading not guilty, forces his victim and others to expose themselves to publicity in a way that brings more discredit upon himself, but the law, in supporting a man's right to defend himself to the utmost, does not recognise that wrong as such, and it remains a moral, not a legal, fault.

It will, however, be helpful to look at the successive lines of defence upon which a man will take his stand. When the first line fails, he retreats to the second, and so on. The four main standpoints may be said to be: (i) that the accused had nothing to do with the crime at all; (ii) that he, if concerned at all, took no part in any criminal act; (iii) that he, in taking part in the crime, was forced to do so, and his own part in it was not willed by him; (iv) finally, if he cannot avoid the consequences of what he has done in any other way, he pleads mental aberration of some sort, now known technically as 'diminished responsibility'.

For brevity, we can name these stages of defence as (i) involvement, (ii) agency, (iii) freedom of acting, and (iv) subjective —or actual—responsibility. It is analytic that, if a man can be said to be in a certain situation, he must be involved with whatever is in question regarding that situation. Also we have seen that it is analytic that if he acted knowingly he must have been in a situation. Are we now to say that if he is to be held responsible, the situation in which he acted must be the one with which he is credited as responsible by his judge, or any onlooker?

This is another way of asking whether the meaning of what he did is the same to him as it is to his assessors, and it clearly is a restatement of Bradley's requirement that a man's intention must be the same as the 'external existence' for which he is indicted. But in practice the two are not, necessarily are not, identical.

At this point we should leave aside the legal considerations, for a man will not acknowledge his guilt during a defence; but in morals it is otherwise, since sanctions are not so severe, and because, as a general rule, the injury itself is not so great. In morals not to admit to a fault is in itself an additional fault and the resulting guilt is the greater. Men do not wish to answer for more than they need, so that in practice apologies are offered and seldom rejected. The remoteness of the agent's world is often expressed by an observer in the remark: 'Wonder what he thinks he's doing', which is usually a form of disparagement; but it is not so much blame as a recognition that the agent is foolish or misguided. It amounts to a doubt as to how far he does realise what he is about.

If we accept such statements as meaningful, we must regard responsibility not as the perquisite of a man as such, but as the result of the disparity between his situation and that of his fellows. *A man is responsible for his actions,* not because he has acted, not because of what he has done, but *because in acting he acts in his own situation, and because he may bring his fellows' interests into that situation, or he may not.* If he does not, and he causes harm to his fellows, then he is responsible for having failed to allow for that harm, for having constructed his situation in isolation, for having withdrawn, we might say, from his proper place in society, for contracting out of his social relations.

The time barrier between the situation of the agent and what is seen of it by an onlooker cannot be over-emphasised. Even if the latter were, through friendship, to identify himself very closely with the agent, he would still not be able to see his situation at the moment when the decision was finally made, for each man would have also in his mind that background of experience which, as we recognised, provides the interpretation of what is perceived from instant to instant. If the agent was able to communicate his situation, as a construct, to his friend, the friend would still see that construct as an object against a different ground. He might also assess it according to different standards. Such a man might indeed be able to say that the agent had acted after very careful consideration, with his eyes open, and this is evidence that is verifiable and acceptable; while, on the other hand, it is impossible from a detached, objective study of a person's behaviour to tell what he does after full deliberation and survey of alternatives, and what he does from chance influences or strong desire. Even in the case of the two friends, it would still be possible for the agent surreptitiously to toss a coin. And it would not, necessarily not, be possible for an observer to halt the process of deliberation at the precise point when the situation was so developed that a certain decision was made. This point might occur, for instance, during the process of deliberation, not at the end: for one can go on turning things over in one's mind, and then accept as final an earlier stage of thought. It is conceivable that decision might result from occurrences in sleep, as it does when 'things look different in the morning'. The agent, when he pauses to reflect, halts time and retains the one perspective until once more he looks at the passing pageant. It is logically impossible for observers B and C to halt the process at the same perspective as the agent A halts it; for that of B and C is and must be an abstraction from a longer process, while that of A is genuinely halted at its furthest point, even if an earlier arrangement of the problem is adopted once more as a basis of decision. Nothing can be at once the end and not the end of the same process.

I am not speaking of a mere difference between one person's world and a generally agreed, or common-to-all world, but of one between a person's situation and any other situation which might be constructed by anyone at all. It is a fact that no one would construct a relevant situation unless he were involved in it in some way. Kant would have put it that an agent, when constructing his situation, could include those others involved in it as ends or as means. If he included them as ends he would have to know something of their interests, that is, he would have to some extent to identify himself with them, to understand, sympathise with them, even if he did not make his decision in their favour.

A man is responsible for what he does to those affected by what he does, or to those who act on behalf of those affected, and thus it is initially by them that he is held responsible. This is merely another way of saying that he is responsible for the results of his actions, and that if he recognises his responsibility as such he will be prepared to take a risk when much is at stake. But the responsibility has import only as a relation between his situation and those of others; and, since he cannot perceive the situations of others, responsibility is in fact a relation within the range of his own perceptions, within himself, as it were. It is not, for example, a margin of chance, or guesswork, or the evaluation of duties and claims; it is not just being a human being; it is not autonomy, for autonomy, as applied to a human being, is a chimera, a dream; it is not a matter of initiative, since this must be limited by suitable opportunities, occasions. Responsibility is a relation within a man, and, as such it is there or it is not there, and does not admit of degrees.

A man is responsible for his actions because it is he and no other who constructs the situation in which action takes place, and in terms of which it carries significance. To mask the distinction between an agent's and an observer's construction of the situation behind an extended and all-embracing concept of action is not only to make every action, for moral purposes, into a particular action which can hardly be brought successfully under any classification of kinds of action, but is also to make it unique. By openly admitting the situation in which the action occurs to be unique, logically unique, we escape the meaningless question as to whether situations recur, or can be summed up and typified. Whatever the situation, if the action can be said to be 'of a kind', then it can be named according to the conventions of language, and precepts and moral rules applied, for the action is then distinguished from the agent, and the agent judged for having chosen it. Otherwise it is hard to see how anyone can apply a rule. But this question may be left for the next chapter.

Nor can responsibility be said to be the difference between 'action' and 'event'. Actions are not events because what is called an action is not, in ordinary speech, called an event. Supplementing what has already been said, we can point to events as distinguishable changes in the world, to actions as changes in the world which are due to human agency; both are logical constructions so far as perception is concerned. But the distinction is that between the inorganic and the organic: for the inorganic is inert, while the organic is active, activity is its essence, for activity is also growth. This is what we mean by "organic". No amount of philosophical analysis will reduce behaviour, as a form of activity, to the inertia of the inorganic. By speaking of stimulus and response one cannot reduce the notion of movement as regards organic bodies to that of the inorganic—for example, the billiard ball. For the movement of the organic *is* activity, and activity may be split up into increments, each of which can be called an action; but it makes nonsense to go on to say that there is any antithesis involved in human behaviour as activity and as movement, as if there were an analogy between physical movement in organic and inorganic matter. If any such comparison or contrast were possible, or thinkable, it would be between physical force and human motivation. It would have to be argued that the latter was based upon the same quantitative principle as the former, that motivation resulted from majority innervation among the purposive systems.[1] Even to say this is no more than to say that if a man wants to do X, then he must follow those pursuits which put X among his strongest motives, which is, of course, just what we all do in following our own pursuits and professions. No one can, for example, be a printer without learning the trade. As for the moral life, a man who wishes to acquire practical wisdom, to act wisely, must integrate within himself those facets of behaviour which the man of practical wisdom, to use Aristotle's unrivalled description, shows him by example. There is nothing here to endanger responsibility.

A distinction that can be made is between man as able to make an ideal construction of his situation, and the other higher animals who are limited to acting in a real situation which is not of their construction, but is pure sense. Animals respond to signals, as sense-data, while men respond to conceptual constructions. It is a matter of opinion which arrangement is the happier. Kant, we gather from pages 12–13 of the *Fundamental Principles*, thought the condition of the animals to be so! But we have no choice, and those who belittle man's reason and say we should try to recapture the instinctive reaction to whatever confronts us are unrealistic to the point of blindness; for if it is by reason that a man constructs his situation, how can he dispossess himself of reason in order to act like an intelligent horse or tiger. That apes seem to have sufficient powers of reasoning to make visual rearrangements of factors in their situations I do not doubt, and many skills in men require this ability, for instance, a musician reading a score which includes transposing instrumental parts, or playing at sight in a different key. Such reasoning is an extension or development of the sensory apparatus, and the final development of the sensory apparatus up to date on this planet is man's magnificent brain, by which thoughts of actions, or incompleted impulses to actions, can initiate the imagination of new situations. Deliberation is a prolongation of the process of perception, made possible by ideation, and requiring the fixation of stages in that ideation by words.

Where man is prone to error is not in using his reason but

[1] What A. Gesell calls "electrotonic integrations". See his *Embryology of Behaviour*.

in that the situation as he constructs it, ideally, does not correspond necessarily to the actual circumstances in which he has to act once decision is taken. It depends upon the type of error he makes in the construction of his situation what kind of mistake he will make in acting, and what further difficulties will then confront him. On this account it is easy to see how lack of knowledge and skill lead back to faulty perception; for since perception is guided by previous experience in the form of knowledge the lack of the one limits the accuracy of the other.

Many philosophers find the notion that reason is limited in its application to what is perceived obnoxious, and prefer to believe that reason is a source of knowledge in itself, on the ground that it has some kind of divine origin. I am not here concerned at all with theological arguments, and will merely comment that it would seem to be an error, if God is both immanent and transcendent, to describe some attributes as "more divine" than others. But there are also arguments based upon empirical observation which are brought in favour of a non-physical or non-natural source of reason, and we may look at two of the main ones.

(i) The first is that thoughts occur, be they calculations or other solutions which are not consciously worked out, at a speed which would be impossible in a neural system of any kind. Against this we can bring two objections.

(a) If when we want a word, we obtain the word somehow without all the paraphernalia of sensory experience by which we learned its use, there seems no objection to supposing that any piece of information which is, either immediately or mediately, inferred from any element in experience is also available without pause or process. If tables of numbers are learned and their relations understood, there is no logical objection to supposing that all extensions of those tables are computed in the brain and are thus available if wanted. That they should be available, or readily available, is unusual, but not in any way inconceivable. Children often amuse themselves by carrying on tables beyond the conventional limits, and since any mathematical process is an analysis of relations in what is given, there seems no obvious reason why mathematical processes should not continue indefinitely. We have no evidence at all that thinking does not continue when we are not paying attention to some problem or train of thought. That it is unusual that the extensions of our mathematical knowledge should be available in practice as are our memories is no argument against that extension as a product of the brain.

(b) Again, unless thoughts are bound to words, they are not limited to the speed at which words can be said or intuited. The most probable speed would be that of the nervous impulse. We have thoughts in a moment of danger which can take up to an hour or more to relate fully afterwards, especially when some action has had to be improvised. Dreams are subject to the same flashing quality, and they, when recorded, have to be stretched out in narration, and embellished by a fair amount of rationalisation before they are even describable, either to oneself or to others.

(ii) The second argument is that, with so vast an amount of experience, it is impossible for that experience to be stored in the brain. In answer to this, we can admit that, if reality is to be thought of as an endless multitude of units, of bits, it is inconceivable that these could be stored up anywhere. But if all experience is qualitative and reiterative, and each successive experience is a rearrangement, needing no more obscure basis than the neural pattern which occurs at the time, then there is no need for anything to be stored up. Our experience would thus be built into our bodies and brains as such, and what we remember is a reference back to a certain stage in the building-up process, a certain integration. An unusual experience would be easier to recall as a distinct experience on this view, than would those experiences which, because very similar to many others, we call "dull" or "ordinary". The very act of asking ourselves what we mean by a word may start the recapitulation of a seemingly endless succession of usages and applications which rises in our imagination, for, when we try to generalise on our past experience, it is usually the imagination which provides the evidence. Those who do not easily make use of their powers of imagination in this way are more likely to become attached to verbal definitions, which somehow at a later stage come to enshrine eternal truths.

It may be that the traditional antagonism between reason and sense is due (1) to the ease with which many people carry out one job while thinking about something else, or (2) to the unpleasant fact that we often find people do not do what they say they will do, but do something different, and (3) to the necessity of controlling and restraining our dislikes and likes in the interests of health and reputation, etc. We tend to identify 'sense' with desire and forget the beauties of the landscape and the harmonies of sound. That we desire an object for the pleasure it will give us is a matter of purpose, not of sense alone; and too much indulgence in sensuous pleasures may not have worse effects than too much indulgence in seemingly non-sensuous pleasures like crosswords, betting, and research. At some point any indulgence ceases to be a pleasure and becomes a compulsion, involving serious denial of other needs. We use our reasoning powers to find out how much of a thing gives maximum enjoyment, and what assortment and arrangement of our purposes or wants, including the simple physical ones, is most pleasing to us, and most likely to exclude waste of time or boredom. Reason does not dictate, as it might be expected to do if it was indeed divinely inspired, but it enables us to deliberate within ourselves about what we are doing and what we would like to do before we commit ourselves in action. It also permits us to make use of a feeling we deplore as a motive for some activity we favour. We use reason in the sphere of the ideal, or conceptual, as we use our eyes to guide our movements in a busy street.

Responsibility is, we have seen, dependent upon the rational nature of man since, to be responsible, he has to construct ideally. And I must now consider and attempt to support the implications of the account of responsibility that I have given. For it could be said that this account has been reached and formulated in a somewhat haphazard fashion. First of all, we should take one or two examples of personal situations which differ not merely logically, but also materially from any reconstructions that can be made of them. In these we shall see more clearly that the only possible link and basis for discussion between the agent and the observer is the action itself.

First let us take a child of about ten who is shown little or no affection by his parents, and who steals money from a substitute person. Now the fact is that he has stolen the money. That is the proper description of his action. But the situation to him is not the same as the situation of the observer: the child's situation is one in which he takes what is due to him, while to the onlooker the situation has quite the opposite meaning. If the motive of the child is established, he does not thereby cease to have stolen the money, but he becomes entitled to different treatment on conviction.

Secondly, there is the too frequent case of a man who kills a child. It is commonly supposed that such killing is done to prevent the child revealing rape, or acting as a witness, or aiding arrest of an offender by recognising him. From the agent's point of view, a man who kills a child may be trying to destroy within himself some inhibited purposive system, some lesion of his brain,[1] which has resulted from bad treatment, or accident, at about the age of the child he kills; or else it may express and thus integrate a lesion of violent jealousy of a sibling or a friend resembling in some way the victim. The attempt to ravish a child may be an attempt to integrate a lost thought-system, to join it to the rest of his thought-processes, for if motivation is interpersonal, it follows that sexual behaviour is in fantasy often symbolic of reunion within the personality. Yet such an account would sound fantastic at a court hearing of the crime itself, and in any case it would be impossible to prove, for the hidden situation of the criminal might fall within any of dozens of such explanations. But at least it can be generally agreed that, in the case of a schizoid, or paranoic, who has reached the institutional stage, it is the impossibility of finding out what situation the patient is acting, or trying to act, in that is the most serious barrier to successful treatment. There is no point of contact between his thought and that of the observer at all. To humour a man by joining in his fantasy is not to contact his thought, but merely to concur in its isolation, and this is particularly the case with *dementia praecox*. It is very difficult indeed, with those of even mild mental dysbalance, to know what remarks will help them, and what remarks will offend and add to their misery and sense of injustice.

In all such cases there is no responsibility because it is impossible for the agent to bring anyone but himself into his situation. His situation, whatever it is, is no longer his construction from what he sees about him, but an invasion of irrelevant feeling and purpose. It is out of the question for him to verify any of the statements he might make about his situation, or in it, and it is also impossible for him to doubt the accuracy of

---

[1] Kierkegaard's expression "the offended consciousness" is in my opinion the most accurate yet used. See his *Philosophical Fragments*, tr. Swenson.

what he believes to be true. While a criminal may admit to his act and say he has no idea why he has done it, the lunatic could not apply any social criteria to the words he uses to describe what he has done. Thus the criminal's responsibility follows from his ability to find out by observing his actions and utterances what his unbidden crime signified, and in this way to bring more and more of his behaviour within the compass of one critical awareness, into that situation within which his reason can be properly employed.

There are many questions we have to face. First, we must attempt an answer to the one put at the beginning of the chapter, as to the relation between responsibility and morality; secondly, we must examine the relation between responsibility and agency; thirdly, we should look again at the reasons why the statements in which a man describes his situation are not verifiable, even though they appear to deal with matters of contingency; fourthly, we must ask how we can ascribe responsibility, or ascertain whether a man is responsible— whether we have a social concept which is also empirical, and if so, what are the positive criteria for its application. And fifthly and finally, we ought to attempt to decide what, if responsibility is, as we said above, either to be applicable or non-applicable to a man, we can say about the concept of diminished responsibility now introduced into English law.

I. RESPONSIBILITY AND MORALITY

If we accept the view of responsibility just put forward, we must say that the connection between responsibility and morality is asymmetrical. A man would not be said to have a moral problem unless he was responsible, but to say that a man is responsible is not to say that he constructs a moral situation, or that he is morally responsible. Whether responsibility is moral responsibility is, it seems to me, contingent. That a man is solving or dealing with a moral problem, that he is in a moral situation, is a sufficient condition of his being responsible, but though responsibility is a necessary condition of morality, it is not sufficient, in my view. With regard to the use of "ought", we shall see later whether it can, just as "ought", be said to be moral or non-moral. Once a man is a moral agent in any respect, it is difficult to refute Bradley's view that there is no area of his life, into which norms enter, that has not been moralised.[1] Once a man's situation becomes a moral situation, it remains so, and *necessarily* remains so.

2. RESPONSIBILITY AND AGENCY

Let us repeat once more what we have suggested as constituting responsibility. A man is responsible for his actions, not because he has acted, not because of what he has done, but because in acting he acts in his own situation, into which he may bring the interests of his fellows, or he may not. I do not mean to imply by this that his action may be selfish or unselfish in the usual sense of this opposition, but rather that a man may consider other people's interests as facts alongside his own to any extent that he wishes when constructing his situation. Responsibility occurs as a relation between a man and his fellows as a result of the impossibility of an identification of perception and thus of interests. Interests may be shared, and to this extent we can speak of common experience, doing things together; but even so, our common experience in one direction will not comprise all our situation, for that we do have common experience in that direction is merely a feature of our personal situation. Green[2] spoke of social interest thus: 'For it is characteristic of this interest that, to the man who is the subject of it, those who are its objects are ends, in the same sense in which he is an end to himself. Or, more properly, they are included in the end for which he lives in living for himself.' Green thus escaped the egoism-altruism antithesis which has haunted moral theory by taking Kant's point that other people should be considered as ends, not as means; but he conceived of social interest as a quality of a man, a tendency to think socially, a habit of mind which Hobhouse[3] described as 'the transpersonal reference' which is a 'constitutive element in the normal personality'.

Social interest in this broader sense is more akin to Hume's notion of 'humanity', and merely indicates in general that feeling of affinity which holds between men and is thought by some philosophers to be a condition of society. What is more

[1] *E.S.* p. 217.
[2] *Prolegomena to Ethics,* para. 200.
[3] *The Rational Good,* p. 102.

important for our present purpose is to distinguish the particular interests of men as the social patterns according to which they expend their energies and realise their ambitions. We must also distinguish between those interests of others about which a man knows by experience, common experience, and those of which he is unaware, perhaps that he cannot know of. The man we call responsible will include the interests of which he is aware as facts in his situation, the man who is irresponsible will perceive interests but disregard them, while the man who is not-responsible will be unable to perceive them at all. And if he does not perceive them, he cannot consider them when acting. We have to see how these conditions affect the relation between responsibility and agency.

Plainly if a man is responsible for his actions, his responsibility is limited to those actions, to what he does. Thus we can say that if a man is responsible at all, he is responsible for all that he does. Yet it seems to me that the relation between responsibility and agency remains contingent. We have to be careful not to assume that by "agency" we mean 'his act' in Bradley's sense of what is ultimately attributable to a man. We are trying to avoid these kinds of assumption. By agency we should indicate a person's behaviour as described in action-words, as the changes in his surroundings that he actually achieves. There is a difference between saying that a man is responsible for his actions and saying that he is responsible because he acts, but it is not easy to be sure where the difference lies. If we say that a man is answerable for the actions that can be agreed to involve his agency, and that his responsibility extends beyond answerability, we approach perhaps to the distinction we want. There is a sense in which responsible men can be said to be responsible for the whole development of their community, yet it would be absurd to try to say in what particular way they were severally responsible for the details of that development. Interaction is not completely explained by dividing events up between those concerned. We could take two examples of what occurs in social relations generally, to illustrate the difficulties of arguing from action to responsibility as distinct from 'responsible' as generally applicable to the agent.

(i) What happens among a group of people who are caught up in a misunderstanding is not usually attributable in detail

to particular members of the group, but results from the interactions of all concerned. It is mainly because such interactions
are not fully understood, or because they cannot be sorted out,
that what a man attempts to do often appears as an act of a
completely different character. It is on account of these complexities that we are ready to listen to a man's excuses. He may
not be disclaiming responsibility, as is evidenced by his readi-
ness to admit he has something to explain, but he tries to show
what it was he was really trying to do, showing, perhaps, that
his fault was due to ignorance of existing circumstances. Over-
plausibility in excuse is soon recognised as the attempt to exploit
the privacy of a man's thoughts, and such explanation is no
longer acceptable.

(ii) There are ways of securing a man's confidence, and thus
profiting by his influence, that are indistinguishable from
ordinary acts of friendship. As examples we can give such acts
as flattery by the offer of publicity, or by pretending to make a
price concession. Such acts may be genuine, or they may not,
but observers would hardly recognise them as the latter unless
there was some statutory offence. Offers and concessions would
assume a different aspect when made to a co-director or co-
examiner, yet the line between friendly assistance and bribery
would be impossible to draw, even in the agent's own thoughts.
In social relations the results of one person's acts, the influence
of one person, is impossible to describe accurately, because a
person is not unified as a person in any one of his social relations: he is simply their meeting place. Yet there is no good
reason that I can think of for saying that an agent, a person, is
answerable for influence that cannot be recognised as particular
actions.

If the relation between responsibility and agency is contingent, then we can easily see why we do not ordinarily wait to
prove agency before judging an act. To be certain of what a
man has really done, as distinct from what he has more or less
been led into doing by others, we might have to wait for a long
investigation, and it would be odd to refrain from judging
actions because we were not sure how much an agent could
'help' what he did. We judge actions that we see, and we utter
those judgments, not because we are thereby charging a man
with an act, or because we hold him solely responsible, but
because we either wish or do not wish to associate ourselves

with the principle of the action. It is, as mentioned above, one function of the moral judgment to make our own position clear, to assert ourselves as agreeing or disagreeing with the performance of the actions in question. In doing this we assert what we believe to be right or wrong, we ally ourselves with, or identify ourselves with a principle, or we dissociate ourselves from it, we repudiate it. And we do this on the evidence before us, we do not wait to satisfy ourselves there were motives, or drives, or irresistible impulses, and the like. When we judge A for doing X we cannot say, as Bradley would require, that A had, previous to his act, X before him as an alternative. Responsibility is not affected by considerations of this kind, if it is freed from identification with answerability. It is a concept based on the conditions of acting, not on the act as such. The difference between judging actions, and praising and blaming an agent is a difference of kind, and it is a difference that is more often overlooked. To criticise an action is to give an opinion on it, it is not also to apply sanctions, though many people will take it as such, and expend so much energy on proving their non-responsibility that they altogether neglect to consider how best to remedy the position.

Those who attempt to show that the use of "action" is the ascription of responsibility in specific cases must logically try to disprove action if they are to disprove responsibility. To do this seems to me to make a mockery of human behaviour: for who can I be if I do not do what is done by me? My dispositions, my interests, my friends who influence me, am I to pretend I am not these, that without them there would be anyone, or anything, at all?

I am not, on the other hand, suggesting that an agent, in putting forward his own view of what he does, can assert his intention and have his statement accepted as valid. His statements of intention are experiential, and are not verifiable. They must be taken as statements by the agent and weighed up with all the other empirical facts. If a man, accused of a robbery, said he was visiting a house nearby to place a bet, when it was known that he had never betted before, and that he could not produce a slip, then his experiential statement as made by him would remain a fact but would not be admitted as evidence of intention.

A man does what can be seen as done by him, and he knows

why he did it, and whether it was done by mistake, or on purpose. He knows whether an act is done on principle, provided he knows what acting on principle is. That responsibility is wider than mere agency is perhaps due to the fact that agency refers to separate acts, and responsibility does not. Choice and agency concern the particular, responsibility the general. We may take one more illustration: suppose a man accepts an honorary post and then finds that his acceptance has occasioned a reshuffle, enabling a disabled employee to be dismissed. He then regrets his acceptance, and reproaches himself that he was not fully aware of the position. Should he find that in fact it would have been impossible for him to have known in advance that he was likely, by his acceptance, to deprive the man of his job, he does not immediately cease to have feelings of regret. He is in a position which is very distasteful to him, and that distaste need not be attributable to what he thinks others might say of him. He feels somehow responsible for the disabled man's predicament, and he will not be consoled by the knowledge that had he not accepted the post as a spare-time interest, no doubt someone else would have done so. It seems to me a fair empirical generalisation to say that those men we regard as reliable and conscientious are prepared to accept responsibility for many contingencies not due either to their agency or lack of foresight; and anyone in 'a responsible position' has to act upon his own initiative in situations which are not at all of his own making, and which he might be prepared to interpret and construct in quite a different way were it not for the interests entrusted to him. In other words, he has to act according to principles with which he is not wholly in sympathy. It is this, no doubt, that Sartre means by "playing a role". The agent knows that he will have to justify what he does in accordance with a code or standard that he himself does not fully endorse.

3. THE NON-ACCESSIBILITY OF SITUATIONS

(i) We have based our account of responsibility upon the inaccessibility of a man's situation, the situation in which he acts. But it could be argued that if men were perfectly honest about their thoughts and intentions, then, since the material of those thoughts and the actions contemplated as intentions are matters of fact, all the statements an agent would make about his situation would be verifiable.

There are two objections to this view. (a) The first is that, as Kant maintained, a man with the best will in the world cannot be completely honest about his principles and motives for the simple reason that he can never know whether he is aware of them all, or whether, of those he does know, he has selected the ones from which he actually does act.[1] If the agent himself cannot be certain, then the statements he makes can hardly be verifiable. For all an observer can see is the completed action in its social setting. (b) Secondly, although it is true that an agent explores the possibilities of his situation by means of material implications from what he sees to be the case, yet since actions are social concepts, there are among what he sees to be the case surmises based upon his experience of other people, in the light of which he foresees what they may do as a result of his action. But in constructing his situation, the agent will base his assumptions about other people's actions upon what he sees of their own situations. As he has not yet acted, he cannot possibly envisage the situation that will confront those others when his action is taken, and thus his description must remain incomplete and unverifiable. For it contains statements about the future which will not be verifiable until the situation is radically changed.

Further, it is by no means the whole story to say that an agent's situation is concerned with matters of fact. For his situation is a construction from matters of fact, it is a selection, it is an abstraction from what is perceived to be the case. It is based upon relevance to a specific problem. And we have also seen that to speak of an objective situation which is available for all to see is alike misleading in theoretical as well as practical affairs; for if a situation is set out to be looked at by all, it is in the nature of data selected for experiment, and apart from such a prepared situation there is no possibility of referring to any social situation which all would interpret in the same way. It is the presentation of the social and political situation in varying ways that marks the political parties and religious sects. Their programmes are based upon different constructions of the facts, or status quo.

[1] *Fundamental Principles*, tr. Abbott, p. 28.

It is important to remember that an experiential statement, whether one of perception or one about a situation, cannot be verified without being taken together with its context, and that, in statements of opinion taken with their authors, all that can be done is to explain why those authors have held that opinion —the opinion itself must be found either to be based upon empirical evidence, or upon a selection from that evidence occasioned by some prejudice or attitude. Moral judgments taken with their authors are certainly verifiable, though it is the man judging in that way that will be 'explained', verified, or established, not the 'truth' of the moral opinion. Moral judgments express the opinion of an assessor, and this opinion is a factor in the agent's situation, and is often foreseen by him.

(ii) Another argument against the inaccessibility of situations is to say that a situation is only constituted of claims, and that such claims are matters of fact. It is true, we can concede, that claims arise in personal and other social relations, and that there have been codes which purport to lay down rules of priority for all claims according to the nature of the relationship. But this argument defeats itself, for no one but the agent could survey all the claims upon him from his unique position as one end of all the relationships giving rise to the claims. And it would be the relative strengths, not of the relations, but of those relations as affected by his contemplated action that would interest him. A hierarchy of claims and loyalties might indeed be compiled, but in itself this would not tell the agent what compromise action would be correct in a complex situation, nor what to do if equal claims happened to be opposed. Also, it must be remembered that one factor in the situation is the knowledge that the agent has of himself, and the extent of such knowledge in itself constitutes some kind of claim, or at least influences the assessment of other claims. The same position arises if obligations or duties are regarded as claims: for their urgency is unlikely to be based only upon the nature of the duty, it is the relationship of the person concerned with the agent which will determine the decision. It is the significance of these duties, claims, and relations to him that *is* the situation. To take them alone is to exclude the agent from his own situation, and thus to make him decide in defiance of his most vital interests. In such a case an agent might locate the strongest claim, yet fail to act in accordance with it.

4. CRITERIA FOR RESPONSIBILITY

Is responsibility, we might ask, to be a matter of opinion, or of fact? If a man is responsible for what he does *because* he acts in his own situation, and if his situation is not only, as existing, a logical construction, but also an ideal construction, then he must, to be responsible, be able to construct that situation. A child may be so identified with another person as to be incapable of constructing his situation: all his actions are subsumptions to a rule. If he cannot find a rule, or where rules seem to conflict, he does nothing, because he cannot assure himself in advance that what he proposes to do will be considered right. Given freedom to choose something, again he does nothing because the absence of direction is, to him, the negation of action. He may wait till someone else makes a choice and then join up with him in whatever he is doing.

Such a child does not recognise his wants and acknowledge them as his own. To be admitted as a want, his desire would have to find a rule by which it was supported as 'real'. He only recognises the demands of others. But since he does not, ideally, in words, see his own wants in a situation and assert them in propositions neither can he see those of others. What others do is what he must do, or should do. Mere conventions are turned by him into categorical imperatives. Accordingly he never constructs a situation in which his interests are set side by side with those of others: he never brings them all into one perspective. Confronted with the need to act, he will look about for a precedent to use as a guide, and although he may look at the varied actions of others, he will select one on the ground that it appears 'safe', or 'permitted', not as suitable, adventurous, or anything else. Its moral nature will be a matter of indifference to him, and it may be that this is why prudence is sometimes regarded as outside morality proper.

At the traditional age of discretion, a child is supposed to have emerged from this stage, and he may of course have been lucky enough to escape it altogether. In his previous years he has not been held responsible, mainly, one supposes, on the ground that he has not enough knowledge to make a competent judgment. Whether he is in fact responsible for what he does is beside the point. If he thinks for himself, as we say, then it can be said that he has learnt to build his ideal situation.

If, according to this, a man, or child, can say what he wants, what he likes, if he can also describe what he sees of others and of their likes and dislikes, he is certainly responsible for his actions. He can communicate with others, he can form personal relationships, and is capable of understanding that people vary in their interests and tastes, and that his actions may impinge upon those interests and tastes. If he can communicate these things, he can construct his own situation. The main consideration is that he should be able to objectify himself to some extent at least, even if only to say what food he enjoys, or whether he dreams at night.

Such criteria as this seem to me to be sufficient for responsibility. But since there is at present a determined movement to establish responsibility as a rebuttable assumption, we should ask what is implied in this suggestion. The argument is that it is, in any particular case, impossible to say whether a man is or is not responsible for his actions by applying positive criteria. So responsibility is taken as a quality of human nature, and if it can be shown that an accused man, on certain agreed grounds, fails in this quality, then he is not blamed for what he has done. I will first comment on this view, and then proceed to discuss it as a view.

We might recall that Hegel believed that to tamper with the notion of responsibility is to infringe upon the dignity of man, and he specifically deplored the idea that psychological conditions such as sudden impulse could take away guilt.[1] Bradley's remark, we can surmise, would have been that, since negative criteria must have some positive ground, it is idle to regard responsibility as at the same time devoid of positive criteria and determinable by negative ones. If we meet this by saying that the positive ground is that a man is responsible as a human being, then we fall under Hegel's accusation that to attempt to disprove a man's responsibility is to attempt to remove his human dignity. In other words, to deny his humanity in some important respect. That too many people do lower their standards of behaviour towards other people whom they manage to convince themselves are stupid or crazy is an empirical fact that supports Hegel's view; but such behaviour usually reflects most discredit upon the agents. The refusal to listen to what a man says in his own defence is a variation on the

[1] *Philosophy of Right,* para. 132.

same theme. And another variation is that many children are intellectually crippled for life as a result of the abusive way they are spoken to by their parents and other adults, including the sarcasm of their teachers. Take away a child's chance of ever forming his own opinions, of ever looking out upon the world with vision unclouded by fear of verbal and other forms of attack, the searing scorn shown in violence and ridicule; then, when he grows up in years, the last remnant of his rights can be taken from him by saying there are no positive reasons why he should be regarded as a responsible person, except that he is just a human unit. Such is the pass we have almost come to. But, on the other side, we must recognise that it is now established as a psychological fact that children, and adults also, learn to co-ordinate their thought systems and their action tendencies by discussion, through, that is, speech that is not mere expression but is also communication: and to say this is to assert that the co-ordination occurs through a personal relationship, that the words used refer to a common experience. Such discussion can be contrasted with those many 'conversations' which occur at all ages, when different people make remarks in turn without taking the trouble to listen to each other at all. Before a child can in fact become a responsible person he must be treated as if he already were just that.

It is time to turn from these somewhat vague comments to a more methodical consideration of the view that there are no positive criteria for responsibility. That the view has found much support may be due partly to the impossibility of applying criteria, such as those of Bradley, in practice, and partly from the awkward fact that once we start analysing behaviour to find a cause, we discover we have no way of knowing when we do have a cause, or of knowing how far to pursue the myth of this suspected entity. If we cannot find a cause without postulating the whole of a man's life, how can we say when a man is responsible for his actions and when he is not: for it is a question that requires an answer in the form of an account of the origin of a specific action. Again, it appears that the analysis both of reasons for and of motives for actions reveals no substantial evidence for speaking of responsibility at all. Nor need this surprise us, for responsibility we have found to be a relation between ideal constructions. Such a relation we should hardly expect the psychologist or the sociologist to come upon, and it is unfortunte that they should assume that, because they have not come upon it, it is not there to be come upon.

We allow that a man is responsible, so the argument runs, if we fail to show that he is not. The emphasis then falls upon showing that he is not. The main evidence brought to refute the assumption of responsibility is not ignorance, or mistake, but is based upon a further assumption that if psychological conditions can be found to offer a sufficient reason of a man's action, then he can claim exemption from the consequences of his acts. Thus from the idea of external compulsion as an excuse there comes the idea of internal, or interpersonal compulsion. Even in the face of Freud's argument that the mentally insecure or unstable are morally sick, it is maintained that they should be morally immune because they are not responsible. But how is a man who is acquitted of responsibility and thus of guilt to discover he is morally sick if he is treated as morally immune? It is the man who gets away with it who is just the man who should not.

We are not dealing with morality in this chapter, so I shall confine the argument to the bearing of psychological stress upon responsibility. We shall then be in a position, we hope, to say something about the notion of 'diminished responsibility'.

If we can explain human actions completely in terms of psychological causes and effects, so the argument runs, the agent must act according to the psychological principles that are exemplified in him. Thus he cannot be said to be responsible in himself for what he does. In a situation he will respond according to 'sets' and the relative strengths of his drive-systems.

We have already dealt with the logical aspect of this. In the first place to explain a man's action is not to give any account of his situation as he saw it. The action is explained after it has occurred, and presumably if the agent had acted differently, that action would also have been satisfactorily explained. For if a process is regarded *as* a process, to divide it up into events to be related as causes and effects is analytically to find an explanation. There is no room for failure: if one explanation does not do, we adopt another that fits in better. We cannot err because there is no room for error: we have the process *as* completed to theorise about. Principles should be tested by prediction, and it is admitted by all but the most bigoted psychologists that no psychological theory has yet reached the stage where general predictions can be made about human conduct. For either the experiment is so narrowly devised that failure is impossible, or else it is devised to cover human behaviour, and it is impossible to find two identical specimens to set against each other. For in behaviour, a chance association in the memory of an agent can alter the whole course of his activity.

The strongest answer to the psychological objection to responsibility is to be found in the nature of psychological theory itself. For it is a feature of theories of personality, as distinct from theories resting upon aesthetic analysis, that what happens to a man when a child conditions what he does when he grows up. If this is so, we are to understand that those tendencies which are inhibited by one means or another during early childhood, and later, will gradually make their way back into the mainstream of personal behaviour. They do this, we are told, by acting in a hidden and subtle way upon a man's situation so that he is led to interpret it and to act upon it in ways that encourage the inhibited impulses to action to find an outlet through the motor system. A man is said to "over-react" when his action expresses not only his act in the present situation or context, but also an inhibited act that should have occurred in a past one. When he constructs his situation partly in accordance with present perceptions and partly in accordance with past ones, he is said to "project". Now, if this process of integration is said to take most of a life-time, and sometimes not to be completed in a life-time, then it seems to follow that the process is a slow one, and that no-one could say whereabouts a man 'is' at any time with regard to it. The inhibitions and lesions are not formal in character, but material; they concern content, and thus are, necessarily are, personal, unique experiences. How then can any generalisation cover them? The fact is that if a man derives his compulsions, as 'oughts', from his subconscious material, then neither he, nor any observer, can say when these 'oughts' are compulsive in character and when they are not. A man, as we saw above, can compare his situation with what his friends see of it, and smooth out any obvious incompatibilities. He can obtain the opinion of others upon his actions. He can contrast his unexpected results with what he foresaw would happen. But at the time of decision, if he has a strong bias in favour of an action which, unsuitable in the present, yet has value as releasing the tensions of the past, he has the right to decide in favour of this bias against the advice of all his friends, and even with a partial realisation that he is being foolish in doing so—using "foolish" here as imprudent, as against his obvious interest. He may even see that his reason for acting is totally inadequate to justify it, and yet he proceeds, saying that he knows it will turn out all right in the end. And it may do so. If the psychologists are right, the individual person must have more, not less, freedom to act as he thinks he should, and be credited with the responsibility for his own decisions. For it is only thus that he can find himself out. If he is to construct his situation with greater accuracy and competence as he matures, the psychologically handicapped person must have freedom to try himself out, and to be able to see, through moral censure and the attribution of responsibility for what he does, what is unsuitable in his handling of his affairs and what is genuinely relevant.

For this reason, I find the notion of responsibility as a rebuttable assumption an unfortunate step towards the loss of all meaning by the word. 'Responsibility' may become a mere conventional excuse for conditioning citizens to the life that other citizens assign to them.

5. 'DIMINISHED RESPONSIBILITY'

Responsibility, we said, does not admit of degrees; yet diminished responsibility is now adopted as a legal concept, and the very use of the expression will establish it as meaningful. It is a device to exempt a criminal, or convicted man, from the full penalties assigned to certain crimes. There are, admittedly, many criminals who fall between the stools of responsibility and the McNaghten rules, which in effect specify insanity, and there is no way of avoiding the rigour of the law without forcing a man to relinquish his rights as a person. It is easy to say that these difficulties arise because we have capital punishment and thus have to find an excuse for preserving the lunatics and hanging the sane. So long as the concept of diminished responsibility is limited in application, as it is now, to murder cases, it may have little effect upon our thinking in moral issues;[1] but

[1] It should, however, be noted that Lord Kilmuir, when he spoke, on the second reading of the Homicide Bill, of the grounds upon which degrees of murder

the danger is that it will spread its illusive tentacles into other categories of criminal processes. It was mainly because members of the Gowers Commission doubted that the concept could be limited in application to one class of offences that they did not recommend its introduction into English law in their Report.[1] There is a growing field of strict liability, and it is conceivable that this will gradually extend, although at present it is in practice based upon a presumption of knowledge or skill in some occupation, and is likely to remain so. It is the fact that death turns a murder charge into the equivalent of strict liability on conviction yet without any presumption of standardsthat has occasioned the introduction of an alleviating measure.

Let us see what the concept requires and achieves. The Act[2] itself speaks of diminished responsibility as 'impaired mental responsibility'. When it is proved, the description of the crime is reduced at the conviction stage of a trial from murder to manslaughter because the agent, while fit to plead, has been found to be unable to prevent himself doing what he recognised as a crime, and/or incapable of understanding the enormity of what he did. Consequently, the description of the crime is made to tally rather with the requirement of the agent's situation than with that of the community or the victim. But the crime is in fact just as it was: a murder. For murder is deliberate and unprovoked killing, unprovoked in the sense that the killing is not done in self-defence against an attack. It is true that a man may believe he is acting in self-defence when he has no need to do so; either because he wrongly believes an attack upon himself to be imminent, or because he mistakes a gesture. It is likely that such illusions arise more frequently in the mentally unstable.

There is the question of deliberation: for if a man is not responsible, if he cannot construct a situation even remotely related to his present circumstances, then he can hardly be said to deliberate. But in this case he is not responsible, his respon-

---

were to be introduced, admitted that the government had abandoned the principle of moral heinousness in allocating the death penalty. See Hansard, *House of Lords*, 21 Feb. 1957, col. 1167.

[1] *Report of the Royal Commission on Capital Punishment 1949–1953*, Cmd. 8932, paragraph 413.

[2] The relevant statements of the law are clauses 1-4 of Section 2, Part I of the Homicide Act, 1957.

sibility need not be said to be lessened. If he can deliberate about what tie he will wear, provided he has more than one, or in what place he will buy his food, he can deliberate about his situation, whatever it is.

What provision is there for impressing upon a man whose crime has been reduced, by official misdescription, that his guilt extends over the wider crime? Kant held that punishment must be exacted, since it is the measure of guilt. Bradley thought punishment to be the assertion of right, and the suppression of 'a standing assertion of wrong' in the person of the offender. It is difficult to apply such notions to capital punishment, for if, as Kant seems to have thought, not to execute a murderer is— if he has been condemned to die under law—to share in the guilt, it is hard to regard such guilt as personal.[1] Yet if guilt is not personal, but social, or interpersonal, it is surely absurd to suppose that society is expunging its guilt by killing the murderer. To say that it is, approximates to the old notion of a scapegoat. However, if guilt can be held to be social, or interpersonal, then the punishment of single persons must inevitably and often involve serious injustice.

It is here that we come up against a logical objection to analogies between morals and law; for the law must decide in favour of one party or the other, while in morals it is possible to distribute the blame. Again, however, the moment one admits that blame may be bi-personal, or multi-personal, the path is opened for a long series of causal explanations extending back into the life histories of all concerned. After this research, each person involved might feel satisfied that, if there were guilt, it was certainly not *his* guilt. The situation, in such a case, becomes complicated beyond redress or solution of any kind, and we come back to the essential one-ness of the situations in which each man did act. To revert to this single situation, we can ask an agent 'Did you kill *B*?' He replies 'Yes.' We then ask him 'Why?' But he has no reason, for him the killing was meaningless, or perhaps he has a reason that is patently insufficient. Somehow it has to be brought home to this man that what he did was called murder by the community, yet he is told it is counted as manslaughter. The idea begins to germinate that

---

[1] Bradley, *E.S.* p. 27. Kant, *Metaphysic of Morals,* tr. William Richardson (1799) Public Law, General Observation E.1. This passage is also translated, presumably by Bradley, in *E.S.* p. 28.

perhaps after all it was an accident. Again the man, in learning to deceive himself, is becoming more skilled at deceiving others.

The problem of impressing upon another person that his is not the only situation, that his values are not the only values, that his ways are not the ways of so-called good men, is properly concerned with morals, and fortuitously brings us to the next chapter. But the problem is not, so far as one can see, helped towards a solution by 'diminished responsibility' as a legal plea, and it is unfortunate that the absence of a positive account of responsibility should have left the critics of the adoption of the concept as a plea without a strong argument in support of their opposition.

XI

ACTING FREELY:
REASON AND MORALITY

'MORAL'

It appears that 'responsibility' is a wider notion than 'morality', it has a wider application. To act morally a man must be responsible, but to be responsible it is not necessary for him to be moral. On the other hand, it seems that a man who does act in a moral situation must be said to act always in a moral situation, since morality extends over all a man's actions if it is applicable to any of them at all. If a man is a moral being, then of necessity there is a moral element in all he does.

Moral philosophy is a theoretical study dealing with practical situations. Like any other theory, moral theory should contain the conditions of its application. If an agent is to decide that an action is right, he must at some point be sure that he knows how it is to be done, for who could decide on an action without knowing what it is? To say that he must know precisely what he is to do and how he is to do it is to ensure that he knows whether he can do it or not. Many philosophers have endeavoured to provide a logical connection between morality and freedom, and, having achieved this to their own satisfaction, they ignore the problem of fulfilment. Since the logic of practical morality is the logic of facts, of making inferences according to our knowledge of facts, then if we are to act in a certain way in a practical situation, the actual means of carrying out the action must be present before us in that same situation. If a man conceives his action as an end he must also conceive it as a means to that end. In saying this I recognise that it implies that vague expressions of principles of justice, benevolence, tolerance, self-love, and so on, cannot be commands, or even contain commands as to conduct. At best they suggest ways of assessing actions, with no indication of the nature of what they purport to contain. As described above, they are usually applied piecemeal when constructing the agent's situation; for he will deal with the claims upon him as, apart from the material of the claim, claims for just, kind, tolerant, consideration. The word "claim" could be used for the tensions that arise in social relations, the obligations, the conventional interpretations of relationships, or it could be used in the moral sense as the requirement that certain interests of others should be fairly taken into consideration. But it is here that the practical danger is most subtle: for the unjust man *is* unjust because he sees the unjust act as just, the unfair trick as straight dealing, or 'serving someone right'. He does not set out to be unjust, and he usually makes a glib use of moral principles in replying to adverse criticism.

In chapter VII we assumed that the situation under discussion was a moral situation, and we have yet to find the differentiæ of morality, if there are any to be found. If we say that a situation is moral when a man asks what he "ought" to do, we have still to explain why "ought" signifies morality. If there are alternatives, then to ask which action "ought" to be done is to ask which action is to be preferred in terms of practical value. We can at least agree that value cannot of itself emerge from facts, since value is a relational word requiring a subject-object complex; yet, as a man constructs his situation, it can be said that the construction *as* a construction—as a pattern, an arrangement—reflects the relevance of his present perceptions to his past ones, that it is in the light of his past experience, as cognised, that he selects from the present; and included in that past experience are valuational expressions with certain concrete associations, so that those valuational expressions will recur in connection with the recognition of similar phenomena. On *any* psychological theory of perception this is bound to be the case; since if a situation is a construction from available evidence, it is analytic that what counts as evidence, what is perceived as evidence, is perceived as relevant to the present problem. If some features of the landscape round about a man, as he constructs his situation, are disregarded, it does not mean that they are not there in the physical sense, but that they do not enter into the situation, they have no significance so far as this problem is concerned, they are irrelevant. How often do we hear a man say: 'I am not taking that into consideration,' or 'I am not going to let that influence me.'

Action is change, and if an agent is going to make a change he is either going to alter the situation by getting rid of some features of it he dislikes, or he is going to introduce some new features, or he is going to effect some re-arrangement of the old. In other words he is going to produce a situation which suits him better, and which he can see, at least in part, as distinct from the present one, to be desirable in some way. He prefers the later situation, one might say, to the present one, and the difference between the two, and that he desires that difference, are his reasons for acting. If he acts because he desires the change in the situation, the situation in which he acts is a moral one. He is acting on the principle that the new situation will, at least for him and in his view, be 'better' than the old. It is analytic that to be able to say 'X is better for me than Y' is to value in terms of some notion of good, even if only as 'good for me' and where the advantages can be fully listed. Similarly if A fulfils a promise to B because he has promised, then he recognises his promise as binding, and if he is bound and knows it we can speak of obligation. Promises are deferred or interrupted actions: we can promise because we can shape the future in idea. To promise is to make either a decision or a prediction about the future. To break a promise is either (*a*) to change one's mind, or (*b*) to fail in a duty. A man who does (*a*) in the case of a promise may not recognise his act as (*b*). This may be said to be what is involved in recognising an obligation as such. If A later decides that his promise was wrong in some way, his proper course is to seek out B and ask to be released, giving his reasons, for only between A and B can the promise be rescinded. Hume's account of a promise as a form of words for which a man can be held accountable emphasises the nature of a promise as (*b*) above, but, as Hume was exclusively concerned with morals, it disregards the fact that the same form of words is used frequently in a predictive rather than an obligatory sense.[1]

It could be argued that to comprehend a law fully is to recognise it as binding, to regard its observance as 'right' in general and in particular. Obligation and duty, when accepted as such, are things that it is 'right' to fulfil. It must, I think, be conceded to Prichard that in applying 'right' in this way we need not look for any reason beyond the obligation itself.[2] But philosophers are uneasy about agreeing that it is superfluous

---

[1] *A Treatise of Human Nature*, III. II. 5.
[2] See ch. I, page 6, above.

to ask a further question as to why the obligation should be fulfilled. It may be that it is the wrong question to ask, and that the question really should be why we see an obligation *as* an obligation at all, and not merely as something someone has suggested we might do as a way to pass the time. There seems to be, somewhere, a condition by which an obligation is an obligation and is recognised as such. Obligations may collide, and then we must look for other factors in the situation to help us choose between them. If we appeal to moral principles, or to theories of ultimate value, we need not be looking for a link between doing our duty and the ground of that duty, but for an additional reason for fulfilling the one rather than the other. The seeing of an obligation as an obligation, it seems to me, depends on the context, upon the fact that the agent, the one who sees it thus, is in any case a moral agent. He sees the world as a world of moral implication.

Let us approach this question from another side. If a man recognises an obligation as such, then he brings another person into his situation. For obligation is certainly a social concept. But other persons may enter into his situation without the recognition of any obligation: in the example of the promise, we said that a man might break his promise just by changing his mind. In this case that he 'broke his promise' would be an assessor's account of his action, but not necessarily his own. For he might merely find himself doing something else, since to do that something else seemed to be indicated by whatever events preceded it. The promise was nothing more than an interim proviso to fill up a certain period of time in a certain way. The convenience of the promisee did not enter into it. Had he nothing better to do, however, he might have kept the promise because it was the way he had intended to fill up his time. Now the promisee certainly was taken into the agent's situation if there was a chance of his keeping the promise, but the promise was not recognised as constituting a claim, a *reason*, for priority. The promise was merely a fact in the situation, it had occurred and been noted. There is no subjective aspect, no relation between the agent and the promisee to provide a source of value. Had the agent felt his relation with the promisee to be of value to him, then the promise would have constituted a claim in respect of the value of the personal relationship. But the promisee in this case is irrelevant, he does not matter.

Here I should say that the agent was certainly responsible for his actions, but that his situation was not a moral one. He merely acts according to the facts in his situation and if he makes a promise and does not keep it, it can only be said that he made a prediction and that it turned out to be incorrect. Asked, he might explain that he did not keep the promise because he did something else. If it was desired to influence such a man, it would be necessary to argue only from material facts, and to leave matters of principle entirely alone.

If a man acts in one way rather than another because to do so seems to him best, he is, even though he cannot give any other reason, certainly acting morally. So too if he meets an obligation because it is an obligation. Such a man has a notion of good in both instances, because no one fulfils a duty because it is recognised as such without assuming it is better to do so than not to do so. This pertains also if he acts out of fear of the law or of the claimant. Such a simple use of "good" and its degrees is often inexplicable in less vague terms; its inexplicability does not stem from its being a name for a simple, unanalysable, indefinable quality, but from the fact that it is the net result of calculations and assessments which the agent cannot express in words, partly because the processes take place subconsciously, and partly because it is mainly a matter of feeling. When, for instance, a man weighs up his situation and decides that the facts of that situation indicate he should act in a way X, he gives his reasons for acting, if asked for them, as an account of those facts. An assessor can extract principles from that action, because he may be aware of principles as principles. But it does not follow that the agent is acting on any principle but the one that he should decide what to do by looking at the facts.

Again, an agent may not deliberate before acting, but may wish to be able to give his own act a retrospective assessment of approval, and if he understands that it is important to him to feel he has done right, then his situation is certainly a moral one, and he a moral agent—even if, proceeding on this principle, he acquires but little wisdom and an uncomfortable air of selfrighteousness.

Have we analysed the situation of the agent in sufficient detail to enable us to find material or observable criteria for the moral as distinct from the non-moral situation? If an agent's statements and reasons are examined, along with himself as context and reference, it should be possible to determine whether he acts morally or not. The account I have given makes a distinction between the man who sees his action as producing a change, and the man who moves about without pausing to consider the nature of what he does, or its relation to what other people do. Other people may not appear to him as other people having rights. It would seem useless to require of such a man that he should organise his life in accordance with ends. Whether he commits any crime or not may be largely a matter of the coincidence of motive and opportunity; for such people act as occasion offers, without considerations from past or future, which means also without thought of retribution, and with whatever motivational force meets the chance of action. The former man, however, has a choice because he sees the situation ideally before and after acting, and however he makes his choice, the action must necessarily exhibit some principle. Otherwise he could not choose.

The feckless man, our second supposition, lacks the ability to put two actions over against each other, which is the condition of choice. We can assume that others have encouraged him to do so, and that he has been himself judged morally from time to time. I do not think it can be assumed that because a man hears talk about 'good' and 'bad', he learns to apply the notions in any way that falls within morality: for the uses to which the words have been put in his hearing could have been so conflicting and varied that he never acquired their meanings as concepts at all, and thus remained unable to use the words meaningfully.

Mere acquaintance with certain words does not seem to justify any inference as regards the moral life. As a man's experience alters from day to day, so must he, if he *is* as a person what he has experienced, alter also; and, on any account of valuing, if the valuer alters, so must the values given, for it is analytic that a valuer, if he is a valuer and not merely a 'rubber stamp', in some way constitutes the standard by which he values. If, as maintained by Freud, values are acquired from the relationships of early childhood, then it must necessarily follow that, in principle, values can be acquired through any social relationship, and here again is the idea of identification with a 'role', a social self, that which acts 'properly'—suitably on a certain social occasion or set of occasions.[1] We speak of a man who is "too easily influenced", and we mean that he has no resistance to other people's standards, that he can offer no strong set of his own values to ensure a balanced judgment. 'Good' and 'bad' might vary with every different companionship or chance acquaintanceship. Such a man does not assert himself in his judgments in a consistent way, and this again is tantamount to saying he has an unstable character, if he can be said to have one at all.

CONSISTENCY

Are we to require that a man, to be moral, should give some consistent sense to the expressions of value that he uses? Is this what 'acting on principle' implies: that the principles are consistent and reasonable? For if a man acts upon consistent principles, or consistently upon certain principles, on the theory that he becomes what he is by his actions, he should thereby acquire a stable character. If a man is unaware of his principles, yet acts consistently according to them, he should sooner or later become aware of them as constant, or formal, features of his situations. We can thus ask whether morality, to *be* morality, does not involve, besides the construction by himself of the agent's situation, also the inclusion within it of the stable disposition towards the right which is Aristotle's definition of the condition of virtue. We look for some structure in the dimension of growth as well as a succession of decisions in widely varying circumstances.

A man might be forced to pay attention to the principles upon which he acted, we have said, by noting constant features in his situations. Failure or error in the results of his actions at some point might indicate an unsuitable principle. For this, as Nowell-Smith has pointed out,[2] he would have to have already an attitude in favour of questioning his principles, his pro-attitudes. Yet without going so far as to set him down deliberating upon his principles, he could become more wary, more

---

[1] See also Butler, *Analogy of Religion*, Part II, ch. 1. 'By reason is revealed the relation which God the Father stands in to us. Hence arises the obligation of duty which we are under to him.' Duties arise from the relations 'themselves, not out of the manner in which we are informed of them', Butler continues, with reference to the other two persons of the Trinity.

[2] *Ethics*, ch. 20, para. 6.

observant through his unpleasant experiences: for to become aware of mistakes of principle is not, in itself, to be willing or able to change those principles. It is unlikely that a man could change his principles, his attitudes, if aware of them, unless he had the necessary knowledge to do so. Such knowledge would have to be scientific knowledge, applied to the self. Self-knowledge as such makes no contribution to action unless a man puts that knowledge as knowledge of fact into his situation on a level with his knowledge of others. Yet it seems reasonable to suppose that as soon as a man begins to criticise the principles of his own objectified and assessed action, he either has to lie to himself or recognise any disparities and inconsistencies. If self-knowledge is not a sufficient condition of altering the self, it is certainly a necessary one, for one cannot change what one does not even perceive.

It is probable that such a man would find a disparity between those principles he believed himself to act upon, and those principles he found actually in his actions. He could then try to act upon a principle deliberately chosen and suitably applied. He could, for instance, say, if asked, that he had decided upon his action because it seemed to be the one indicated by the facts, that his situation demanded that action, that the action was the most sensible way out of the difficulty, whatever it was. He foresees how the situation may develop, and acts to further that development. If his insight is right, correct, his action will be successful, leading to that development which seemed to him to be the one that should occur: if he is wrong, something unexpected will happen which may not please him. An agent can see what, in the situation he constructs, is inevitable, beyond his power to influence, and what can be moulded by himself. To make use of his knowledge in both these respects is to act deliberately, and to have the sense to confine the application of his standards only to those features in the situation which are under his control. It is often pointed out, in the course of discussions on determinism, that it is only by making use of causal sequences that a man can plan his actions according to his principles. It is here that the distinction between logical and contingent possibility is relevant (see pages 75-6 above).

From the assessor's point of view, it is clear that only from a series of actions by an agent can that agent's principles of action be discovered, more properly as 'character'. Thus an assessor has no means of determining whether an agent is aware of the principles upon which he acts or not. He can ask him, but the answer may not be accurate. The agent's account of his reason for acting may be based upon his idea of what he does rather than on the actuality. The principles an agent believes to be manifest in his actions may not in fact be so.

The main point is, for us, that he has a reason, and that he believes he acts upon a certain principle. This is a necessary condition of moral action. It must be so, since if he acts on a principle it is analytic that he acts because his act is a certain kind of act, even if only the vague "best". He must accordingly be aware of his particular act as an instance of that kind of act, even if he is mistaken. In a man's situation, if he is to act morally, there must be principles, for if there were not, he could not act on them. If he says to himself that he should consider what he had better do, then he has at least one principle in his situation. His notion of 'right' and 'good' supply the content of the principle. Thus we can say that since those notions, as concepts, are derived empirically, the normative element in his situation *is* the family of propositions upon which the concepts rest, or from which they are abstractions. Thus Hegel derived the 'judgment of the notion', and Bradley the 'moral ideal'. These two philosophers had a tendency to present the facts of our experience in a complicated way, but there is nothing remote or obscure about the facts themselves: for they are the common sense requirements of all our social intercourse, even of the use of language itself. The facts of our experience, the sequences our reason perceives within the compass of those facts, enable us to assert ourselves as judges assert themselves in competitions by selecting what is best from what is presented to them.[1]

REASON AND INTUITION

Reason, or reasoning, is that part of sense concerned with the consistency of perceptions and the probability of future states of affairs; it is at once a condition and a test of knowledge. We do not speak of knowledge if we doubt the validity of the statements in which it is presented. But just as our perceptions of the natural

---

[1] For an elaboration of these points, see the Appendix to this chapter, on 'Values and evaluation'.

world are given us in a form which appears to have little relevance to the means by which they are acquired, so our perceptions of how we should act may be given us as intuitions which offer no clue to the factual conditions upon which they are based. Philosophers try to distinguish between intuitions based on inadequate premisses and those which seem to give gratuitous information, calling the former by the name of "insights". "Insight" used in this way is something like the result of thinking described by Wertheimer as a new arrangement of elements in a problem (*Productive Thinking*). The reservation of 'intuition' for the supposedly self-evident proposition, and the immediate inference, far from establishing 'intuition' as a special source of knowledge vouchsafed to philosophers and theologians, merely supports the view that our reasoning powers transcend the formal processes we devise to express them. We think we test our thinking by logical conventions, but in fact we test the logical conventions by and in our thinking. Otherwise we should not have such a profusion of notations in mathematical logic.

The purposes or aims of an action may not become known to the agent until after the action is completed, then when he sees its full effects, he also becomes aware of the features which, it seems to him, must have commended it to him. An agent who acts because he 'knows' it is right, but cannot give an explanation that satisfies him, can be said to be acting on the principle that decisions made in a certain way turn out successfully, as against decisions taken in other ways, for example, the first thing that occurs to him, or on strong feelings of some sort.

There are many differences in the way an agent may make his decisions, and select his reasons for acting. The misconceived opposition between intuitionism and other accounts of morality results from failure to recognise that in different persons different portions of the thinking processes occur consciously. It is our awareness of these processes that varies, not the processes themselves. Our awareness may vary from decision to decision, from year to year, and as affecting decisions in different social relations, with respect to different interests. *To act on intuition is to act on a principle that the intuition is reliable, it is not to disparage the claims of reason.* If the intuitionist supports his action by saying that he has a moral sense which perceives an objective good in the action contemplated, he may be right; for the moral sense in this instance is the practical reason which is guiding him, and the perception is that cognisance and comprehension of the facts of the case which has failed to reach those areas of the brain essential to awareness. We could put it that subceptions have been computed with the known evidence and the total result communicated to the consciousness of the agent, who, by experience, has learnt to trust to it. It would be hard to maintain that decisions influenced in this way were irrational or even unreasonable, since a man who is reasonable does not act on intuitions unless they relate sensibly to the conscious construction of his situation.

When a man constructs his situation, the situation in which he must act, he thereby limits his actions to those which meet that situation, or which arise out of it. An irrelevant suggestion which was intuited would hardly fall within this limitation. To act upon a sudden impulse would not be to act in his situation at all. Yet if the agent is able to construct that situation when faced with the necessity of acting, he does not escape moral responsibility if he does act on an irrelevant impulse, for he is then faced with the necessity of constructing another situation in which he manages to find an excuse for his action, if it has led him into difficulties. But if he describes his action as an assessor describes it, he will be able to see that the lack of cohesion between what he saw as his problem and the action he took to meet it reflects the irrational nature of the impulse.

ACTING FREELY

A man, we have said, is responsible because he acts in a situation which is his own, and which is inaccessible to others. He constructs that situation himself, ideally, from his perceptions, and according to his abilities. In doing so, he may merely confront it as an opportunity to further his interests, and those interests may or may not include the claims of others upon him. He may construct his situation in such a way that what he knows of himself stands before him side by side with what he knows of others, so that his decision treats all those concerned in the problem according to the force of their claims, giving no preference to his own (see page 289 below). But if, as we have seen, the influences brought to bear upon a man in his early years must be worked out and integrated after his youth, and as a condition of maturation, then at certain times and in certain circumstances it will be important to him to work them out even at the cost of seeming to neglect the claims of others with whom he is closely associated. He may from time to time act because he feels impelled to a certain action although there are strong arguments against such a course. But if he decides that his feeling is such that he should accept it as a motive, then who is to say he is wrong? He is not abrogating his responsibility, he is not necessarily acting selfishly, for the results of his action may be that in the future his decisions are the wiser for this earlier concession. If a man is responsible for his actions because he constructs and acts in his own situation, his practical freedom consists in his recognition of that situation as his own, and in a similar recognition by others who are interested in his action, that he is acting in a situation of his own. Where a man may be said to be responsible on simple, physical criteria for his actions, he may be said to be *morally* responsible in recognising and accepting his responsibility for his actions. Thus his situation, as he constructs it, is said to be a moral situation, and the problem of how to act is a moral problem. Responsibility must be actual and ascertainable for moral responsibility, or morality, to occur, and practical freedom must also be a fact. Morality requires acting on principle, which means that a man acts knowing the kind of act he does and why he decides to do it, even if he only decides to do it because he wants to do it. That he, when asked, gives the wrong reason deliberately, through shame or diffidence or perversity, does not remove his moral responsibility for what he has done or for lying about his motives. And when a man is aware that he does not know why he acted as he did, and makes up a reason, he is admitting that he knows he acted, or should have acted, on principle.

Acting freely is acting in the relevant situation according to the logic of that situation, which is an ideal construction resting upon statments of fact. Ability to act freely is thus not affected by limitations of perception. Freedom from what Spinoza called passive emotions is a personal state, and as such belongs to description: it has nothing to do with freedom of action. If a mind is so dominated that it only acts in the situations constructed by another, then the agent is not responsible, and the question of morality does not arise at all. We have seen that such a condition occurs sometimes in childhood, and that it may recur later in life.

FREEDOM

We have arrived at the position that responsibility is the relation that pertains between a man and his fellows, each and all of them, in virtue of his ability to withdraw from society or from those by whom society is constituted for him, and to construct his situation as a background for his action without referring to them; and that practical freedom is the recognition of a man's responsibility for his actions by himself and by others. Morality may be described as the use a man makes of his responsibility and of his freedom. If he makes unsuitable use of them, he is called irresponsible, if he makes no use of them at all—through, for example, inertia—we say he is feckless. He may make a casual use of them, and the most cursory glance at the facts may be all he does by way of constructing his situation; or he may take meticulous care to ensure that nothing relevant has been overlooked. A man who takes responsibility for all that he does, and regards the convenience of others as constituting claims upon him, even though these may not be describable as duties, is said to have a strong sense of duty, and it would be tempting to suggest, as some philosophers do, that the existence of many claims upon him reduced his freedom. But it is incorrect to regard obligation as an actual restriction, it is only seen as an obligation because a man is a moral agent, and because he uses his freedom to assess and reconcile the claims of others. If he overdoes his devotion to others, we should not speak of his freedom as curtailed, but of a dysbalance in his judgment, the too ready application of a particular principle.

If an agent finds himself in what appears to be an *impasse*, and has to take action in a way that he dislikes, or which is to his disadvantage, it need not be said that his freedom has been lost or impaired; for he may make desperate efforts to extricate himself from his predicament, and, although he does not succeed, the efforts he has made greatly increase his command over, and understanding of his circumstances in the future. His practical freedom is relative to his situation, and in his desperate situation he has made good use of it. It is incorrect to suppose that freedom is the ability to put *any* idea into practice, for such an account of freedom would be a mere fairy tale of wish fulfilment. In a situation of extreme danger, some near-miraculous deliverance would certainly not be a manifestation of freedom. A man's freedom is not a metaphysical ticket to another world, but an opportunity to make what he can of this one. Freedom is sometimes spoken of as if it must be some capricious, unmotived decision: but the facts show that such a freedom is inconceivable: for if I make a decision and I look back upon my making of it, it makes no sense to say that I was only free in making it if I could have acted otherwise; since I cannot prove that I might have done something else, I cannot prove I was 'free'. The 'I' that made the decision would not have been the same 'I' if the decision had not been made as I made it, and if it was not to be 'I' that made it, then who else? If I had not chosen as I had, there would in fact have been no one to make a decision at all.

Let us look again at this practical decision. It has been asserted from time to time that freedom of decision means that at the time of decision there is no reason why one action should be chosen rather than another. This, it has been argued, follows from the fact that, if there were such a reason, the choice would not be free since a rational man would be bound to accept the reason. This is a 'philosopher's argument', resting upon purely formal grounds, and excluding all question as to the urgency of 'the reason': all we assume is that there is some reason for choosing one action rather than another, and if so, there can hardly be, it is alleged, said that there is a choice, since, when the reason is recognised as such, the choice might be said to be already made. I propose to argue against this view.

First I will state my view thus: that the statement 'I have a real choice between X and Y' does not entail the statement 'There is no reason why I should choose X rather than Y.' If I am to choose X or Y it is analytic that I must do one of them and I cannot do both. If I deliberate, and survey all the features of the situation, including the reasons that might be given as justifications for X and Y, there are three alternative positions that I may reach: (a) on balance, and other things being equal, I would enjoy X rather then Y; (b) I can find no preference in myself either for X or Y; (c) on balance, and other things being equal, there is a claim in Y which I prefer to meet over and above the others.

We are dealing with this decision entirely from the point of view of the agent. Now on the statement we are considering, (*b*) is a real choice, while (*a*) and (*c*), since there are reasons for doing one action rather than the other, are not. But to say (*a*) is not a real choice is to say that my enjoyment is a sufficient reason for doing X rather than Y, and that to have a sufficient reason is to be unfree, determined. A decision is merely the final victory of one side over the other.

On (*a*), if 'myself' as free is to be a mere formal abstraction, the fact that the reason was 'my enjoyment' would be anomalous, since a formal abstraction could not give a sense to 'my enjoyment' as mine. If my enjoyment is to be a reason, it must be a reason for whoever makes the decision. If the 'I' that chooses is a different 'I' from the one that anticipates enjoyment, we have the case supposed above, and it makes no sense to speak of *my* choice. So that to interpret freedom as some kind of abstraction from circumstances is to say that in effect freedom has nothing to do with choosing at all. It is even not so much a matter of not choosing as there being nothing and no-one to choose, to make the choice.

For by choosing we mean someone choosing, and without a person there is no choice, formal or otherwise, free or determined.

To choose is to be aware of the choice and to be aware of what is being chosen and why. But to know why one action is being done rather than another is to have, or know of, a reason for doing one rather than another, even if the reason were that one was being impelled, or compelled. Choice is rational or it is no choice, and to know why a change is being produced is to understand it; this again is to see why one produces the change. If a choice is made, it can only be made in terms of reasons, *even if* the only reason were that I decided to toss, and heads it was.

This brings us to (*b*). I have to choose X or Y, and I have no reason to prefer either. I can either toss for it, which gives me a reason for doing one or the other, but which is not of itself choosing. Or I can vacillate, and in the course of thinking about one or the other of them, I can initiate action in accordance with the one in my thoughts at the time. But again there is no choice, because what I have done is to follow one course and do that in the absence of an alternative.

(c) There is no preference here as regards my act. But I am able to go behind the acts as such to the claims involved in the situation in which acts arise as possible, and hence to decide the issue on emotional grounds, which I may have regarded as formally irrelevant. Does this change the act? One could say it altered the construction of the situation so that one action appeared more suitable. But it cannot be said that it nullifies the act as X or Y, for to do this would be to say that every newly perceived feature in a situation would alter the nature of the acts possible in it. And this would bring us back to the wider use of 'action' in which its whole context is contained. As we have seen, such a usage complicates 'action' beyond application. Confronted by X and Y I can surely analyse them anew without altering them. Suppose then I find a further reason for one of them which refers to the relevant strengths of dispositions or attitudes rather than to the effects produced by the action. I feel that in doing Y I shall meet an intrinsically higher or more intimately personal claim than I would in doing X, but rationally I cannot justify it as a ground of choice. None the less my feeling becomes my reason for choosing Y.

So far from negating my choice, this remote reason is the only means I have of exercising it. I am free to choose it as a reason and I am free to act. For if we can disregard a motive or claim as a reason for acting, we can also select a motive *as* a reason.

It can be argued that acting freely does not rest upon a purely formal choice, but upon the fact that a rational being (or will) has grounds that are different in kind from the dispositional; for to act consciously on an affection is not to be conditioned by it. To know is to be able to disregard. In a determined world 'my enjoyment of X' is an integral part of the situation; in a free world I can say 'my enjoyment is something in the situation that I can remove from it if I wish, and act as if it were not there'. The same can be said of undesirable feelings. If we are aware that we have certain strong hates and desires for revenge, and so on, we can so manipulate our affairs that the drive to harm is made use of as energy in a better cause. This possibility lies behind the notion that competition produces better work, and so long as the competition is kept within reasonable bounds, it is probably a prominent means by which the moral agent rids himself of his less attractive impulses.

If I read him aright, Hegel's account of the will which is 'absolutely free'[1] is a rather abstruse way of saying that a free will can admit every determinate factor and not lose itself in any of them. We are to be able to contemplate all the more unruly impulses, and shoddy desires, our fears and loves for others, and yet remain unimpelled by any of them. It is the subservient will that fears compulsion and influence. Certain formulations of the freewill doctrine have aimed at expressing this independence, but have only succeeded in producing a logical absurdity, by substituting abstraction for transcendence.[2] The will is not something non-personal, unreal, which floats about above the world, or at least hardly within it; it is not a formal arbiter, but a flesh and blood person making a flesh and blood decision, and knowing it to be so. It is interesting to note that Bradley, on page 48 of *Ethical Studies*, remarked that people are misled by the doctrine of an arbitrary will, and are encouraged to believe that they can act as they wish. Accordingly, they pay too little attention to the facts of the case, believing themselves to be 'free' of these considerations, and as a result their actions are determined by circumstances which they have failed to observe, nor troubled to understand.

The account I am giving of practical freedom is not the account of a 'free will', nor is it an account of a self-determined will, since self-determination, like autonomy, is an illusion: no creature whose very existence depends upon his co-operation with other creatures can speak of self-determination without such stringent qualifications that it ceases to have meaning. But what I wish to stress is that a person is free as a person to choose his actions as limited by his material circumstances, and here within 'material' I include dispositions, which are, it cannot be denied, facts. If *A* is disposed to act in a certain way, then it is a fact that his dispositions are such and so on. If he is aware of his dispositions, they are facts in his situation and have to be reckoned with, like debts, or wet weather.

A further attack upon the notion of acting freely comes from the metaphysical doctrine called determinism. This is opposed to freewill in such a way that the two appear as polar concepts,

---

[1] *Philosophy of Right*, introduction, and paras. 34–6.
[2] Abstraction takes from the facts, and is then limited to what it has taken; transcendence accepts all the facts, but passes to a new account of them, or manipulation of them.

that is, determinism—indeterminism. Whatever else may be said of polar concepts, they are certainly the extremes obtained when positive and negative terms are adopted for an identical series of states. Given two sticks of unequal length, it is a matter of indifference whether we say one is shorter than the other, or that the second is longer than the first. The same temperature will be called warm in winter and cold in summer. By extending our normal range of variables we reach a postulated, or ideal, extreme. Thus determinism is the extreme of unfree, and indeterminism the extreme of free. Since if anything were completely unfree we should have no means of distinguishing it as a thing at all, and, on the other hand, if a state were completely free we should have no means of contact with it, so that to all intents and purposes it would not exist, we can regard these two extremes as ideal and entirely without reference so far as practical freedom is concerned. But this is not to say that freedom itself is to be scaled: for a man is free in his actions as a logical consequence of certain matters of fact, and freedom as here applied does not admit of degrees (see also the Appendix to this chapter). If, however, it is said that determinism and indeterminism are principles, then it is true that they cannot both be principles in respect of the same things. Evolution may be said to be a theory of life which excludes both, or includes both, for it allows the encounter of determined pressures to result in a new configuration.

Still more misleading, and logically unsound, is the argument from prediction. If, it is supposed, we could predict exactly what is going to happen in the future the statements in which the predictions were made would be incompatible with any statement asserting freedom. This argument is based upon logical possibility, but the statements it purports to refute are contingent. Although we have already covered the ground upon which the argument can be shown to be faulty, we should briefly recapitulate it here.

It would be analytic that, if it could be said that a complete account could be given of everything that would occur upon a certain evening, even that a man would see a sunset in a certain way, then there would be nothing about him that could not be known by all. And if there could be nothing that was not open to all, then he could not, it is alleged, be said to be free. Why freedom should be thought to involve some kind of secrecy one need not ask; but presumably it is the future where the secrets should lie. As a logical impossibility, it would not be possible to predict a future scene in detail, since the observer's dimensions could not be adjusted to accommodate it; he would have to have the knowledge in words, and the dimensions of words are not the dimensions of things. In any case to say that a complete account could be given, and that since it would include actions, those actions could not be said to be free, is so obvious a confusion of viewpoint that it hardly makes sense. It confuses not only the viewpoints of a man acting and an observer looking on, but also those of the future and the past. For when we say that such and such a thing will happen, we cannot look at it in the way that we can look at what has happened in the past, that is as a series of particular and unique events. Consequently the kind of account that could be given of the two is logically distinct.

Even yet it does not follow that what a man does is unfree because someone knows about it, or can know about everything he does. That an agent will act in a certain way on a certain day does not exclude the possibility that he will in the meantime be tortured with doubts as to what he should do, or ought to do. And his doubts do not become irrelevant because the issue has been decided in advance. The man who acts is the man who has doubted, not the observer who has predicted, or the agent would not have had the doubts. The action of the man who doubts is not the action that is seen by the onlooker: the one is a decision, the other a deduction.

To say what a man is thinking about is to say nothing about the form of his thoughts. We cannot deduce from any account, however detailed or accurate, of a process of thought, what precisely were and are the thoughts at any particular time. We never catch the whole particular as such in a general account, since, as Bradley continually pointed out, words are general while objects of immediate experience are particular. No description, however exhaustive, could ever give us the complete experience; for one insuperable difficulty is that making statements takes time whereas in experience we have the whole object before us in one moment, one glimpse. Also words are used to refer to things, from which it follows that the things are logically prior, so that any future occurrence which contained anything not reducible to our present knowledge could not be communicated. And it would be a bold man who maintained that our knowledge did not increase. The citadel of a man's thoughts is even more unassailable. That, for instance, philosophers tend to express their thoughts in syllogistic or analytic forms of speech does not tell us anything at all about the way those thoughts occurred or occur in the first place. We have to arrange arguments in conventional ways so that tests of validity can be applied, but such tests are of social origin, they represent interpersonal decisions. To be able to predict that a man decided to act in a certain way at a certain time in a certain situation could necessarily not include an account of how his thoughts appeared to him, or of what account he himself would give of those thoughts. No prediction, however precise, of an observable situation could serve as a premiss for conclusions about the form in which that situation was constructed by anyone aware of it, that is to those concerned in it. For in prediction of the kind we are supposing, every observable detail would be observed, but no unobservable details could, by definition, be observed; and, while what passes as images and the content of thought through a brain is observable in principle, what is 'there' to a person, what is noted, attended to, is not: for, apart from the time necessary for attention to details, we must repeat our contention that a personal situation is a construction only out of what is sensed, while a predicted situation is deduced from principles based upon empirical and experimental data, data, that is, which is not only looked for in the light of hypotheses, but which is available for any observer who wishes to test it for himself. A personal situation can be communicated to a greater or a lesser extent, but it can never be observed by more than one person, nor can anyone else be certain of the principles according to which a man collects his impressions. It is logically impossible to look at a personal situation in an impersonal way. The positivist criterion that statements are only verifiable if they can be reduced to statements of the kind of experience that anyone can have is a conclusive argument against any valid account being given of the personal experience as such. To try to maintain that experience is limited to what can be expressed in statements would be to place truth as logically prior to what could be truly expressed. And this, one hopes, is absurd.

There is no reason to regard freedom as a mere absence of

compulsion. Those who fear to lose freedom in admitting the principle of uniformity have in mind that this principle involves compulsion by circumstances. In practice it is the juxtaposition of the factors in a personal situation, the relative strengths of claims, the dispositions, and so on, that leads to decision. In dealing with practical affairs, the principles we find in them or apply to them must be practically applicable. If we, for example, invoke common sense in morals we invoke what the ordinary man feels to be the case in an ordinary situation. To attempt to refute the statement of an agent that he is confronted by a choice of actions by saying that he cannot be so confronted because actions follow the laws of nature, is to make the same sort of nonsensical statement as, for example, to tell a man who says he has lost his way that he cannot have lost his way because the road he is on goes somewhere. And in any case he would not get there unless he continued to travel, which, by an obvious analogy, is a sufficient answer to those who say that to believe in a predestined decision is to destroy incentive for effort.

Such talk is unrealistic, for no one could deny that decisions influence the course of events. Certainly the decisions of an institution affect the future of that institution and of its members. But it can be conceded that they only do influence subsequent events because it is recognised that they should be made in the way that they are made: and this is what I mean when I say that practical freedom is dependent upon the recognition of responsibility, whether by an agent himself or by those who draw up constitutions. For it is what he does in the light of that recognition that is effective, not what he merely stumbles into.

Practical freedom may be said to have two aspects, one conceptual and one empirical. The former is the ability to find and see alternatives, and is the construction of a situation, while the second is the ability to follow a decision when made. Knowledge is the prime condition for both of these, for it is by knowledge that the results of actions can be forecast by reasoning, and it is by knowledge that a man carries out his plans. A child, for instance, has no clear notion of giving, and may not be able to carry out a decision to give a present, though he may realise that the occasion calls for this. It is the remarkable achievement of the human being that he can make an intellectual decision and also invent the means of implementing it;

the more he knows of his own dispositions and abilities, the more opportunity he has to manipulate them to produce the desired effect, and he can if he likes exploit his tastes and character according to a pre-arranged plan to produce in himself motives and tastes which are not there already. If he understands, for instance, that motive is generated through personal relationships, he can strengthen motives he finds insufficiently strong by increasing the number and quality of the social relationships which contribute to them. In effect, this is part of what is meant by organising or systematising one's life. Unfortunately very little is yet understood of the many ways in which this can be done, and in general, men are afraid of such experiments.

Before closing this chapter, some attempt should be made to review the main theories which have recently been put forward to explain what is meant by 'moral', whether applied to principle or to judgment. My view may be said to be supplementary rather than alternative to these, and it may be that the others have advantages that I have overlooked. My view of the moral situation is that it is one in which an agent recognises his responsibility for what he does, and is thereby enabled to look ahead, to deliberate, and to condition himself by his actions. Once he has recognised that his relationship with his fellows is essentially one of give and take, so that he can make his decisions with regard to more or less of the one or the other, he can include in his deliberations any moral precepts, religious commands, codes, and so on, that he happens to come across, and for which he finds he has respect. These are, on our definition of 'situation', but additional facts in that situation. They are not absolute or categorical imperatives unless he accepts them as such. At times he will have to choose between them, as between any other claims, and the status of such claims will be dealt with in the next chapter. For the present let us review other accounts of the moral element in the judgment.

First, I shall reinforce my position by giving the view of C. H. Whiteley who, in a short, forthright paper argues that 'there are no words or expressions, no uses of words or expressions, no types of proposition, which are distinctively moral or ethical.'[1] He points out that 'words like "good", "right", "ought", which are used to evaluate and to recommend in the discussion

[1] *Analysis* (June 1960).

of moral issues, are also used, without change of meaning, in the discussion of other matters'. He finishes this gem of pertinence and brevity with the words: 'There is no type of reasoning or persuasion in place in moral contexts which is not equally in place in admittedly non-moral contexts. Thus the "moral" is not a subdivision either of language or of logic.' So much for the verbal approach. We are left with the facts of evaluation, moral or non-moral, in whatever context, and with the fact of the judgments we make about other people's and about our own actions. We must be clear about these fundamental distinctions: for the judgment of fact, the judgment that asserts a description is not a moral judgment, since a moral judgment evaluates an action not merely as a kind, but as a kind done by someone. If A knocks B down by way of retaliation, C might say (a) that A retaliated by knocking B down, or (b) that it served B right to be knocked down by A. The first assertion is merely of fact, it contains no suggestion of evaluation, and we would want to know more of the incident before making a moral judgment. But (b) justifies A's action, and implies that B 'asked for it'. It is usual to distinguish between the factual or descriptive and the evaluative elements in a moral judgment, but it is incorrect to include the two elements on equal terms, for if a judgment is moral, there must be an evaluation of an action, and that there is an action is a necessary condition of there being an evaluation of it. In most formulations of the moral judgment, the factual element is rather suggested as inference than stated as fact; it is the evaluation that is asserted.

It is sometimes said that actions as such are pronounced good or bad, right or wrong, and then, as a kind of extra, praise or blame is applied to the agent. But this is somewhat confused: actions, we saw in chapter VII (page 165), are social concepts and thus descriptions of actions are interpersonal in their reference. If an action seems bad to us then whoever did it is to be censured, whether we know who it is, whether he is present or absent, and so on. In any case we need to be sure we have the correct description of the action before we condemn it or blame the agent. We need to know what happened. Our knowledge of what did happen is the situation in which we act morally by asserting our opinion, by expressing the judgment. I am sure Hare[1] is correct in saying that one of the purposes for

---

[1] *The Language of Morals,* II. 8. 2.

which we make moral judgments is to make known our standard, for, I would add, without standards we make no impact in our social life, we hardly can be said to exist.

We have now to consider current answers to the question: what differentiates the moral judgment from any other judgment? It must be a distinction of kind, since the content of the particular does not supply us with what we want; we must find a formal difference, one that applies to every instance of a moral judgment as against a non-moral judgment of sense or other statement of opinion. We will consider the following answers that have been put forward: (*a*) universalisability, (*b*) overridingness, (*c*) relative importance, (*d*) remorse, and (*e*) having a certain background.

(*a*) The thesis of universalisability in its simplest form is that a judgment is a moral judgment if it implies that all acts of the kind called good or bad in the particular context would be good or bad if done by anyone at any time. That is to say, particular conditions make no difference to its character, it is intrinsically good or bad, not relatively so. We have already considered the main argument against this view: namely, that if an action is described in simple, recognisable terms, it is so common an action that there would almost certainly be occasions upon which it might be justified and others upon which it might not; while if it is described in such detail that we can be sure it would always be right or wrong, we make it almost certain that it would not be found to refer to more than a very few instances. If the implication is logical, then it could be said that my present argument does not hold, but in a practical matter, one should surely be practical. Is there any point in saying that actions of a certain kind would always be right everywhere, if there could not, contingently, be more than a few instances? This is only, after all, to say that ethical values are objective.

(*b*) When a statement of a principle is a statement of a moral principle, then it is such that it will over-ride any other principle which it meets in a practical situation. Thus the argument that a principle is moral when it is over-riding. It is upon moral principles that people take their stand in a way that they do not take a stand upon non-moral ones, and if they are prepared to go to great lengths to assert it, we say the principle is a moral one. This difference is not, however, merely one of degree, it is held that the principle is, because a man will take his stand upon it, different in kind from other principles, for example, those of skill.

There is certainly a core of truth in this argument, since as we have also argued, men are prepared to assert the principles they believe in and accept, even in trivial contexts, because in doing so they assert themselves *as* themselves, as people of a certain kind. And if 'over-riding' be taken to mean that a comparatively small matter can be accorded an importance beyond that given to matters of real moment, then we can agree. But are we saying here that it is the over-ridingness that differentiates the judgment? Are not men as quick to draw on, for example, technical questions? Or are we to say that, if so, it shows that they take moral responsibility for the protection of their technical integrity? On such an argument, any firm stand could be brought into the moral sphere.

The obvious objection to this view, apart from the fact that it would be very difficult to instance cases which illustrated it, is that it does not so much show the strength of a moral principle as reveal the strength of those who wish to assert themselves and their moral opinions. It would be hard to say, in any instance, that a man took his stand because a moral principle was involved, and not because his prestige and reputation might gain from the stand he was taking. Principles of any kind can be used as moral principles by a moral agent, and the moral element comes from the agent and not from the principle itself.

(*c*) Again, it is argued that principles are recognised as moral when they deal with matters of moment. Plainly, this differs from (*b*). It might even be said to take the whole point out of it. For if importance only is to be the criterion, how can there be a difference in kind between moral and other principles. We are merely dealing with degrees of importance. And it is obvious that some people make a great fuss about trifles while others take serious crises in their phlegmatic stride. So who is to say what is important, and to whom is it to be important?

The argument suffers from triteness, for it is a truism to say that we usually deliberate more carefully about those things that are important to us. There is nothing specifically moral about this. To call issues moral issues just because we spend a long time and expend a lot of energy over them would be absurd. To the moral agent, the moral aspect of his life may be the most important aspect, but to say this is to assume that the moral judgment is a moral judgment because a moral agent makes it, and we have no need of any further argument.

(d) If a man feels remorse in retrospect, the argument goes, then the principle upon which he acted—wrongly—was a moral one. From the occurrence of a moral feeling it is deduced that the situation was a moral one. My objection to this view is that, since remorse is retrospective, the agent could hardly have acted on the principle at the time, or else he would have recognised it as a moral issue then. If he did not act on it, then he can hardly be expected to feel remorse on its account. To say acting morally is a necessary condition of remorse does not make remorse a necessary condition of acting morally though it is sufficient, and the argument presupposes its conclusion. Again, if remorse signifies a moral situation, we must have a moral agent, since the remorse as feeling is his feeling, and a non-moral agent would hardly have a moral feeling. It is probably easier to make mistakes about the nature of feelings than it is to make mistakes in recognising moral judgments and principles.

(e) Finally, P. R. Foot has argued that moral principles and moral judgments require a certain background, that they are not self-sufficient in some way. This suggestion does not go very far, but I am sure it is correct. Moral judgments and statements of moral principles appear to reach back, to belong elsewhere, to be attached to some context of their own without which they are incomplete.

I have no right to assume that Mrs Foot would agree with any of my views, but it seems to me that, if we accept moral judgments as experiential statements requiring their author as a reference, then we can understand exactly what she says about the 'background', and why it is she finds it so difficult to say what it is she requires of this background.[1]

This sketchy account of views which have been put forward at length and with skill may appear churlish, and I can only plead that this is not a moral treatise, and that we were only led to the consideration of the criteria for 'moral' because we could find no other way of disentangling its application from that of 'responsibility' and 'freedom' than to locate differences of reference. Since we did raise certain difficulties with regard

[1] *Ar. Soc. Suppl. Vol.* (1954).

to ethics, or moral philosophy, at the outset of our inquiry, we are perhaps justified in giving some account of it, and in any case we have not pursued our inquiries beyond the formal grounds of morality, its prolegomena.

In conclusion, to leave moral principles where they belong, we should remark that moral principles are reasons—good reasons—for acting in a moral situation, the situation of a moral agent. Thus it is always the practical situation which is logically prior; and without it we should never think about principles. But when we do think about principles, we are not, by definition, thinking about the moral situation. We turn away from it. Perhaps the difficulties of finding a criterion for the moral 'ought', and, further, for finding a logical rule by which the principle gives rise to the practical decision, is due to the fact that there could be no such rules, and no such differentiæ. The 'moral' element refers back to the agent and the principle does not of itself give rise to any decision.

APPENDIX TO CHAPTER XI

VALUES AND EVALUATION

Ethical discussion may concern itself with ethical concepts, with 'good', 'right', 'obligation', etc., or it may deal with non-valuational terms like "intention", "reason", "excuses" and so on. Here I have mainly considered words in the latter group, because I have been attempting to establish their relations by giving them a reference to fact. Properly speaking, to deal with ethical questions is not within my terms of reference in this book. But since I am finding that the concepts I have tried to elucidate tend to point back to the agent, I have also to recognise that in thus pointing back to a particular agent and to particular situations, I am left with very little opportunity to generalise: for the emphasis is thrown upon the experience of a moral agent, and the content of that experience eludes analysis. I have to limit myself to formal provisions.

If morality is the use a man makes of his freedom as a responsible person, then in that use he may be said to be a source of values. When he assesses he creates values, and since psychology has as yet little to say about this faculty of man, philosophy is within its rights in offering an account on the evidence available from any relevant science, or from aesthetics, always bearing in mind what those thinkers who had unusual insight into their thought processes had to say in their writings.

Comparatively little attention is paid to evaluation itself at the present time. That the moral judgment is evaluative, that evaluative concepts are this and that, is all moral philosophers have to say. This may be because to speak of values suggests either that one is resorting to metaphysics, or that 'value' is a mere inference from the psychological concept of 'attitude'. Again, it might be that the epiphenomenal world of values described by N. Hartmann has alarmed philosophers. But "value" is still the same simple everyday word that it was before the axiologist commenced his somewhat pretentious investigations.

Values are relational: they require a valuer and at least one object. If the valuer has already a standard he can apply to the object, one object will do, for others are present by implication. If, on the other hand, he has no standard, then he must have two or more objects before him, with some features in common, so that he can derive a standard from them. The notion of value is puzzling, because it is a link between what is essentially intensional, as meaning or significance, and what is extensional, or part of the world. The word is little used in current philosophical writings, because it is the fashion to distinguish sharply between logical and contingent possibility, yet value contrives to link these notions: it applies what conceivably might be to what actually is. And what is remarkable is that it does so meaningfully. Let us take an example from pages 27–34 above.

In speaking of the determinist and indeterminist doctrines, we said that these were based upon ideal extremes which could not be found in fact. The false argument from determinism to the negation of practical freedom is thus the attempt to apply an ideal possibility to a matter of fact, and allow the former to annul the latter. As an ideal possibility, determinism is matched by its contradictory, indeterminism, and the two form an antinomy: for, being ideal, reason can find as good an argument for the one as for the other. But although the argument of the one can always be matched against the argument for the other, the denial of practical freedom cannot be put against its assertion, since this latter question is a factual one, it is a matter of proof, or evidence, not of argument; it demands scientific method, not conceptual analysis. There is no way of bridging the gap here between the ideal and the actual, and, in argument, to take them as comparable, as in asserting that determinism refutes freedom, is fallacious as there is no middle term. But value does manage to be a middle term by which the conceptual is applied to the actual, the existent, and thus to the particular. If we act according to our values, it is absurd to say that values are unreal: for if they emerge from the world and then influence the world, they are necessarily part of it.

We may ask how this comes about. When we acquire a concept we acquire a set of propositions which govern the application of certain words as names. If I have acquired the concept of a wood, I shall be able to distinguish in a practical way, as well as in idea, between a wood and a copse on the one hand, and between a wood and a forest on the other. There will be instances in fact when I hesitate between the words, but in general certain types of woodland can be correctly designated. Suppose now I speak of 'a beautiful wood'. I do not only distinguish the object as a wood, but also as woods go I assess this as a beautiful example of a wood. This means I must have a standard of grading for woods and kindred things according to which the particular wood in front of me stands very high. Of another wood I might remark that it was gloomy, meaning it stood low on the scale light-dark, which would lie in the background as a standard. We could say that aesthetic values, or grading, imply a hinterland where many similar things previously experienced, but varying in respect of the aesthetic element, lurk half forgotten.

When we pronounce a certain action as good or bad, or describe it by names for virtues or vices, we apply to that action a scale that we have acquired from experience of actions of all kinds. The concepts of 'good' and 'bad'—or 'right' and 'wrong'—are acquired from sets of propositions about actions just as any other social concepts are acquired. We apply them according to their meaning for us, which in turn is a reflection of the meanings others have given to them, and from time to time, as in the case of an empirical concept, we may hesitate about their application. We should remember that the propositions from which we derive our ethical concepts differ from those which give us material object, or concrete, ones in that they contain, as reference, the person who uttered them. Our moral concepts we obtain, not from a number of expressed opinions, but from persons having or asserting those opinions. Opinions by themselves cannot set up conceptual schemes, for by themselves they say nothing tangible. But someone making a judgment, giving a moral opinion, these are facts, and from our perception of such facts we acquire certain concepts of classes of actions which go to make up our standard of what is proper to social relations and what is not. It could be said, then, that when we make a moral judgment, and utter it as an assertion, we apply the concepts we have empirically acquired. Our moral judgments are thus relative to our experience in the same way as our other perceptual ones.

Why then, it may be asked, do our moral judgments remain so obstinately objective? We say 'X is bad' not 'I think X is bad'. Of course it could be said that it is plain that we do intend 'I think X is bad', since if we give an opinion and are honest, we must hold it as an opinion, as *our* opinion. But from the form of our speech I think it is fair to say that it appears as if when we make a moral judgment we assert that X *is* good, and that anyone should be able to see that it is so. Yet in making a valuational judgment, it is clear that we are not, in fact, making statements about kinds of acts which are intrinsically good, whenever they occur; what we are doing is to recognise a certain action as of a certain kind, valuationally. When we see that action, we apply the concept 'good' or whatever it may be. We do not say: 'It is an action of kind X, so, as I think all X's are good, this action is good.' Valuational judgments are *not* mediated by judgments of perception, but merely by perception. We make our moral judgments upon the facts as we see them, and the facts as we see them are that the action we see is good or bad. From this arises the difficulty in finding criteria to distinguish description from evaluation.[1] Evaluative elements in a sentence may be said to be a protrusion into it of former descriptive statements.

I have no doubt that the confusion upon this point is mainly due to theories of ultimate goodness and rightness. Whether there is an ultimate 'good' or 'right' is utterly irrelevant to our everyday moral judgments, and if philosophers think they are going to find out anything about these ultimates by analysing ordinary language, it is hard to suppose they will not be disappointed, if, that is, they ever complete their analysis. It seems to me to be immaterial whether, with Ewing, we use "right" or, with Moore, "good" or "best" in the practical situation: both are plainly indefinable as we ordinarily do use them. What 'goodness' and 'rightness' *are* remains, and must remain, the proper study of philosophy and distinct from that other proper study, the formal conditions of acting in accordance with whatever values we wish to adopt. There *is* an objective element in 'good' and 'right', etc. as applied to actions in that it is the action that evokes the judgment, and it is what we actually perceive that we judge. There is also a subjective element, since the judgment rests on standards we acquire from others. Again, we are in practice much more likely to feel that we should assert our moral opinions than that we should display our feelings. For we do not usually accept our feelings as the last word: we need, as is often pointed out, to conceptualise those feelings before we assert ourselves in accordance with them. Sometimes we doubt them, and wait to see if they have been wrongly aroused owing to some illusory perception.

But if we can say this, can we not also say that moral judgments are the conceptualisation of our feelings? Then it could be argued, with Westermarck among others, that we have a moral sense which manifests itself in moral approval and disapproval at the sight of certain actions; and that moral good and bad can be said to be the tendencies of certain actions to rouse those feelings in the majority of mankind?[2] Again I think there is confusion here between what is occasioned by an action and what is directed towards an agent. For it is when we recognise an action as bad that we feel an urge to intervene on behalf of the victim. Or, when we recognise an action as good, we feel an urge to intervene with congratulations for the agent. We want to clap him on the back, or write to the papers, or something of the sort; and our desire to do these things is our desire to assert ourselves as approving of the action, as recognising its character. We wish to identify ourselves with the agent, for we would like to do such actions ourselves, had we the opportunity and the strength. On the account I give here there is no room for any special moral sense. We use our ordinary, or common, sense to recognise actions of the kind we approve or disapprove, we use the paraphernalia of action to make this known, and, in so doing, to establish ourselves as having the character and tastes we wish to have. What philosophers overlook sometimes is the difference between the recognition of an action as good or bad, right or wrong, and our attitude to the agent as a result of our own desire to intervene in some way, to express our feeling of being involved. For the former is the application of standards to what we perceive, while the latter is our practical decision to act. Both find their expression in the moral judgment which is itself, when uttered, an action. When an agent judges his own action in retrospect, he attempts to keep it with him as part of himself, or to thrust it from him.

[1] E.g. G. M. Matthews, 'Evaluative and Descriptive' in *Mind* (1958).
[2] *The Origin and Development of the Moral Ideas*, chs. 1, 2.

XII

THE AGENT:
THE CONCEPT OF A PERSON

CONSTRUCTING A SITUATION

The man who is morally responsible recognises his indissoluble kinship with his fellows together with his ability to withdraw from the group, from society, to a greater or a lesser extent. Recognition of his responsibility and the freedom this recognition brings leads to problems of conduct which, for him, are moral problems. When a man does not recognise his responsibility, supposing him to be responsible, he can perceive when others require something of him, such as maintenance, or the physical efforts he has to make to earn his living. It does not occur to him that he should not act on his feelings, and he would be very angry if anyone suggested he was not responsible for his winning pools coupon. Such a man is responsible for what he does, but not for anything that he might have done, or does not do. The question, that is, of wilful thinking does not apply to him. His situation, in which he acts, is mainly constructed out of material wants of his own, or demands from others that he does not particularly wish to meet, though he may have little ability to resist them.

Let us look now at the way a man constructs his situation. Suppose we have an agent, *A*, who has a problem. What is he to do? He has to decide, let us say, a matter that affects *B* and *C*. Thus *B* and *C* are both in his situation. But what about himself? Is he in it too? And if he is not, how can he make a decision about *B* and *C*? For is it possible for him to know *B* and *C* except in relation to himself?

The construction of a situation is not the simple matter we might suppose from a definition. If *A*'s action is to maintain right relations between himself and *B* and *C* then it must surely also maintain right relations between *B* and *C*. But *B*'s relation with *C* is something that *A* cannot experience, he can only guess at it from the evidence available to him. He cannot, for instance, judge easily whether his own relationship with *B* is of more importance to *B* than, say, *B*'s relation with *C*.

This may seem an odd matter to raise. In practical matters it is, however, of supreme importance, for the main source of conflict and turbulence in social relations is the failure to allow for loyalties in which one is not directly concerned. The emphasis in moral theory is always on justification by an agent of his act, or on the building of his moral self, on, that is, the personal problem as such. But could it not be said that responsibility should be used not only for attempting to act rightly oneself, but also for acting in such a way that others are enabled to act rightly as well? If an action produces a misunderstanding, or hostility, between others more remotely affected, then even if it appears to be right to an agent, ought he to do it? All such difficulties lie concealed within the sophisticated use of "action" against which I have repeatedly argued. For such 'actions' are supposedly subsumed to moral rules or principles, and between the principle and the action the practical complexities escape notice.

When moral philosophers make the stipulation that part of the notion of 'right' is to know when to apply certain principles and when to disregard them, they unwittingly betray themselves into an admission that moral principles are only in the situation as possible guides, as reasons to be selected from, as part of the furniture of the moral problem, saying nothing at all about the nature of that problem and about how it is to be solved. Principles are not to interpose themselves between an agent and his problem, but are to be seen in their proper place among the constituents of it (cf. page 165 above).

If an agent is to regard himself as bound to respect relations in which he is not personally involved, then it is necessary for him to enter into the situation he constructs in the same way as those others who are in it. Only thus will he be able to compare his relationships with the persons concerned with the relations between the others concerned. For, as remarked earlier, it is impossible to compare what is not objectified in the one perspective. Let us look at the issues involved in what we are saying; and as a commencement we may attempt to do so diagrammatically:

Situation 1   Situation 2   Situation 3

(1) In this arrangement the agent remains outside the situation, and is, as the saying goes, confronted by it. The agent could be said to be 'there' as complete, but in the situation as he constructs it, B and C are only present as related to him, in so far as there is a common experience AB and a common experience AC. Outside AB and AC there is nothing to be known. These relationships are part of A's life, and when he chooses his action, he assesses them as more or less important to himself, more or less significant in terms of his prospects and enjoyments. Those prospects, or interests, form the criterion, since it is by them only that B and C can be valued. In any situation in which the three are involved, claims arise out of the social contexts of the relationships, and the actions seen as possible depend mainly on different relative assessments of these existing claims. A, wishing to preserve his relationships with B and C, will be careful to avoid any action that will injure these, but apart from this, he will meet his claims according to the hierarchy or the priorities of his own position. If he finds he must risk offending B or C, he will make sure he has some adequate reason by which to excuse himself to them.

(2) Here A constructs his situation as containing himself; he objectifies himself as he objectifies B and C. He still sees them as he knows them, but he is aware that, apart from his relations with them, there is much in the situation which concerns him alone. He is thus able to assume that there is much in the lives of B and C which does not concern him, and if he has doubts about their interests, he can consult them. Since all three are in the one situation, A can appreciate that what he regards as a suitable solution may not appear so to them, for they are also able to construct their own situations, and may reach different conclusions. He recognises the incompleteness of the situation as he sees it, and he can remedy this at will.

(3) Lastly, there is the situation which A constructs as if he were on equal terms with B and C, as if his relations with them were but items in a total of relationships. Thus he assumes

that B and C's relationships, which are unknown to him, are loyalties which give rise to claims in the same way as his own various relationships do. He will accordingly not only take care not to injure his relationships with B and C, if he values these, but he will also take care not to injure that between B and C. If B and C should be hostile, A will take care not to act in such a way that the hostility is aggravated, or that embarassment will be caused by their being forced into a position where they are expected to co-operate. In this way A is accepting the fact of the claims arising from the relationship BC just as he accepts the fact of the claims arising out of AB and AC. In doing so, it is plain that he must be so well informed about his own feelings for B and C, and about his own ends and desires, that he is able to place the claims they impose on a level with those he perceives in B and C. He then devises his action to meet all the claims concerned in such a way that he satisfies not only his own values but those of B and of C as well.

Situation 3 might be varied thus:

(a)   (b)

In (a) equal status is given to AB, BC, and AC. Thus X, as an action, is right, if "right" means, for example, just, and "just" refers to proper relations. In (b) the relationship AB is of more importance than the relationship of A and B with C. Y, on the criterion given for X, is 'wrong' because biased, though it is possible that it might, outside A's and B's knowledge, suit C.

It could be said that 3 is another version of impartiality. Impartiality is a negative term; it suggests we should not put the claims of one person above those of another. How then should they be assessed? Not according to persons, we suppose, but according to the claims themselves. But claims have to be seen as claims if they are to form, and objectively form, a hierarchy. So it still remains a matter of what claims are seen, or recognised as claims. I am avoiding the word "duty" because it implies more than I here mean to imply. The less we

are able to put ourselves into the situation, the more our unrecognised present intervenes to shape our situation; yet, on
the other hand, the more we objectify ourselves, recognise
what in the situation pertains to us and not to others, or to
'chance' or 'luck', the more clearly we see *our* part in it as the
action we must take, the change in the facts that the facts
themselves demand, the claim that is the leading issue about
which all the others group themselves. To speak thus is not to
say anything about impartiality. Yet if we admit the feelings,
interests, aims etc. of others along with our own in making a
decision, we do, presumably, take a remote view, and one that
could be said to be impartial. If claims, duties, etc. are seen as
instances of the relationships, social and personal, in which
they arise, then their review in one perspective enables the
reconciliation of interests which, when seen in the subject-
object dichotomy, range themselves into egoism and altruism;
if the subject-object relation is abandoned, the egoism-altruism
opposition also vanishes.

But, it will be objected, it is impossible to put the whole self
into one's construction of a situation, since there must still be
the self which objectifies, the self which decides the issue after
all the preliminaries; for there must be decision, and someone
who decides. Certainly we can admit that there is a decision,
and that there is someone who decides; but since the situation,
even with the self included in it, is a personal situation, it is
analytic that it is the person who decides. The situation may
be said to be constructed of all the facts relevant to the problem
that are perceived by an agent, the situation is what he is aware
of when he is forced to act—for we must regard action as
forced on him, he *must* do something, even if that something is
just to go on considering what he should do. If it is impossible
in principle to put the whole self into the situation, then we
must content ourselves with saying that a man puts in as much
as he can see of himself. When solution appears to be reached,
it is his solution because it is his problem and he is considering
it.

Again, it may be said that a person cannot put himself into
the situation he constructs, because what he knows of himself
is a miscellany of traits, interests, likes and dislikes, hopes and
fears. All these are the things a man finds out about himself,
we may reply to this objection, and in finding them out they

go into his situation. Whether they stay there, or for how long, is another matter. A man who substitutes for self-knowledge a set of beliefs about himself, mainly based upon moral precepts, and puts these in his situation is in the position of a man who argues that because he is virtuous, his acts must be virtuous, so that there is no need to look critically at them.[1] He himself is not in the situation at all, he is merely confronted by it, distorted as it is by a false premiss about himself. A man has to find out about himself. He does not know what he likes and what he does not like until he tries it out, and if he tries it out he gets to know through his action. Nor is it sense to say that a man has or has not a certain trait, or ability, if he has never acted in accordance with it. We mean by "trait" a characteristic feature of a man's behaviour. It is only in his actions, in what he does, that a man exists at all; if he did not act, we should have nothing to say about him. If he lives in secret and no-one knows him, he does not exist as a person at all, as witness the appalling results on a man who has been confined to one room and denied any life of his own by a crazy parent. Such 'people' are found from time to time, and their condition is a clinical fact. Similarly, a man cannot tell what he could do or what he might do unless he knows what he has done; for, without a most extensive knowledge of physics, economics, political science and psychology, he could not deduce what activities were possible for him from the size, shape and power of his body, and some intelligence tests, etc. Even then he would get no knowledge without doing the tests and asking to be measured. What a man believes himself to be capable of is a mixture of what he has seen himself do, and what he believes he could do if he tried: unfortunately, what he believes himself capable of is too often the reflection of what he has seen others do rather than based on a genuine assessment of his own powers; for to know what one can do is to have tried to do it and either to have succeeded or to have failed to achieve it. A man who makes a statement about what he could do must produce evidence, and the evidence is, inevitably, an account of what he has done.

Since many men do not look at what they do, but make assumptions from what they would like to think they do, they

---

[1] Cf. Sartre, *Huis Clos*: 'Tu as rêvé trente ans que tu avais du cœur; et tu te passais mille petites faiblesses parce que tout est permis aux héros.'

need some sort of verification if they are to attain a true account. This is provided by the accounts of others, their criticism, their judgments, the sanctions of approval and disapproval offset by his own estimate of their reliability. From taking note of these, a man can anticipate them and include them in his situation, thus applying a kind of publicity test to what he intends to do; for if there is any sense in morality, an act is not influenced in its rightness or goodness by the contingent fact that it is publicly and not merely privately known about. No moral fault, when there is one, is 'worse' *because* it happens to get into the papers. No good deed is of less value unpublicised. Thus the man who has some notion of moral progress may acquire the ability to assess himself, by supposing what could be said about what he proposes to do. There is no arguing from principle to fact here, but the deliberate scrutiny of a mere proposal from other supposed points of view, in order to be certain as to its objective significance.

How do these considerations affect our account of 'person'? According to our method, we can attempt to answer this question in three stages:

(1) How do we learn to use "person"?
(2) Does 'person' necessarily imply 'consciousness'?
(3) Does 'person' include a notion of personal identity?

I. THE USE OF "PERSON"

We do not learn to use the word "person" until we have learned to differentiate between persons. That is to say, it is because we individuate, because we distinguish *A* from *B*, that we have any notion of a person. Thus it can be said that we acquire the concept as we acquire that of other material objects, by experience of individuals. So far the concept of person is concrete. Persons differ mainly in that they look different and in that they act differently. And it must be admitted that from the fact that they act differently we infer that they feel differently about things that appear similar. By "action" I also indicate speech-acts. But sooner or later we discover that our inferences often turn out to be incorrect. Much later we learn that what appears to us as *xyz* can appear to someone else as anything but *xyz*. It is then that it may occur to us to ask what after all we do mean by "a person"? And we return to the position where all we can say is that we know *who* certain persons are, but not *why*.

It is a necessary condition of naming that there is something to be named; and in using proper names we must know something about the object to which we refer, otherwise we could not use the name. If we mention a name but do not know to whom it refers, or that it does refer to anyone, we are not naming, but repeating sounds or guessing. When we use a name meaningfully, we must know the object named. Looking at a crowd, we could say that if we selected whatever person was standing on a particular spot, that person would have a name, but we could not say anything else about him or her. In contrast to this, when we speak of someone by name, it does not matter where he is, we indicate him quite successfully wherever he may be. Thus what we name when we use a personal proper name is some object in social relations, not merely a material object. In naming a person we individuate socially, we refer to a social fact. "J.T." is the son of "H.T.", and he lives in— Street, in —town, and his occupation is . . . etc. As a concrete concept, 'person' is the same as 'man', 'woman', etc. persons as material objects are just 'certain persons'; 'person' as we apply it to people with names is a social concept, and, as such, it has its verifiable or empirical aspect, and also its conjectural, or normative, one which governs its application, and the bringing of instances under it.

By using such expressions as "that table", "this", "his hat", we individuate in the world of things; by calling an individual man Tom, Dick, or Harry, we indicate a social being, we say nothing about him, but we acknowledge him as socially significant.

If a proper name must be applied to something distinguishable, it follows that we cannot use a proper name unless we can distinguish its bearer. Accordingly we must have some relationship with the bearer, even if only knowledge of him as a public figure, or as the friend of a friend. We have some relation in that we have an attitude based upon other relations that constitute our knowledge of society. A proper name does not individuate in the physical sense, for it tells us nothing about an individual human being that we do not already know. We do not as a rule say: "The one with the beard is Joe" with particular reference to the beard. It is not that we are interested in the feature, but that the beard provides an easy method of recognition, so that other characteristics may be correctly attributed to Joe. It is by this means that we do not write a report on Joe which really should refer to Harry. It does not make sense, then, to use a proper name unless a social distinction is either to be made or is already there in our thoughts. With regard to Joe, the name was substituted for the beard, and the beard was used as a flag which marks a site. But now we have to ask: What happens on the site? What is it we locate? With what are we related?

By extensional analogy, we may say that a relation implies two terms, as a line implies two points, and to speak of two points is to speak of the relationship between them. The point has no extension, but the relation between two points has, and also exists in time: for both points must exist simultaneously if both are to have location. If two points both succeed in indicating a third, then there are three points and three lines. Each point has two lines. Extensionally this is a triangle. By analogy, if two persons can indicate a third, there are three persons and three relationships. Now a point has no extension but that of its relations. One angle cannot determine more than one point, so that to speak of one person and two extended relationships is meaningless.[1] It is one of those facts which puzzle philosophers that, although points have no extension, yet without points there can be no extensional relations, that is, lines. To speak of a number of points is to speak of their relations. To speak of a single point is self-contradictory, for to individuate is to locate, to postulate a relation. In a 'relation' of identity, there is no individuation, only identity, which is the negation of relation, although philosophers do not admit this. The same difficulty arises with regard to equality, and if equality and identity are said to be relations, the relations are ideal, and formulations about them in language have no reference.

If by a "person" we indicate a social point, a point in the complex of social relations, it is meaningless to speak of one person only. To use the word "person", or to name a human being, is to postulate two social points and a relation between

---

[1] Readers should compare this figurative account with that given by Bernard Mayo in *The Logic of Personality*. He bases his analogy on the resemblances between our relations with other persons and our relations with things, and it may be that the reader would find his argument more fruitful and illuminating.

them. It seems to follow from this that what we mean when we speak of a person is the content of his relationships.

In support of this view, I venture to refer to Strawson: In *Individuals*, page 100 and elsewhere, he argues for the interdependence of the concepts 'myself' and 'others'. Also I can quote Bradley, who wrote, on pages 166–7 of *Ethical Studies*: 'If we suppose the world of relations, in which he was born and bred, never to have been, then we suppose the very essence of him not to be; if we take that away, we have taken him away; and hence he now is not an individual, in the sense of owing nothing to the sphere of relations in which he finds himself, but does contain those relations within himself as belonging to his very being; he is what he is, in brief, so far as he is what others also are.' I am going further than either of these writers, but the main difference is that I have omitted from my argument the notion of individuality that they both include, and from which Mayo also fails to cast himself loose. If we omit the 'individual', we are left with a social being, a person, who relies on his relationships. As a physical organism, he does in any case rely on others, for that is a condition of birth and survival, but in surviving, he acquires his personality, his social being; it is in respect of this that he is responsible, and he is responsible for the expression he gives of those relations of which he is constituted.

If the meaning of a person is the content of his relationships, the word "person" does not refer to an entity. To speak of a person is to indicate social existence, which consists in the interplay of the relationships concerned in it. But to say that a person is a point in a social complex is to say that he is, since he has many relationships—some to other people, some to institutions—the one point where all the relationships begin or end, that he is the common end of many diverse relations; it is he who is in some way modified by the social influences that the relationships represent. We may say he is the focal point of those influences, the place where they all converge. And to say that he is a focal point is not to say anything at all about what happens at that point—at the site of confluence.

What does happen is what a man does, and what he does must be an assertion of himself in accordance with the content of those relationships. If the influences, the content of his relationships, should conflict, each demanding assertion at the same time, the agent must, since he has only the one physical means of expressing himself, come to some arrangement whereby he can reconcile the conflicting influences by finding appropriate expressions and other means of assertion. But as he has no social existence apart from them, he has no criterion by which to decide between them, or to reconcile them, which is not also derived from one or other of them. Accordingly he will be forced to act by means of those forms which, owing to the strength and stability of the influences or relationships which have generated them, have become well established, that is, habitual. But we have seen that when a man constructs his situation, he can construct it differently according to his particular problem, and thus bring it to contain a different selection of influences. By remembering the situations he constructs he can include in one of them the habits and influences which pertain to another if he so desires. It follows that if a man is aware of what he is doing and of how he does it, he has the means so to organise himself that he alters or modifies his habitual behaviour. He can decide and carry out his decision to assert a relationship or act on an influence which he would not otherwise have asserted or acted upon in a particular situation.

As an example of this, we can say that to act in accordance with relationship M rather than relationship N is to give the action which relationship M would suggest precedence over that which relationship N would engender, or indicate.

This may appear to be a simplification, but it is at least formally correct. For if A is nothing apart from his relationships, he has no means of surveying his situation, of constructing it, except from the material of one or other of these. His situation can only be what he makes it because of what he himself is and has been. Interpretation of his situation in terms of possible actions is confined to his experience as included in one relationship or another: it is basically interpersonal.

It is meaningless to speak of a relationship except with reference to the common experience of the persons concerned. There may be any number of persons concerned in a relationship, however. Any joint or shared activities constitute the relationships of those concerned. It follows that society is *not* a relation, nor an organic whole; if we can ever speak of 'a' society, or of 'a' community, we only refer to the complex of personal and institutional relations of which it consists. The feeling of solidarity which is characteristic of membership of any group comes *only* from actual shared experience. Speaking and discussing is a form of joint activity, and the subjects, with the associations of those subjects, which are discussed will be marked with the social influence within which they were activated.

When a person acts, he asserts himself socially in terms of the influences of which he consists, and it follows that there can be no stable self, or basic dispositional complex.[1] The individual, as organism, can only act from or by means of acquired social forms, being conditioned by convention from birth. The physical mechanisms involved in all activity are subjected to varying control, interpersonal direction.

Thus it may be said that acting in accordance with one set of habits rather than another, choosing one kind of action rather than another, with some systematic reconciliation of conflicting influences, is to have a standard of behaviour, or a formal criterion for assessing values. The establishing of such a criterion involves choice and decision.

This account of a person will bring objections from those who regard a 'self' as essential to the concept of morality. The requirements of such a self are usually thought to be that it is something that endures through change, that is predicated of and predicable, that it is impinged upon and acts upon, and that it is at once static and metamorphosed in growth. The language of moral theory has long been dominated by this requirement, and psychology may be said to be almost strangled by this notion. Agency and responsibility, according to Bradley, would require 'self-sameness' as a necessary condition, yet he himself failed utterly to find any principle upon which such a self could rest. He postulated 'a good self' which was to be the result of right acting. But what is meant by an acting self, which may be good or bad? Is it just another name for a habit? It is seldom realised how difficult this concept is to establish: for when we act, we pass from the potential to the actual, and cannot point to any precise moment at which the change takes place. Have we to wait until the action is completed? But *when* can it be said to *be* completed? Looked at from the traditional standpoint, the acting self is but the point

---

[1] Wells, in a thesis included in '*42*—'*44*, spoke of the unity of the human personality as a 'biologically convenient delusion.'

of intersection of thought and action, their overlap, perhaps. Suppose I have a strong wish for revenge, and one day a way of indulging it occurs to me. I think it over, but I know that I shall not carry out the suggestion. After a time I forget all about it. What are we to do with this kind of event, for event it certainly is? In its psychical aspect it is actual. The notion of an acting self is quite inadequate to deal with such a problem. But if we can say that such occurrences are concerned in the construction of the situation in which a man acts, then we can cope with those changes that occur only in ideation. For it will be part of the way the situation is constructed, a stage in the process of deliberation, some development having an effect upon the action which eventually occurs, but not forming part of behaviour. It is absurd to suggest that thoughts are not subject to manipulation and control in the same way as we control external objects. Without a thought before us we could not perceive a relation of implication.

The self that acts is, for the agent, the agent himself; for the onlooker, it is an abstraction from the social phenomenon he sees before him in action. If a person can only execute one action at a time, it follows that he is integrated differently at different times while doing different actions. His purposes vary, his interests may conflict and have to be kept from each other, and the severance in fact tends to generate a severance in thought. Disloyalties cannot be permitted to meet on the same stage at the same time, and so on. The only common denominator is the physical executant, bereft of purpose. And this is not what is meant by a self.

We might say that the self could be an integration or co-ordination of all the 'I's that do different things; but then we suppose something outside all our purposes and skills which does the co-ordinating. This could only be a principle of subjectivity which, by definition, had no content. If it has no content, then in co-ordinating, it has nothing to implement the co-ordination. It is a mere arbitrary distinction between subject and object. Why should I, when I go swimming, be different from the swimmer? My decision to go swimming is a decision of the swimmer. My decision to learn something is a decision of the learner, the untaught who will be taught, not a something that is both untaught and taught, or both, or neither. For if the self is to endure through change it must be predicated by opposites, and to be predicated by opposites is to be self-contradictory, to be logically untenable.

Why should we require a 'self' to be the repository of goodness, badness, and agency? If we say that we have selves that are a kind of remote control system, somehow distinct from our bodies and brains, what becomes of our feelings? If 'my' feelings are part of myself, do my feelings 'cause' my actions, or do 'I' consider my feelings when deciding to act? If my feelings are not part of myself, how do I know what they are like: for by feelings we mean modifications of ourselves, an immediate way of perceiving what is occurring to us, the indication of experience and the condition of awareness. But if feelings are part of the acting self then when I feel, I am what acts, not something that merely decides that I shall act; and if feelings are not part of myself, how do I recognise them as feelings, and as mine? Feelings are sometimes held to be assessments, incipient judgments of value or import: but how can I assess, if I am at the same time what is being assessed?

We have seen that critical awareness of different sets of values within us results from awareness of different relationships: for if relationship X is different from relationship Y, by memory I should be able, when I *am* relationship X, to criticise relationship Y that I was yesterday afternoon, and assess its significance in the light of what I have now become. In some ways we could, since experience is like an ever-widening landscape, say that values change imperceptibly but steadily from hour to hour, for we are never exactly as we were the previous day, and we never or very seldom become so completely identified with our surroundings that we cannot compare them with other experiences we have had. Such comparisons, logically resulting from a changing viewpoint, are, far from being a negation of the moral life and of ethical achievement, its very life-blood.

2. CONSCIOUSNESS

We have now to ask whether, when we use the word "person" we indicate a personal consciousness. The question is important, for a man might be at the point of confluence of many social influences, and yet be merely swayed by the strongest; he might never reach a level of comprehension where he recognised alternatives of response to those pressures to be open to him.

I propose to leave the word "conscious" alone for the moment, as the necessary element in 'consciousness' is awareness. To be aware must mean to be aware of something, but awareness does not include that something as specific. To be aware, for instance, of stillness is not to be aware of the absence of sound and movement; for to connect the stillness with their absence is a thought beyond that of the stillness itself. To be aware cannot logically include being aware of what is there, for it would be impossible to draw the line between what we might perceive and what we do perceive, since everything cannot be perceived at once. But should we speak of perceiving? Does it make sense to be aware and not to perceive anything in particular?

We can rule out at once the scientific notion of 'simple awareness', in which the mere fact that an organism reacts in some way constitutes awareness, sentience. Instead, we can look at language: for language is a form of behaviour, and its proper use depends upon experience. We can expect that there may be certain propositions that can only be expressed in language if awareness is present.

The expression of an opinion gives no indication as to how it has been reached. A man may quote two or three lines from a newspaper, without understanding what they say. Their relevance may be assumed from the presence of one word-form. If a man gives an opinion or an item of information, he should be able to produce the premisses upon which his opinion is based. If a man can justify his opinion to another, then it is analytic that he can justify it to himself. The premisses of 'p' are the premisses of 'p' whoever is concerned. To say "I know that 'p'" is not to array reasons, but to be in a position to array them if required. They may not come immediately to mind when wanted, but there is a kind of vista which opens along the route by which they will come eventually. This may lead a man to say he "just feels" that 'p', especially when he has a long record of relevant experience. To "feel" in this sense is the equivalent or accompaniment of being satisfied discursively. Similarly, if a man feels a hypothesis to be wrong, he may be said to be aware of an incongruity between the hypothesis and his knowledge or experience.[1]

[1] Cf. Aristotle, *Nichomachean Ethics* 1143b.12.

It is sometimes overlooked that thinking is the exercise of a skill,[1] and Ryle's comments on 'knowing how', in *The Concept of Mind* certainly apply to it. In thinking on a well worn theme we have so systematised our knowledge of it that the knowledge constitutes a criterion, a standard, and it does so as a whole, immediately. It is thus that we become resistant to new ideas as we get older—so it is said! This also is how we run, jump, swim; it is how we make sentences when we have something to say, the selection of words is a process of which we are only partially aware, and many sentences, as we think, write, or speak, come as a surprise to ourselves. We may think so hard about what we wish to say that we do not consider the means at all unless we reject a phrase and pause to find another. In thinking, our knowledge is implicit in the process of thought itself, in the logical development of the subject of our thought. We cannot have our thinking proceed towards an end, and at the same time explicitly survey and marshal the factual knowledge upon which our ideas, the ideas we are thinking with, are grounded: when we make use of a concept we are not aware of it as such, we are only aware of certain permissions and vetoes, a kind of colour signalling by which we pass along several avenues at once. As we go, we have glimpses of other avenues which will have to be explored later. When we stop thinking and try to support our conclusion, the story is different: we have to find suitable premises, and, waiting as it were at a crossroads, justify our choice of route. We then make our logical processes explicit, using recognisable and conventional forms, and if the premises are not immediately available, we have to look for them. If they are not even then forthcoming, we have to abandon that particular route.

'To have a feeling that' is, I said, 'to be aware that'. But this awareness is the simple awareness of reaction. It is the response to a suggestion. I do not become aware that I have a feeling that '*p*' is untenable, I feel that '*p*' is untenable. Some time later I do not remember that I became aware that I had a feeling that . . ., but I remember that I had a feeling that . . . I may, however, remember that the feeling was very strong, and to say this is to say something very significant: for if I can say that my feeling was strong, I must have compared it with others, and

---

[1] A notable exception to this oversight is the lively article 'The Stream of Thought', by D. W. Hamlyn, in *Proc. Ar. Soc.* (1955-6).

used an adjective of intensity. If all our feelings were strong, we should not know the difference between strong and weak feelings; but if they vary, and I can find differences of intensity among them, it is analytic that I have compared them. Since a feeling is what I feel at some moment, and is a whole, it follows that if I can compare such wholes of feeling I must be aware of different feeling contents at different times: in other words, my awareness is one in that it covers different contents of experience and can set the one against the other. To compare my feelings at different times in respect of intensity I must not only have had those feelings but have been aware of them at the time; and, further, the awareness of them persisted and overlapped. Thus I suggested in chapter vi, page 150, that we can say another person is a conscious being, that is, that he has a 'mind', if he can compare his feelings and express these comparisons in words. For questions about comparing feelings would have no meaning for a man who was not a conscious being. But we should consider feelings further in connection with awareness.

Feelings may, as in the example of 'feeling that . . .', constitute awareness, but awareness of feelings is necessary for knowledge, since feelings must be conceptualised before we can speak of knowledge. Feelings may be perceptive in character, but of themselves they cannot contribute to knowledge, they can only indicate where we should look for knowledge. We perceive the feelings, and this perception involves a second awareness. What is important is that the two awarenesses occur simultaneously: the feelings could not occur, then stop while awareness of them occupied our attention. Our feelings may appear to occupy our whole attention, but if we are wondering about their nature, we have both the feelings as awareness of something, or reaction to something, and our deliberations.

It does not make sense to speak of two awarenesses that are simultaneous. Two awarenesses might exist in connection with one organism, but not simultaneously, for if one were aware of the other, the awareness would be unified. What must occur is that in our awareness at some time we distinguish feelings from our perception of them and from our interpretation of them. And it is analytic that we would not be said to "have" feelings if we did not perceive them, and perceive them *as* feelings. If our awareness can enable us to reflect upon feelings which, at some given time, have entirely carried us away, then that awareness must be *one* awareness and not two. Feelings, if they are to be called awareness, are so in that they alert us, or call our attention to certain things which have significance for our welfare. Without feelings, we could say, we would not be aware at all. To attempt to say that judgment of a feeling as strong or weak is, for example, a purely conceptual affair, is to carry philosophy into a limbo of not-being; to judge a feeling as strong or weak is to feel strongly or weakly and to perceive that it is so. The strength or weakness is not a mental state, but is the whole reaction of the person as he is at the time. The words used to express anger, pleasure and so on are part of a person, they are not part of him looking at another part. If he should say: 'D——, I wish I wasn't so angry' he is still one with his anger, while if he says: 'Oh, no, I'm not really angry' he is a liar.

It does not follow that, when a man makes statements about his feelings, he is objectifying himself in any way, he may just be expressing himself. Two or three hours later it is possible he may not recall anything about it at all. Pressed, he can reconstruct the occurrence, and observe that at the time he was angry. But not necessarily so. To make such an assertion does not in itself imply self-knowledge, although to be able to make such remarks is a necessary condition of self-knowledge. It is thus conceivable that a man does not know he has been angry because he did not perceive it at the time. It is also possible that he did not perceive his anger because he had a bias in favour of the statement 'I never get angry', and an assertion of his anger would contradict this. Here again there is no question of two awarenesses but of one limited one. The contradiction is not allowed to occur, and it cannot occur unless the anger is verbalised, since the contradiction must occur on the level of verbal thought or speech. Factual anomalies can exist side by side.

The incongruity of speaking about two awarenesses in connection with one thinking being may be adequately shown by the fact that to be aware of something is to be in contact with it, and for two awarenesses to be in contact is to say they are in fact one. It is only because we cannot be sure that a certain person *A* has the kind of awareness that we have that we can speak of 'other' minds: for if we were directly aware that they were aware we should fall within the one awareness. This, indeed, is what Kant meant by the 'common sense', that our critical awareness of things is 'the same'. The world of reason is undivided.[1]

If we can say that to compare feeling states with regard to intensity indicates they are contained within one awareness, we can apply the same argument to inference: for while a man may not know why he makes a certain statement, or holds a certain opinion, if he can follow the steps by which he reached it, or remember how he acquired it, then his awareness covers various periods of time, and is thus capable of being used for checking the validity of what he says. He can check memory statements by reference to his experience at the original time of occurrence. In the human being, awareness is a necessary condition of what we call knowledge, since situations *are* what they are in virtue of our previous experience, and we see them through a categorial scheme which not only arranges but limits our present perceptions. It is not a sufficient condition of knowledge, since what we see cannot be accurately reproduced at will: it must be related propositionally to other perceptions: and this process constitutes, not merely awareness in the conceptual sphere, but *reason*, the organised use of past experience in comprehending the present and anticipating the future.

There is little justification for distinguishing between awareness and consciousness. By saying the human being is conscious, we often mean to indicate that purpose and understanding are so inseparably concerned with awareness that they seem together to form the very existence of a person. They give individuality by the uniqueness of their content. But it would be incorrect to suppose that awareness, or consciousness, has any real part in this: a person is what he is because he is aware to a remarkable degree of the circumstances in which he finds himself, and this because his reasoning powers present him with an extensive account of his abilities and potentialities. So far as awareness is concerned, if a human being is with us, acts relevantly and gives an account of himself, he is conscious. If his awareness is limited, it is not a necessary, but a contingent, limitation.

---

[1] *Critique of Judgment,* part I, book II, para. 40.

3 PERSONAL IDENTITY

We use the word "person" to indicate a social being who is the focal point of many social influences, usually in the form of relationships with other people. The statement '*A* is a person' does not, we have seen, imply the further one '*A* is conscious', except when "conscious" is used to say that *A* responds to pokes and punches and rude remarks. *A* is not, on this account, necessarily aware of any thoughts. Consciousness, or awareness, enables us to retain what *has* happened and to place it alongside what *is* happening; and further, it permits reason to analyse that past and present, recording what occurs in words for purposes of verification and tests of validity. To do this involves the application of standards in judgment, and the result of these processes is our knowledge. Knowledge facilitates the combination of propositions into theories. A man is conscious, we say, if he can assess his feelings quantitatively, or produce a reasoned argument that he has not learnt by heart. We can also say that *A* knows what he is doing if he can not only give an account of what he does, but also predict what is likely to happen.

In all these assertions, we have to do with a man as and by himself; but, as already pointed out, a man is a person and is not a hypostatisation of consciousness or of reason. Being aware, of itself, gives no guarantee of continuity in either the person as aware or in that of which he is aware. The only criterion of continuity *is* the awareness, and since what we are aware *of* changes constantly, we cannot infer continuity from changes. To be conscious and rational is not a necessary condition of being a person, although it is sufficient; for a person does not stop being a person when, for instance, he is asleep, nor does Smith cease to be Smith when in such a rage he can neither speak nor think.

To deal with the question of personal identity, I propose to distinguish between being a person and being an identical person. The first is an empirical affair, but the second requires a principle. The notion of self-sameness belongs only to the former, though there is a variation in its sense as applied to oneself or to another. I am myself, am a person, because I have a unique position in respect of all my social relationships, my experience and knowledge of material objects, my abilities and my preferences. My identity consists in, and only is, the uniqueness of my position. Unique access, not privileged access, is the meaning of a person. That others are similarly placed, uniquely placed, is an inference from what they do and say. To speak of the self-sameness of others is accordingly a matter of recognition, of contingency. Ayer, in 'Individuals', makes the point that in practice we continue to give descriptive statements about a person until our interlocutor is satisfied he knows about whom we are speaking.[1] This is how we individuate personally. We can only speak of individuals if we can recognise them, otherwise we refer to numbers of human beings, ten, twenty, etc. Given that a man is aware of what he is doing, that he is responsible according to our criterion, and that we can recognise him either by direct experience or by account, then the question of self-sameness is settled: for if, as an agent, a man tries to evade answering for something he has done by saying he was not himself at the time of acting, it is (i) up to him to make sure that he is himself when he acts, and (ii) up to us to make him aware of the nature of the agency he is trying to reject. If a man is not aware of what he is doing, he has still the possibility of increasing his knowledge to include it.

On this pragmatic definition of self-sameness, a man, as a person, should be able to combine in one awareness all the various roles or relationships that he asserts in his judgments. There seems no reason why several value systems should not exist and persist in connection with one body. There would be varying viewpoints. Yet since we are, in the absence of a common or central self, either one or other of our relationships at any time, we can only combine these by bringing them all under or into one of those relationships. This might be effected by admitting one code or set of values into all the others by acting in accordance with it in all our roles, thus maintaining one standard of behaviour in all social relationships. These would come in time to be included in the one viewpoint, they would all be available for purposes of comparison and assessment, and would all influence the construction of any new situation and assist in the solution of new problems. If one role has generated the adopted standard, its values must extend gradually over the whole field of experience and effort. And this is in fact how most people live, working out in practice some

[1] *Philosophical Essays.*

of the values given them in early training, yet often conserving some role or roles in which the same standard is not applied.

It thus seems that only by acting in certain ways can such an inclusion be achieved. To do it, a man has to become aware of his standards, deliberately identifying himself with certain of them. As emphasised above, the moral judgment is the instrument by which a man asserts himself as the person he is, both to himself and to others. Moral judgments are one sub-class of experiential statements which, with a human being as their reference, assert the social fact of persons. A man seeks to gain confidence in his dealings with others by ideological assertions just as he seeks to command credit in business through advertisement. In both cases he may do so honestly or dishonestly.

Finally there is the question of an identical self. At first sight, the subjective "I" might seem to offer some hope of a principle, since if we say that a person has access to all his situations and experience, surely we must concede that the very construction of his situations implies some overlap. But by definition, the subjective element in the construction of a situation cannot enter wholly into it in any particular instance, and thus could not be the organiser and systematiser of all that goes to make a person.

If we say that to be a person is to be able to combine all that occurs 'on the site'—unique in its multiplicity—into one awareness, we seem here to have at least a formal ground of identity. "To be able" expresses possibility, it necessarily here involves consciousness. The principle of personal identity would then be the possibility of unification, not its occurrence. Restrictions of time and the trivialities of life in a highly sophisticated society plainly preclude paying attention to all that one does, and this alone, even without the usual adherence to habit, would be sufficient to rule out complete unification. But I do not see why we should not regard the possibility of such unification of outlook, purpose and means—actions—as supplying us with a necessary condition of personal identity. There is no facet of our lives, as experience, of which we might not become aware, even though empirically we could not become aware of every one; and thus, since the totality of our experience is unique, a statement of the complete unification of ourselves as persons would formally imply a statement of our uniqueness and thus also of our identity.

XIII

IN CONCLUSION:
THE GROUNDS OF RESPONSIBILITY

In the three chapters just completed, I have ventured to suggest definitions for the expressions "responsibility", "moral", "practical freedom", "action", "situation", and "person"; and I reached these definitions by analysing certain features of our attempts to solve our moral problems. I could not avoid giving a phenomenological account of these attempts, and it may be that few thinkers will agree with this account either as an account of the moral experience, or as a suitable basis for the conclusions I appear to have drawn from it. Inevitably also I have had to attempt to describe the place of reasons and reasoning, principles, conventions, and values in our everyday efforts to deal with practical problems.

Here, once more, are the definitions.

Responsibility. A man is responsible for his actions because in acting he acts in his own, unique situation, into which he may bring his fellows' interests, or he may not. He may withdraw from his place in society if he so desires, and thus his responsibility for what he does in society is a relation between his own situation and those of others who are affected by his actions.

Situation. A man's situation depends upon his perceptions; it is thus an ideational construction from the facts relevant to his problem. It is logically inaccessible to anyone but himself.

Practical Freedom. If a man recognises that he is reponsible for what he does, that he is in relation with others, and that he can construct his situation in his own way, and if his responsibility for what he does is recognised and allowed for by others, then he is free to choose whatever actions are feasible in the circumstances.

Moral. An agent who is responsible need not be a moral agent. If he recognises his responsibility, and has practical freedom, he is a moral agent in the use he makes of his freedom to act on principle.

Actions should be taken as social forms, and described in such a way that they can easily be recognised by observation, without knowing those motives of the agent which are not apparent in the occurrence *as* an occurrence, without any moral significance.

Agent or Person. What a man is, what is seen and known of him, his opinions, the principles he asserts, and so on, constitute his social being. As a person he has unique access to a certain fund of facts and experience, and as agent he is a focal point of social influences, all of which he can combine, through knowledge, into an integrated way of living.

Problems occur because a man's relationships overlap and conflict and have to be reconciled. A man has a problem when he has to act in his situation and is undecided how to proceed. It is the particular problem which provides the criterion of relevance by which he abstracts from his circumstances and knowledge and constructs his situation.

THE QUESTION OF REFERENCE

Of these, "responsibility", "practical freedom" and "moral" are applicable generally to an agent, or they are not; they rely on conditions of the agent. Problems, situations, and actions are particulars.

If we can find out whether a person constructs a situation, we can say that the expression "responsible for one's actions" refers; "person" also refers, since the word is socially significant; names of actions are words for what we can see people doing, and they too refer. Practical freedom is dependent, conceptually and actually, upon the recognition and admission of responsibility, and can only be called a derived term, in respect of reference.

Difficulties abound with regard to "situation" and "moral". It could be argued that if responsibility is based upon the construction of a personal situation, and if we can know when men do construct their situations, then "situation" should refer. But I do not think we can make this passage. That a man does make or construct the situation he appears to act in may be ascertainable, but it is not ascertainable that he does act in it, and we can not know what it is like. To some extent "situation" is similarly placed to "intention" which I have wished to discard. I could be charged with shifting the difficulties of the one on to the other. It is partly, however, on account of this that I decided to omit "intention" from my account; for it is easier to determine what we mean by situation in terms of perception and of the actual problem in connection with which it is constructed, than it is to locate intentions. And, since actions are recognisable, we can give "problem" a sense as the concrete occasion on which action must occur.

"Moral", relates to an agent, and cannot be pointed to on some one occasion. If a man is a moral agent, so long as he is not forcibly prevented or coerced, he is morally responsible for all his actions, in whatever social role they occur. It is possible that his practical freedom only occurs in some of his relationships and not in others. But here a moral agent would endeavour to build his life of those social relationships in which he was able to act on the principles he regarded as right or good.

THE GROUNDS OF RESPONSIBILITY

In the account of the moral experience given in the preceding chapters, we should be able to distinguish principles if they are there to be found, and if we have made a suitable choice of descriptive expressions, so that they relate to fact as they were intended to do.

As a formal ground of man's responsibility for his actions I should suggest the uniqueness of the situation in which he acts. It may be said that this is merely another version of the statement, intelligible in previous centuries, that a man's consciousness is free, and thus he is responsible. I have given my reasons for regarding the word "consciousness" as misleading, and I will not enlarge on the subject. Being inaccessible, the agent's situation is unique, since it is not available for comparison. The question is whether inaccessibility, which is not a necessary condition of uniqueness, can be said to be sufficient. On a pragmatic view, it is, though an idealist might not accept the relation. But if man is a social animal, and if his situation is inaccessible, then it means at least that it is inaccessible to any other man, and thus in the context of society it is sufficient for uniqueness. I attach value to the concept of uniqueness here, because it supports a further argument that a man is responsible because no-one else could be, and this, it seems to me, is the kind of argument that could be used against determinism.

If the uniqueness, and/or the inaccessibility of a man's situation, is the formal ground of his responsibility for what he does, the best candidate for a material ground, if we want one, is the ability to construct a situation, and the fact that a man does so. We have seen that, in the case of the complete domination of one man by another, the material ground is lacking, and we say the man is not responsible. This state is usually only found in children, or in the pathologically tyrannised.

My arguments on this point are, however, open to a charge of circularity. For I have laid it down that we cannot know what a man perceives of the world around him, and then that he constructs his situation of the facts he sees as relevant to his problem. But his appraisal of the facts—how he sees them—follows from his past experience, and his habits of perception. So could we not content ourselves with saying that responsibility follows from selective perception?

The answer is that we cannot simplify the matter in this way, because of the definition of person that we have adopted. If a man is a focal point of social influences, then his perceptions must, both in theory and in fact, vary as those influences become stronger—through reinforcement by presence, etc.—or weaker. His relationships give rise to claims, and it is the claims he finds relevant to his problem that in part produces the uniqueness of the situation. A man's choices may be strongly affected by his adherence to a certain principle, but the adherence itself must also be attributed in a final analysis to some social influence. The argument remains valid under all these conditions and variations.

Again, to say that responsibility is based on selective perception makes responsibility a quality rather than a relation. Now it can be strongly argued that to distinguish between qualities and relations is, in this context, a quibble; but I think it can be shown that to disregard the distinction here is very misleading: for it would conceal that the relation occurs between people, or qualities of people, whereas the quality, as such, would only apply to one person. And this would extinguish the whole value of my study of responsibility, which emphasises its social origin and yet avoids equating it with mere ascription. It is true that I have said that responsibility relies upon or issues out of a relation between situations which, because perception is limited to single viewpoints, occurs within a man rather than between men; yet it is inconceivable that any man, living in society, should not at some time in his life, be aware of others as having the same kind of problem, the same need to construct a situation in taking care how he committed himself to action, as himself. And this awareness of others as finding themselves with problems is not what we have called a direct awareness, but results from experiencing the behaviour of others when they are, in fact, busy working out their problems. At a simple level, a man can tell when another man is considering buying him another drink, or offering him a cigarette.

I am not interested in arguing for a subjective state of affairs where a man is, or feels himself to be, responsible for his actions to a postulated inner and ultimate self, or to a deity; for I am convinced that increasing numbers of people escape the strictures of conscience because they soon decide that their answerability to God is a myth, and have been given no strong principle based on social structure to take its place. It is commonly overlooked that in these days of general education, every section of a community requires reasons for what it is urged to do. If there is little chance of increasing the sense of responsibility by religious doctrines, then instruction in the inter-relations of men could act as a demonstration of a man's power to manipulate his social relationships, as instruction in simple anatomy and physiology enables him to safeguard his health. For responsibility is a state of affairs arising out of society itself. And it is not a question of society projecting itself into the individual by what is called introjection or the acquisition of ideal selves, but is inherent in the very structure of society—in men living together, no matter how. That society itself depends for its persistence upon this responsibility whereby a man mixes up, as it were, his own interests with those of others in making his decisions, goes far beyond mere ascription in import.

INDEX